ECM Solutions
What you need to know

Bill Forquer
Peter Jelinski
Tom Jenkins

This book is dedicated to the staff, partners and customers of Open Text Corporation and its subsidiaries. This book is possible due to their collective effort, innovation and vision.

We would like to thank the staff, users and partners of Open Text for their contributions to this book.

Special thanks go out to the contributors

Suzanne Allen Chiovitti, Evelyn Astor-Hack, Randy Baird, Jeremy Barnes, Virginia Bartosek, Steve Best, Scott Bowen, Cameron Brennan, Don Brown, Adrian Butcher, Charles Carter, Chris Churchill-Coleman, Malcolm Cohron, Tara Combs, Katherine Dunfield, Lisa Dekker, Joe Dwyer, Grant Edgar, Rick Elassaad, Peter Fischer, Patrick Giesa, Nick Gilbert, Christopher Ginder, Dietmar Grillhoffer, Luc Haldimann, Scott Hardin, J.P. Harris, Adam Howatson, David Howatson, Anton Huenermann, Toby Jenkins, Carol Knoblauch, Walter Köhler, Agnes Kolkiewicz, Melanie Landry, Thomas Lederer, Steve Lett, Julie Mandell, Bruce Marquardt, Jennifer McCredie, James McGourlay, Roland Meier, Darren Meister, John Myers, Peter Near, Tony Niederer, Mark Nusca, Russ Pandel, Donna Pearson, Cynthia Prescott, Thomas Probst, Kirk Roberts, Maurice Rodriguez, Jacky Saayman, Jennifer Schumacher, Robert Skanes, Jared Spataro, Martin Sumner-Smith, Claudia Traving, Renée Tremblay, Doug Varley, Annemarie Vander Veen, Chris Vassalotti, Dave Wareham, Kathleen Wilcox, Neil Wilson and graphic artists Janet Catipi, Sabrina Prudham and David Rees.

Specific resources are accredited in the Bibliography and the Innovator Case Study Bibliography.

Forquer, Bill
Jelinski, Peter
Jenkins, Tom

ECM Solutions

Fourth Printing, July 2008
Printed in Canada

ISBN
0-9730662-6-1

$29.00 U.S.

Published by
Open Text Corporation
275 Frank Tompa Drive
Waterloo, Ontario, Canada
N2L 0A1

(519) 888-7111
info@opentext.com
www.opentext.com

WHAT YOU NEED TO KNOW

Enterprise Content Management (ECM) represents a critical new stage in the advance of the information age. Never before have companies been faced with such daunting challenges. On the one hand, technology has allowed companies to create every type of content imaginable, from documents to presentations, from spreadsheets to digital media. On the other hand, the volume of content being generated continues to grow by leaps and bounds, making it more difficult to manage. In particular, this situation has been exacerbated by the general take-up of the Internet and the ubiquitous use of email. Add to that the potential legal consequences that could occur from not properly managing content and you have a time bomb in the making.

To provide readers with a comprehensive understanding of ECM, we have created a three-book series called "Turning Content into Competitive Advantage." It can be read easily as a trilogy, or selectively, depending on the reader's depth of familiarity with ECM and area of interest. No prior knowledge of ECM technology is required to understand this material. *ECM Solutions*, the first book in the series, examines how corporate enterprises are applying ECM as a key element of their business strategy to gain competitive advantage. Many industry solution cases are used to support the solution concepts presented. *ECM Technology*, the second book in the series, provides the reader with a solid foundation in the principal technology elements that make up ECM. It includes many Innovator Stories, which illustrate the use of each ECM technology component in practice.

ECM Methods, the third book in the series, presents the reader with methods and supporting case studies of how companies have successfully deployed ECM. The case studies provide a practical illustration of the best practices used in successful ECM deployments.

This book, ***ECM Solutions***, sets the ECM stage by introducing ECM business needs, ECM technology elements, ROI, and the emerging importance of Compliance and Corporate Governance. If you are not very familiar with ECM, refer to the first four chapters in Part 1— they provide a good overview of the ECM industry.

In Part 2, we examine the use of ECM technology as applied in specific functional departments within an organization. We have chosen a simple approach and assumed that every organization has functional departments that drive the majority of operational matters. Their name and scope vary dramatically from organization to organization, but can be generalized as the department that plans the department business, the department that takes the product to market, the department that develops the product/service, the department that physically makes the product, the department that services the customers and the department that tracks of all the other departments. In a word, these are commonly known as:

- Enterprise
- Sales and Marketing
- Research and Development
- Manufacturing
- Services
- Administration

We have organized this book around needs in each of these functional departments, and how they have put ECM technology to use.

Part 3 examines how ECM is applied in the real business world as driven by requirements that are specific to an industry segment. The industry segments we have represented in this book are:

- Media
- Government
- Education
- Pharmaceutical and Life Sciences
- Energy, Chemical and Utility
- Insurance and Financial Services
- Telecommunications
- Architecture, Engineering and Construction (AEC)
- Automotive

In Part 4, we expand our scope further and consider the highest impact of ECM solutions deployment, and the least understood—servicing cross-functional, organizational, extended-organizational, and online-marketplace requirements. ECM solutions uniquely have the ability to drive alignment between functional areas of the organization that have traditionally operated as islands. We most often see these systems launched from Program Offices within the organization that cannot be functionally aligned with any single department.

You can also use this book as a reference resource. In the Table of Contents, we have provided some Innovator Stories listed alphabetically, as well as an alphabetical list of many of the solutions featured in the book. We have also included a solution grid that shows how to locate solutions based on major industries cross-referenced against the major department and enterprise types of deployment. This grid is provided for ROI (productivity) solutions as well as compliance-based solutions.

In today's business world, ECM is about more than managing content. Society is now demanding higher standards for the accuracy and availability of content.

> *In the two years following 2001, more than 20 new laws were enacted throughout the world that impacted how organizations gather and disseminate information. Government reaction to events such as 9/11 and Enron have been to demand greater transparency in collaboration and content. Regulators are relying on recent advances in electronic content management technology to provide this transparency in an efficient manner.*

In the past few years, more regulations were passed in some industries than have been written in almost a century. From the Patriot Act, to Sarbanes Oxley and Food and Drug Administration (FDA) regulations, government regulations are creating more secure living conditions for consumers. Across many industries, individuals and companies have already been penalized for not complying with these regulations and mismanaging critical business content.

In a business climate that demands structure and control, ECM creates a safe and transparent environment for organizations to foster innovation and growth. ECM leverages the power of the Internet to transform the way people interact. It creates secure and regulated environments, ensuring that protected content remains behind closed doors. At the same time, ECM unlocks the true potential of the enterprise by enabling people to transform content into knowledge, creating new possibilities and business opportunities.

We hope you enjoy this story about the application of new and exciting technologies and solutions, and will be encouraged to make your own journey to bring ECM technology to your business.

Bill Forquer

Peter Jelinski

Tom Jenkins

Open Text Corporation

CONTENTS

Part 1: The Business Case

Part 2: ECM Solutions by Department

Part 3: ECM Solutions by Industry

Part 4: Extending ECM Today and Tomorrow

Innovator Stories

Compliance Grid

Compliance Solutions Map	Gov	Pharma	Energy	Finance	Mfg	Services
Research	U.S. Army S 111	AG S 221	Energen S 231	UBS S 76	Holcim S 271	LMU S 205
Admin	Fluor Hanford S 59	Aventis S 219	Vintage M 58	LVA M 142	Sony M 21	Translink T 119
Mfg	Northrop Grumman T 65	Genzyme T 238	Sasol M 98	Winterthur S 247	Arup S 269	Johnson S 74
Services	Calgary S 199	FSMB S 195	PG&E S 237	Shenandoah Life T 233	CAS S 279	Giant Eagle M 186
Enterprise	GD S 291	Roche S 215	South East Water M 158	EIB T 265	Distell S 6	ISO S 297
Extranet	FMI S 187	Aventis S 219	Kerr-McGee M 216	OSFI T 54	DMJM S 267	LMU S 205

M = Methods Book
S = Solutions Book
T = Technology Book

Company Name	Page Number

For information regarding additional solutions please go to: www.opentext.com/solutions/map

List of Solutions

ROI Grid

ROI Solutions Map	Media	Gov	Edu	Pharma	Energy	Finance	Telco	AEC	Auto	Mfg	Services
R&D	HBO T 29	U.S. Army S 111	FOIC S 109	AG S 221	Murphy Oil S 235	NERA T 58	HP S 47	Miller T 167	Volvo Aero S 121	Distell S 6	TRL M 164
Admin	CBC S 23	ILR S 185	Broward T 225	Novo Nordisk M 134	PG&E S 237	LawPRO S 13	Sony S 21	M+W Zander T 177	BMW S 119	Reebok S 43	Translink T 119
Mfg	TWBG S 169	Northrop Grumman M 200	Turner T 75	Roche S 215	Energen S 231	Alte Leipziger T 185	BT S 259	Holcim S 271	Fiat S 281	Miele S 123	SKM S 40
Services	TSR S 173	DRC M 228	Emory U. S 209	Aventis S 219	South East Water M 158	Barclays T 148	T-Systems M 92	DMJM S 267	Daimler T 7	Owens Corning T 145	Mercer S 151
Sales	EA T 201	Lockheed T 164	LMU S 205	Novartis S 155	Sasol M 98	AGVA S 245	Siemens S 85	Johnson S 74	Audi T 85	Siemens S 85	Swiss Air M 71
Executive	TSR S 173	Fluor Hanford S 59	Clark S 207	Roche S 215	Shell S 229	UBS S 76	C&W S 81	Holcim S 271	Fiat S 281	Whirlpool T 205	Dow Corning S 143
Enterprise	Standard T 223	USPTO T 68	Open U. T 220	Genzyme T 238	Kerr-McGee M 216	Shenan-doah T 233	Motorola M 232	Arup S 269	CAS S 279	Motorola S 83	CARE M 112
Extranet	20th C. Fox S 171	USAF T 240	Broward T 225	Novartis S 155	Shell S 229	Federated Investors M 178	Cisco S 257	M+W Zander M 206	BMW T 124	Unilever M 170	ISO S 297

ROI Solutions Map

M = Methods Book
S = Solutions Book
T = Technology Book

Company Name	Page Number

For information regarding additional solutions please go to: www.opentext.com/solutions/map

1

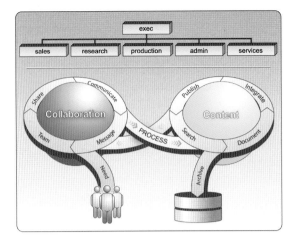

Figure 1.1: ECM Applications

A sign of organizational maturity occurs when multiple departments carry out their work with a single application platform. It is obvious that everyone in the company wishing to spend money should use the same Purchase Order System. If each department had its own system for authorizing purchases, it would be chaotic. Yet most organizations are doing just that when it comes to Enterprise Content Management (ECM) applications. The deployments tend to be isolated in pockets within departments of the company. But increased pressure to comply with new regulations is forcing organizations to consider ECM more strategically.

Take the Sarbanes-Oxley Act (SOX) of 2002 as an example. This regulation is designed to restore (or maintain, depending on your views) the confidence of investors in public markets. Compliance to Sarbanes-Oxley is cross-departmental by its very nature. This type of cross-departmental application highlights the need for companies to invest in applications delivered by a common set of technologies. This chapter focuses on how ECM enables organizations to lower their total cost of ownership by delivering an enterprise data model and core applications that provide an infrastructure for additional business applications.

CHAPTER 1

THE BUSINESS NEEDS

The primary objective of any business is to generate wealth. Businesses are continuously examining ways to become more efficient than their competitors. This is the premise upon which the free market economy is based.

To succeed, companies need to manage their organizational assets. Systems to manage human, capital and financial assets have been part of the IT landscape for the last 40 years. Systems may have existed to manage the information assets of an organization but many have been rendered woefully inadequate by the sheer exponential rate of information creation. How can a company use the information and content that exists within and around the organization? What information should they know? How do they establish an infrastructure that enables them to understand their content?

Enterprise Content Management is technology that provides a means to create, store, manage, secure, distribute and publish any digital content for enterprise use. ECM is not about numbers; it is about words. Much of the IT industry in the past 50 years has focused on back-office databases and their management in Enterprise Resource Planning (ERP) systems.

ECM is unique in that it was developed to manage the proliferation of non-numeric content such as documents, Web pages, spreadsheets, diagrams and images, all largely driven by the pervasiveness of the Internet.

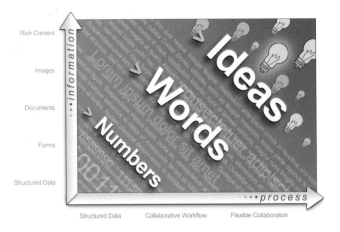

Figure 1.2: Working With Information

For ECM systems to be widely adopted, they need to emulate the way people work without disrupting their daily routines. This involves creating a digital place for people to work in much the same way they work together in departments or at office locations. For ECM to be effective, it needs to automatically capture the content produced as a by-product of this work. The very best ECM solutions deliver applications that integrate content management invisibly within the very act of collaboration. The transparent combination of content and collaboration benefits organizations tremendously by providing a place where simple ideas take root, are nurtured and finally mature into market-leading innovations. This critical point is one we will explore in detail in this book.

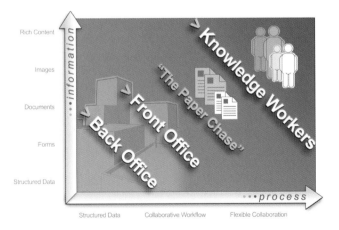

Figure 1.3: The Evolving Challenge

People work together within a particular line of business or work group. Companies are normally organized by departments around these lines of business, such as sales or manufacturing or administration. Typical ECM applications are built to meet the content management needs of a particular department and are driven by the specific needs of a line of business manager facing a particular productivity problem. These departmental solutions provide the foundation for subsequent larger enterprise installations.

ECM as a set of departmental applications is most effective when supported by a common data structure and a combined set of technologies. To put it another way, each departmental application typically requires the same basic technologies and infrastructure, but has a specific set of needs that are unique to that line of business. ECM systems that can be easily adapted to meet each department's unique needs, while maintaining a common data model, are inherently more flexible and future proof. Implementing ECM applications on a common data model results in lower total cost of ownership and faster implementation, leading to greater productivity and higher returns on technology investments.

Content-Based Applications

Consider group-level applications that are closely aligned to the way people work. The following represents a typical organizational chart for a company:

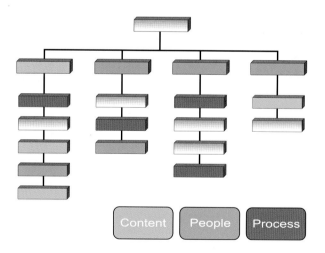

Figure 1.4: Typical Organization Chart

> Distell Limited

DISTELL

South Africa's premier producer and marketer of fine wines and spirits, Distell Limited is a multifaceted organization whose activities range from grape farming, winemaking, distilling, maturation, production, and distribution to the international marketing of trademarks. Facing rapid content growth, Distell needed a solution that would stream-line content-specific business processes and ensure content availability throughout the enterprise.

Enterprise Content Management (ECM) at Distell provides enterprise-wide document and project management support, while an ECM-based Quality Management System ensures that Distell meets the requirements of Quality Management regulations such as ISO and International Food Standards. By automating business processes and ensuring easy information access, ECM has streamlined their quality management, production innovations, and product change request processes.

Integrating the ECM solution with the corporate ERP system has enabled Accounts Receivable and Accounts Payable to scan and later access customer and supplier invoices using the ERP system. This has resulted in improved customer service, as proof of delivery documentation can be faxed to a customer from within the ERP system instead of having to be retrieved from the file room first, copied and then faxed. ECM data archiving also controls the data growth of selected ERP tables, another benefit of the ECM solution.

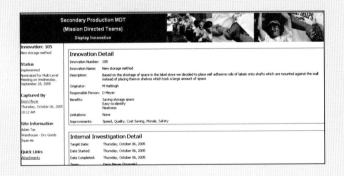

Figure 1.5: A Production Innovation Tracking Solution at Distell

Companies consist of many separate departments—Accounting and Finance, Legal, Administration, Marketing, Sales, IT, Research and Development, and so on. Each department has specific requirements for content management. ECM business solutions have been designed to meet many of these requirements and solve problems specific to a particular department. Typically, these solutions are driven by the need to improve efficiency or save money. Examples include: purchase order processing, invoicing, project management, claims processing, FDA compliance, product lifecycle management (PLM), and sales readiness, to mention a few.

ECM solutions often support core business functions. That is, if the solution were to be used inappropriately or did not exist, the business would not function. In the Pharmaceutical industry, for example, the development of new drugs must follow a regulated content management and approval process known as 21 CFR Part 11. The entire corporation is at risk if this process is not precisely followed. ECM business solutions for Pharmaceutical companies must therefore support 21 CFR Part 11. Other industries such as Financial Services and Healthcare have very similar needs controlled by their own industry regulations.

Figure 1.6: ECM Architecture Simplified

Once an application has been deployed at the departmental or group level, the IT Department involved in implementing the first application can use the lessons learned to solve content issues in other departments. While the first deployment may take place in the Sales Department, the next deployment may occur in the Manufacturing Department, and so on. Some of the most advanced ECM-enabled organizations in the world today have more than 20 distinct department-level applications supported by a common underlying suite of technologies and a common data model.

Figure 1.7: ECM Applications

Some of the solutions that have been developed for ECM include:

- Accounts payable administration
- Bid management
- Content management
- Court case management
- Customer care centers
- Customer due diligence
- Derivatives management
- Digital asset management
- Engineering change management
- Government publications management
- Vendor communications
- Human resources
- ISO 9000 quality assurance
- Managing marketing extranets
- Manufacturing processes
- New hire induction/Education
- New product development
- Policies and procedures
- Project collaboration
- Records management
- Vacation time management

As organizations move to leverage the same infrastructure for process improvements company wide, finding the best solution often leads to a long-term strategic Enterprise Content Management solution. This involves deploying a complete series of applications across an entire organization. In order to make these applications simple to deploy and cost effective to replicate, a common set of technologies with the same content model is required as an underlying infrastructure. This means that the suite of technologies must be sufficient to deliver all applications across the enterprise.

Hundreds of ECM solutions are implemented in the leading organizations of major industries throughout the world. This book profiles many of those ECM success stories.

As deployments of ECM reach critical mass within major corporations, ECM applications are finding their way into every department. At the time of writing this book, there were more than 100 different applications using ECM technologies known to the authors.

On average, a single enterprise-wide deployment of ECM involves more than 20 unique solutions, ranging from Engineering Departments using ECM applications for new product development to Accounting Departments using ECM to track changes to contract bid documents.

Inter-Departmental Requirements

In many applications that are critical to the operation and success of an organization, collaboration requires cross-departmental cooperation. In many companies, achieving this cooperation is the very basis for long-term competitive advantage. For example, when planning and implementing New Product Development (NPD) within a research group, the interaction between this group and manufacturing and marketing is vital to the success of the project. This implies strong cross-functional cooperation and collaboration, plus the sharing of critical documents among all three departments.

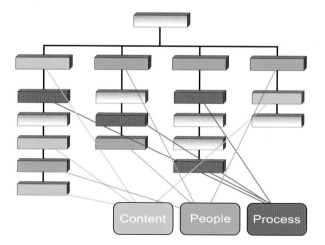

Figure 1.8: ECM Crosses Departments

> E-Plus MobilFunk

e·plus⁺

A subsidiary of the Dutch company KPN, E-Plus is the third-largest cellular phone network in Germany. This innovative organization is continually offering its customers new services and expanding its network; as a result, speedy business processes are essential at E-Plus. A powerful inventory system was needed to keep track of the vast inventory in the 150 E-Plus shops.

The ECM system links the shops with the central ERP application so that sales personnel can use the intranet to directly and in real time access the ERP application when submitting an order or handling inventory. Prior to this, E-Plus employees had to synchronize this data daily with the ERP system. "The new solution has enabled us to significantly reduce the cost of inventory control," says the project manager at E-Plus.

Customized system features have considerably accelerated business processes at E-Plus, enabling the staff to respond immediately to the customers' needs, significantly reducing costs and producing a quick ROI. However, the E-Plus customers are the real winners as their orders are now processed much faster — the processing time has decreased from five days to 30 minutes.

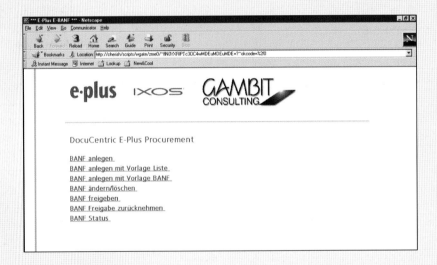

Figure 1.9: Procurement Management at E-Plus

The issue of cross-departmental functionality raises two important concerns for the ECM architecture. First, for diverse departments to collaborate or work together efficiently, both business and IT people outside of a particular department require infrastructure support. Secondly, an underlying common data model is required to let people in different departments share information contained in separate applications at a cost-effective rate. While it can be argued that some applications can be delivered within a department, most ECM applications need to be enterprise-wide in nature so that they can be accessed easily across departments. Otherwise, organizations are fragmented into isolated islands of information and critical content remains buried. Departmental implementations are limited in scope and are eventually replaced by similar applications based on a broad underlying set of technologies that scale the entire organization.

Industry Requirements

ECM customers are looking for a solution that provides a common technology for many different applications. Departmental applications have evolved by adding elements that address specific vertical market needs. Many ECM vendors today are delivering solutions in specific industries based on their initial success in developing solutions in one or more markets. An organization's pain points are often specific to a particular industry, so customers prefer a vendor that has expertise in their particular industry. An ECM solution gains traction in an industry when one organization begins to use a solution and other organizations look to this solution to resolve their issues as well.

Within many industries, managing content is absolutely critical. Pharmaceutical companies have been early adopters of ECM because managing documents is a regulatory requirement for doing business. The New Drug Application (NDA) challenges organizations to provide detailed information about what happened during clinical tests, what the ingredients of a drug are, the results of animal studies, potential adverse effects, and how a drug is manufactured, processed and packaged. The integrated document and records management, collaboration and workflow functionality of a comprehensive ECM solution enables pharmaceutical organizations to detail the lifecycle of a product from start to finish. Using a comprehensive ECM suite, pharmaceutical companies can seamlessly review new drug targets, deploy personnel and resources, manage drug discovery projects and accelerate time to market.

Productivity Gains

ECM has its roots in document management. In the early 1980s, the benefits of investing in a document management system were lower print or paper costs, reduced storage needs and increased productivity. Today, ECM is evolving into a blend of proven technologies designed to solve a variety of content and process-centric problems. It follows that customer investment is moving from departmental solutions to entire enterprise infrastructures that promise return on investment on many levels.

The key to success of the earlier implementations has been the recognition of collaboration and its role in creating context for content. It is simply not enough to know that content exists, without being aware of how, when and why it was created. Collaboration provides this context since it records what was happening at the time of content creation. This provides far greater insight into the relevancy of information.

The current trend in collaboration and content management is toward departmental or group-level solutions. Currently, the Internet is still new and very technically driven. In the future, companies will hide the technology beneath purpose-built solutions. Functionality will be there but virtually transparent. Internet software will evolve in the same way and ECM will lead the evolution in collaboration by making solutions easier to use, without users needing to know anything more about the Web than how to click on a hyperlink.

While many organizations still regard content management solutions as self-contained solutions, they will increasingly deploy technology with an enterprise-wide ECM strategy in mind. Leading ECM solutions will evolve into comprehensive infrastructures offering fully integrated collaboration and content management functionality deployed at the departmental level and then rolled out to the entire enterprise. More and more customers will embrace an ECM approach that is aligned with business needs on many levels. Companies will be encouraged to grow their ECM solution—whether by improving corporate governance, streamlining processes or effectively managing content—as their business requirements evolve.

> LawPRO

LawPRO™

Lawyers' Professional Indemnity Company (LAWPRO) is an insurance company that is licensed to provide professional liability and title insurance. The organization, which relied heavily on paper, sought an alternative to this inefficient, innovation-stifling medium for storage and communication.

Workflow improvement effectively reduces paper usage; it offers tracking functionality and can work on diverse systems — spanning, organizing and connecting them. Automating paper-based processes using a centralized data entry and repository for documents has pulled business processes from a variety of systems into one cohesive unit at LAWPRO.

The solution has caused a profound shift in the original project motivation: the 'paperless office' almost became a by-product, not a goal. Workflow implementation has simplified existing processes and increased efficiency. As a result of the implementation, LAWPRO has realized benefits far beyond initial project expectations.

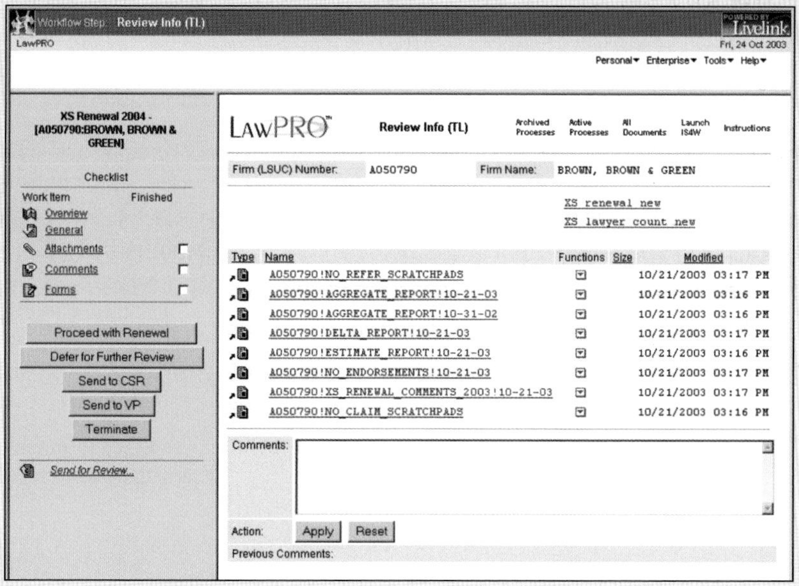

Figure 1.10: LawPRO's Client Review Workflow

Figure 1.11: ECM Technologies

From a more academic standpoint, a new market is emerging which addresses the higher-level needs of the knowledge-intensive organization, namely, how to increase overall organizational effectiveness in a volatile business environment. In order to realize return on investment in technology—and to adhere to new regulations and legislation—smart organizations will move toward implementing an underlying infrastructure that supports many repositories and combines key applications.

Vendors will offer customized views and applications for specific departments and processes that are cross-industry applicable. The infrastructure will have to scale and support new technologies. Customers of ECM solutions will become interested in newer technologies and expanding these systems to support more content types such as email and rich media files.

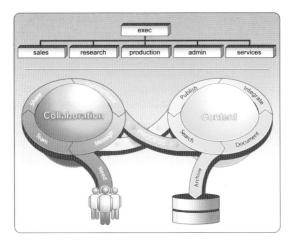

Figure 2.1: ECM Technologies

ECM technologies are all about connecting the right people to the right information in the right context. Historically, most ECM adopters have done so on a piecemeal basis – focusing on a specific business pain point and single technology solution. But this approach is expensive when you consider that achieving compliance with today's new regulations requires visibility on processes that span multiple departments and functions. These processes cross multiple systems, and each one of these cross-over points represents a potential point of failure, additional manual labor, expensive and customized integrations, and additional internal controls for safeguarding. Progressive organizations are adopting ECM as a strategic platform to avoid these unnecessary costs. Nevertheless, understanding each of the component technologies is important to develop a more comprehensive ECM strategy.

ECM TECHNOLOGIES

During the 21st century, companies in the Enterprise Content Management market will dominate the Information Technology agenda as corporations seek advances in technology to better manage content, people and processes.

We can trace the evolution of ECM by examining major developments in the industry as early as the 1960s. At this time, companies such as Honeywell and IBM were major vendors. Their mainframe computer systems automated basic computations previously made by floors of workers.

In the 1980s, the introduction of the personal computer (PC) started the client-server revolution and personal productivity drove the creation of digital content. This content, created mostly by knowledge workers, complemented the automated generation of content that belonged in the mini-computer era. Intel and Microsoft became major vendors in this era.

	1970s	1980s	1990s	2000s
Who	IBM	Microsoft	SAP	Open Text
Why	Clerical Productivity	Personal Productivity	Departmental Productivity	Org. Compliance & Productivity
How	Data Processing	Email; Desktop Publishing	ERP	ECM
Computing Environment	Mainframe	Personal Computer	LAN	Ubiquitous Computing

Figure 2.2: Eras of Computing

In the 1990s, Enterprise Resource Planning (ERP) programs further automated transactional business processes within organizations, allowing more efficient management of numbers through a database. Companies such as SAP and Oracle were leading innovators in this era.

ECM suites are made up of a number of technology pieces working harmoniously to manage the complete lifecycle of electronic documents, from creation to archive and eventual deletion. You can compare ECM suites with other suite-based software products, such as Microsoft® Office. Microsoft Office includes different tools that work together to provide personal productivity for office workers. Likewise, ECM suites offer a set of tightly integrated facilities for searching, managing, distributing, publishing and archiving electronic documents to achieve organizational productivity.

Unlike Microsoft Office, ECM suites require little to no software to be installed on a personal computer. ECM software leverages Internet technology to deliver services to people, meaning that accessing the software requires only a Web browser, a username and a password.

ECM suites provide secure access, storage, publication and archiving of large volumes of business content. ECM allows organizations to manage the processes for working with different types of content, while tracking and controlling content changes. Content management is not confined to organizing computer directories; it involves exploiting your business know-how to avoid critical failures, to operate more efficiently and to become more productive and profitable.

Structured vs. Unstructured Information

To introduce the technologies that underpin ECM, it is necessary to understand the difference between structured and unstructured information and why managing unstructured information is such a challenge.

Structured data is based on numbers organized into tables. These database tables can be quickly manipulated to find data that refers to the numbers in the table. Unstructured data is not as easy to organize and retrieve. Words, an example of unstructured data, are organized into tables similar to an index found at the back of a book. Because the data model for words (unstructured data) is fundamentally different from the data model for numbers (structured data), the technologies that support each must differ. Computers have fundamentally changed the way we work; most office workers today require a computer to do their jobs. Managing payroll, processing orders and invoices, inventory control and financial accounting all rely heavily on the numeric processing capabilities of computers. Computers are exceptional at crunching numbers, but the challenge for ECM applications is to use information technology to manage documents and pictures, or what is termed "unstructured data."

Individual productivity tools such as word-processing systems, spreadsheets, presentation tools, Web editors and email have created an explosion of unstructured data that must be managed. Organizations need to store this information, make it accessible and ensure that it is up to date and secure, as well as appropriately distributed, published and consumed.

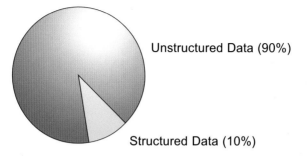

Unstructured Data (90%)

Structured Data (10%)

Figure 2.3: The Ratio of Structured Versus Unstructured Data in an Organization

The reason why unstructured data matters is the shear size of this information and its recent growth rate. While this is important, what makes unstructured data the focus of IT for the future is the astounding growth rates of digital content that are being reported with main stream adoption of the Internet. It is estimated by various industry observers that large corporations are doubling their unstructured data every two months! Even if this rate slowed to every three months or every six months, it represents an enormous change in the type of information that is available for use within an organization. This exponential growth is shown in Figure 2.4

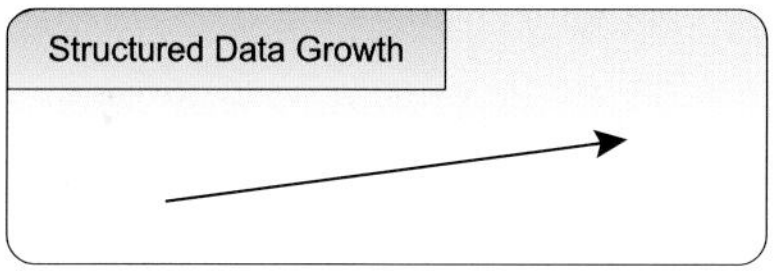

Structured Data Growth	Unstructured Data Growth

Current Structured Data Growth is Linear 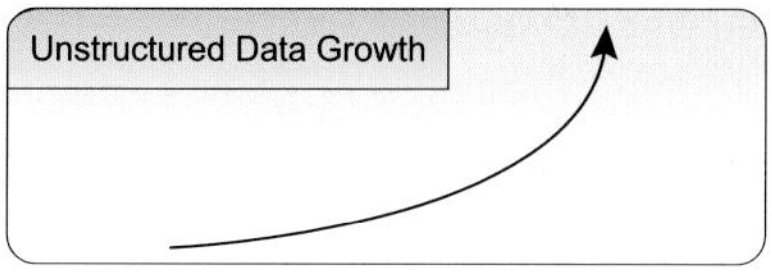   *Current Unstructured Data Growth is Exponential*

Figure 2.4: Structured Versus Unstructured Data Growth

Think about this rate for a minute. Consider all of the digital information created by corporations since the start of computing and then consider that all that information will be created all over again in the next few months!

Our every-day experience suggests that this is happening when we consider the incredible growth in the size of our email inboxes and the scope and scale of the public Internet.

As a comparison, consider that unstructured data probably tracks transactions and that tracks the economy. A very strong global economy grows by an average of 4 percent per year and ERP growth is commensurate with that and probably in the 10 percent range or linear as shown in Figure 2.5.

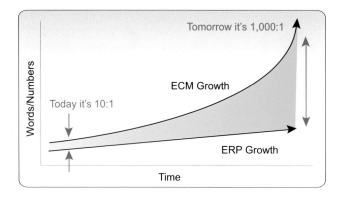

Figure 2.5: Estimate of the Relative Growth Rates
of Unstructured Data and Structured Data

Now consider the two growth rates together. Today unstructured data is probably about 10 times the amount of structured data but consider the impact of even a few years of hyper growth by ECM (unstructured) and steady growth by ERP (structured), the gap will be 1,000 times the size of what it is today. With this rate of growth, whatever problems that IT currently faces with unstructured data it is clear that these problems will only get worse with time. It is better to start early on solving issues with web sites and email management since they will only be larger problems if they are left for another year to grow bigger. Clearly, the ECM repository of web sites and email will dominate the IT agenda for the foreseeable future.

Basic Components of ECM

The quest for solutions to these problems created the ECM market. The following provides an overview of the fundamental technology components of ECM.

Search

It is not easy to search unstructured data—while numbers obey very rigid rules that can be interpreted easily by computer programs (one plus one always equals two), words and pictures have few formal rules and are open to different interpretations based on context. Take the task of cataloging a book called "Lemons." Should the book be cataloged in the

SONY

It is well documented that legacy systems are extremely expensive to maintain, costing enterprises thousands of dollars a year in support, maintenance, location and staffing costs. Faced with the need to decrease costs and comply with data retention regulations, Sony Global Treasury Services (GTS), an internal banking system for the Sony Group, opted to archive data from its legacy IT systems.

A legacy decommissioning solution fully integrated with Sony's SAP system has enabled the migration of over 2 million invoices in less than two weeks using a batch import interface. Remote access to both data and unstructured information ensures that billing documents can be accessed from any location, eliminating the previously cumbersome data retrieval methods.

The challenge of dealing with an array of legacy systems has been fully overcome. All data and documents are now available from a single point of access, delivering significant customer service benefits. As a result of the implementation, Sony has observed a faster and more visible return on its SAP investment.

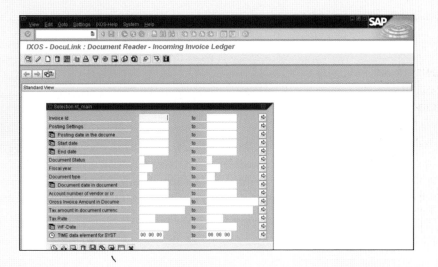

Figure 2.6: An Example of a Legacy Decommissioning Solution

section on cooking, fine arts or cars? Opening the book would immediately reveal to the reader the subject matter and therefore, the correct placement. Computers cannot read yet, so the challenge is to design a system that makes the same interpretations that humans do. If this all sounds too theoretical, try searching the Web for "ECM." Search results will identify more than 800,000 hits, including everything from software products to publishing companies, electronic countermeasures to espresso coffee machines and even the European Crystallographic Meeting in Durban, South Africa.

ECM systems manage huge amounts of unstructured data. Motorola, for example, manages 4.8 terabytes of documents in their ECM repository. The electronic version of this book uses about 0.5 megabytes of disk space, so Motorola's repository would hold 88 million books like this one! ECM systems must not only manage huge amounts of data; they must also allow users to quickly find the documents they need. Modern search tools are able to "learn" concepts that allow them to automatically catalog documents, making them easier to find. Search technology also makes it possible to identify subject matter experts and readers with similar interests by tracking user behavior. Searching unstructured data is the first and one of the most fundamental disciplines of ECM.

Document Management (DM)

We have all experienced the effect on a sentence as it is passed by word-of-mouth around a room full of people. The sentence inevitably changes significantly from person to person and soon loses its original meaning. The same can happen with business critical documents that are mismanaged, with disastrous consequences. Take for example NASA's embarrassment over a space telescope; its giant lens had been improperly ground because of a mix-up involving one team member working in centimeters, meters and kilograms while another was using inches, feet and pounds. As a result, the telescope was out of focus and inoperable. Another case involved confusion between different versions of an aircraft maintenance manual, causing the cockpit window of a passenger aircraft to fall out of the plane at 16,000 feet—the accident apparently caused by engineers using the wrong size screws.

When a document is reviewed by a number of authors, it is easy to lose track of who has the most up-to-date version. Documents can get lost, deleted or fall into the wrong hands.

Document management systems allow businesses to control the production, storage, revision management and distribution of electronic documents, yielding greater efficiencies in the ability to reuse information and control the flow of documents. Managing electronic documents is a key technology of Enterprise Content Management.

Archiving and Document Lifecycle Management (DLM)

The accounting scandals at Enron Corporation made the world aware of the need for records management. When an employee of Andersen, Enron's outside auditor, admit-

> CBC Radio Canada

CBC (♦) Radio-Canada

Canada's national public broadcaster, CBC Radio Canada, provides services to Canadians in English, French and eight aboriginal languages. Dedication to the ideals of public broadcasting has made the organization one of the country's largest cultural institutions. The same dedication has also prompted CBC to implement an ECM solution to enforce consistent business standards and practices across the enterprise.

Custom enhancements to its ECM system provide a number of Web-based solutions including an all-in-one, online contract management system that collects data and generates more than 25,000 contracts a year; an audience relations repository for communications documenting audience reactions; and a collaboration tool that allows various departments to plan programs and add their own information describing CBC's program offerings.

A single system enables the creation of all contract and rights licenses, and one repository holds contracts for all networks. CBC has been able to automate labor-intensive business processes such as negotiation, contract creation, amendments and renewals and obtain support for research of audience reaction. Workflow technology now enforces the use of well-defined business processes across the enterprise.

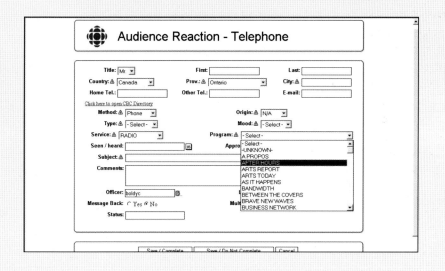

Figure 2.7: Capturing Audience Reaction at CBC

ted to destroying a "significant" number of documents related to the Enron investigation, it made people wonder, "How could that possibly happen?" It happened because prior to the court investigation, the documents were being destroyed properly and according to an established procedure within the company. However, a court order necessitated a change to that established procedure which, evidently, wasn't properly communicated or enforced. Systems today must be immediately adaptable to change and enforce new behaviors, either sternly or delicately, depending on each situation.

Everyone has experienced the sense of panic that hits when a spreadsheet or document somehow gets deleted. No amount of screaming at the screen, banging on the keyboard or shaking the motherboard will bring it back. Now imagine that the document you lost contained proof of an accounting infraction or was the only copy of a sales agreement for a million-dollar order.

Records Management

Records management is the discipline of managing records to meet operational needs, accountability requirements and community expectations. Records management software works by allowing you to attach rules to electronic documents. These rules tell the system when it is okay to delete documents or move them to a data archive, either physically in boxes or electronically on storage devices such as CD-ROMs.

Government offices are superb at record keeping. When we are born, when we are married, when we have children, when we get divorced and when we die, a record is created at a government office. The rules that determine when those records can be archived and deleted are stipulated in government regulations and policies. Records management systems enforce these policies for government organizations, and for the equivalent form of vital records in an organization.

With daily pressure to comply with regulations and with changes to legislation, managing records and the lifecycle of documents have become crucial components of ECM.

Web Content Management (WCM)

How many Web sites does your company have? One? Twenty? These days, there are Web sites for every subject or product and many organizations host at least a dozen.

The first Web sites were created by computer geeks and academics. Because they were used mainly to share technical information, they were text-based and not very visually stimulating. The World Wide Web and its support for graphic images and animation moved the Internet into the realm of art, and graphic designers became the new Web Masters. Corporations soon discovered that Web sites could be more than just a place for casual visitors to browse; they could be used to sell products, attract investors, interact with customers and engage with suppliers.

General Dynamics C4 Systems, a leading integrator of secure communication and information systems and technology, had many methods for distributing news and information across the company. Email was becoming more prevalent, but users were being overwhelmed by volume and spam mail, and distribution lists were getting harder to manage. Also, the Web site had static content. The process was highly manual, decentralized, labor-intensive and inconsistent.

To solve the problem, the organization began taking advantage of the key features of its ECM solution—using news channels and tickers to 'push' information to users and establishing notifications to 'pull' items of interest. Next, GDC4 worked with various departments to help them maintain their own content. Finally, the static Web site content was migrated to a completely automated presentation of general news and information—the GDC4S News Stand.

Visits to the News Stand have increased steadily, while the labor required to post items and keep content up to date has decreased significantly. Archived stories are available for searching, providing an easy resource for people looking for an item of interest they remember seeing.

Figure 2.8: Virtual Community News Stand
at General Dynamics C4 Systems

In today's organization, every department wants representation on the corporate Web site: human resources wants to advertise job vacancies; marketing wants to promote events; sales wants to sell product; and investor relations wants to inform shareholders. Furthermore, the CEO wants to have the site available in seven languages. Requests for site updates can overwhelm a single Web Master and create bottlenecks that result in information not being posted in a timely manner. The solution is to enable Web content to be owned and managed by individual content and authorities.

Web Content Management (WCM) software was created to allow multiple content contributors to make changes to Web sites, removing typical Web Master bottlenecks. WCM systems conceal all internal workings of a Web page, allowing users with little or no technical experience to add and modify content. WCM enables data fragments to be easily reused, so that updating the company's logo involves changing only one or two files, magically transforming the whole Web site. The technology behind Web content management is very similar to the technology required to manage documents. Most ECM suites include Web content management capabilities.

Teams and Collaboration

We have quickly grown accustomed to being able to phone each other anywhere at any time and in a matter of seconds. Cell phones and mobile telephony are so entrenched in our daily lives that it is hard to imagine life before they existed. The Internet has also revolutionized our ability to connect with others. We send documents over the Web and drum our finger impatiently awaiting its delivery. Being able to connect so easily with our colleagues over the Internet has made it possible to work effectively in virtual teams, with geography no longer a concern.

The Human Genome Project began in 1990 as a collaborative effort by research establishments around the globe to identify the 30,000 genes in human DNA. The project required the collaboration of scientists from many fields, including molecular biologists, engineers, physicists, chemists and mathematicians at the U.S. Department of Energy. Technology had a huge role in the project; the Genome Data Base (GDB) is the worldwide repository for genome mapping data. Researchers around the world used the Internet to share research and answer questions. The project successfully concluded in April, 2003 and would not have been possible before the creation of the World Wide Web.

Global organizations are now able to capitalize on Web-based collaboration facilities to empower their workforces, working as virtual project teams to bring expertise from different areas and office locations to tackle business-critical problems. ECM systems include collaboration tools that enable the best minds within organizations to work together more efficiently—sharing information, capturing and preserving knowledge, managing collaborative processes and projects, and resolving issues.

More than one in eight Americans rely on VSP (Vision Service Plan) for eye care health coverage and thousands of companies trust the organization to provide a variety of eye care benefit plans. VSP teams with an extensive network of doctors across the country to deliver both high quality and value, which creates significant challenges in managing information and communications. Some of the affected areas include credentialing/recredentialing, doctor/practice information and frequent communication with doctors. A unified ECM-based system allows VSP to manage the collection and dissemination of information more effectively.

The ECM system consolidates the newsletter creation process at VSP from an idea for article content to final distribution to doctors. Integration with back-end systems auto-mates the process and provides support for creating, revising, managing, versioning, and archiving of newsletter content. The system provides the functionality to generate a newsletter for each office, customizing content based on user request, geography and/or plan participation. It includes a repository for doctor credentials and information that aids with the doctor certification process and has also been integrated with VSP's Web site to enable doctors to change practice information online.

Doctor satisfaction has improved considerably as they now receive a single newsletter and only relevant, preference-based news and information. Automating manual processes has generated costs savings for VSP. Mailing costs alone have decreased tenfold.

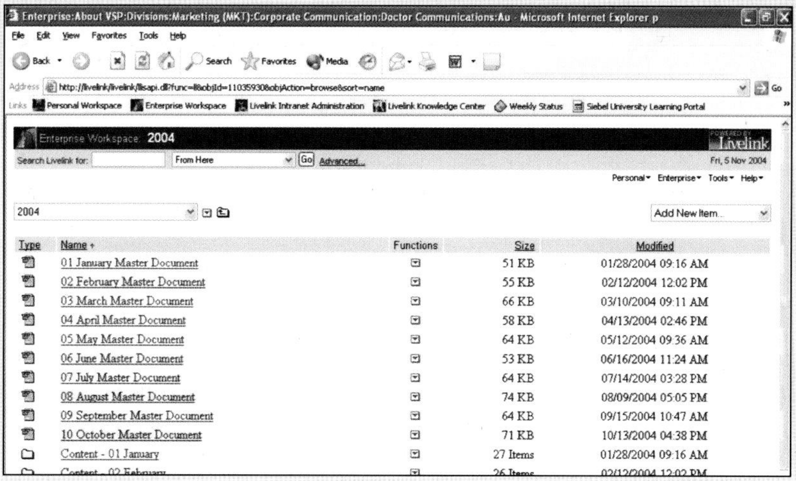

Figure 2.9: Vision Service Plan's Doctor Communication Newsletter Overview

Portals

The word "portal" immediately brings to mind science fiction movies or books in which a portal is depicted as a dimensional doorway in space that connects two or more worlds. Software portals are designed to perform a similar role by providing a place that connects multiple Web-based software applications. Portals are often the glue that pulls all of the various bits of an ECM suite together, providing a contextual shop window to underlying applications.

Portal technology was designed to make the user's life easier by providing all the tools needed in a single, unified Web page. Most of us use portal tools to make sense of the Internet; Yahoo!®, MSN® and AOL® are all portals. They link us to places of interest very quickly, whether to book a vacation, check out the latest movie release or view the stats of our favorite football team. Most portals also let you personalize your experience; My Yahoo!®, for instance, allows you to build your own home page by picking from your favorite places and pages on the Web.

Rich Media and Digital Asset Management

High-speed Internet connections now allow rich media types such as voice and video to be used over Internet connections. Software applications are rapidly emerging to take advantage of this technology for business use. Imagine sitting in traffic on your way to a business meeting and hearing your email messages read out to you over your cell phone. Or picture yourself in an online meeting watching a presentation by a colleague overseas from the comfort of your home office. These are not pipe dreams; these technologies are part of the way we do business today.

CARE Canada, a humanitarian organization fighting global poverty, uses collaborative technology to save lives. When CARE relief workers operating in Kosovo came across an uncharted minefield, they transmitted live video over the Internet back to CARE headquarters to update their pilots on safe locations to drop food and medical supplies.

As telephony networks develop to support unlimited bandwidth, rich media applications will become more popular and integral to conducting business. For this reason, the need to manage rich media within ECM applications is steadily increasing.

Workflow and Business Process Management (BPM)

Business Process Management is both a technology and an approach that connects people and content. BPM helps organizations combine content and collaboration to support structured and unstructured ways of working together.

Every organization conducts numerous business processes each day—from filling out a purchase request, to assigning documents for review and approval: the effectiveness of each and the overall efficiency of an organization depends on business process automation tools. BPM provides powerful tools for defining and reusing business logic, simplifying business processes and helping employees coordinate effectively with both the organization and each other.

ECM solutions integrate with BPM systems to optimize business processes and improve performance. By linking processes with content creation, ECM enables organizations to exchange transactional information and respond more quickly to new or changing business requirements. BPM is a fundamental component of Enterprise Content Management.

Enterprise Application Extensions (EAE)

Enterprise applications such as Enterprise Resource Planning (ERP) and Customer Relationship Management (CRM) effectively perform transaction-based processing. However, data residing in these applications is the result of work that has been completed and, in many cases, cannot effectively support other business processes. Many processes, like contract creation, still require collaborative efforts of employees in multiple depart-ments. To maximize content's effectiveness, organizations need to connect content to the appropriate business processes and make it accessible to people participating in the process. Enterprise Application Extensions provide the underlying business structure that supports these business processes. Allocating unstructured content to business processes puts information people need at their fingertips without searching across many systems for content.

ECM extends enterprise applications by providing links between key processes and transactional information. Making this information secure and accessible across a variety of processes helps companies lower costs and the risks associated with meeting data retention and disposal requirements.

Bringing all the Technologies Together

Enterprise Content Management (ECM) is an amalgamation of the different technologies previously discussed. The component technologies that underpin ECM are shown in the grid below. The grid separates technologies that connect people with people, such as email systems, from technologies that connect people with information, such as search. We have also divided the vertical axis into applications that deal with structured business processes, such as document management, and those that deal with unstructured processes like Web conferencing.

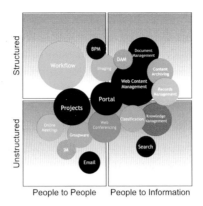

Figure 2.10: ECM Technologies

Making sense of all this technology is a challenge, so let's simplify the picture.

Everything on the left-hand side of the grid describes a technology that deals with working collaboratively. Collaboration technology links processes and individuals across the enterprise and creates a work environment in which teams can share and circulate ideas, experiences and knowledge.

All the information, ideas and data created as a by-product of collaborative work needs to be securely captured, managed and made available to others. The technologies on the right of the grid deal with all content accumulated by business, such as memos, spread-sheets, reports, email messages, images, audio and video files, and transactional data.

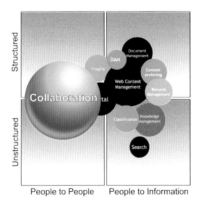

Figure 2.11: Collaboration Technologies

Connecting the content and collaboration bubbles is the genius behind ECM software suites. With ECM, knowledge is automatically captured as a by-product of collaborative work and is transformed into invaluable corporate knowledge. This knowledge is information that enables action, or further collaboration. ECM enables you to effortlessly capture ideas generated during an online meeting or store plans and other documents created by virtual project teams. These knowledge assets are preserved in a secure knowledge repository, where they can be easily accessed, shared or reused throughout an organization. People and content are interconnected by the productive work carried out by the business processes.

The "double bubble" motif is used throughout the book to illustrate ECM's value proposition of combined collaboration, content and process.

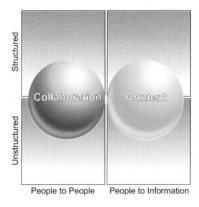

Figure 2.12: Content Technologies

The core technologies of an ECM suite must work together to address a vast range of business needs. While it may be possible to buy each of the technology pieces separately, bringing the pieces together in a suite provides a more efficient way to access and use information across multiple applications—making it easier to move content from one application to another.

Figure 2.13: ECM Value Proposition

ECM Solutions Framework

The diagram below shows the technologies that form the framework for ECM solutions. The framework provides a layer of ECM Lifecycle Management Services that link information workers to an Enterprise Library of information, which integrates content from multiple sources. The ECM Lifecycle Management services include: Collaboration, Content and Process. Collaboration services support person-to-person interaction and facilitate cross-application collaboration, including community and project workspaces, discussion forums, blogs, FAQs and polls. Content services provide a single point of access to all content, either in Web-based portals or the desktop applications with which information workers are most familiar. The ECM Solutions Framework provides access to content across the enterprise and supports storing the content on any mix of storage devices. Business process services deliver a common framework for automating the routing of information and documents, entering information via forms and notifying information workers of critical tasks and events via email. The ECM Solutions Framework facilitates the smooth evolution of existing solutions, speeds the development of new solutions and provides agility for the business to be responsive to change.

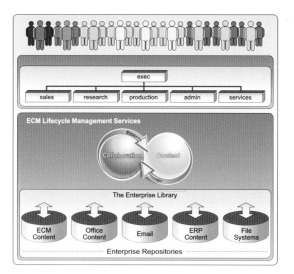

Figure 2.14: ECM Solutions Framework

Now that you are familiar with the fundamental technologies of ECM, we can begin the journey of discovery that led to the creation of a market. The following chapters focus on specific business and industry solutions based on ECM technology. You'll learn how corporate enterprises are applying ECM as a key element of their business strategy to gain competitive advantage. Many industry case studies are included to support the solution concepts presented.

CHAPTER 3

PRODUCTIVITY AND
RETURN ON INVESTMENT

In order to succeed, companies need to know how to use the information and content that exists within and around their organizations to deliver better productivity and achieve competitive advantage. The key questions to be asked are: How do they assess the Return On Investment (ROI)? How do they establish an infrastructure that enables them to understand the impact of ECM on their organization?

Return on Investment as a driver for deploying ECM is identified in this chapter, demonstrating methodologies, measures and gains in productivity that lead to realizing an ROI.

Figure 3.1: Applications that Drive ROI in Departments

Figure 3.1 displays a grid of applications that drive ROI by department. All ECM technologies and applications can be mapped to an organizational chart. The figure shows a simplified representation of such an organizational chart to include Sales, Services, Research, Manufacturing and Administration.

At a macro level, the value of ECM delivered over the Internet was observed by early pioneers such as Robert Metcalf, the inventor of the Ethernet and Mark Andreesen, the inventor of the Netscape browser.

Robert Metcalf's law states that the "value" or "power" of a network increases in proportion to the square of the number of nodes on the network.

Figure 3.2: Metcalfe's Law

Marc Andreesen, one of the founders of the Web, commented that a network in general behaves in such a way that the more nodes added, the more valuable it becomes. We witnessed this with the phone system—the more phones on the network, the more valuable it is. "Federal Express, in order to grow their business, would add a node in Topeka and business in New York would spike. You see it on the Internet all the time. Every new node, every new server, every new user expands the possibilities for everyone else who's already there."

Similarly, every new ECM application can expand an organization's possibilities and productivity, leading to greater ROI.

Simply creating this global network and gathering mountains of information is not enough. To make effective decisions the data must be put into context and turned into information. It must be easy to find, access and share with key decision makers. ECM solutions create value by facilitating all of this and more.

With some ECM solutions, multiple departments work within a single application. This delivers a greater ROI than multiple departments working across multiple applications. The increase in ROI highlights the need for companies to invest in ECM solutions that deliver a variety of technologies to the organization through a standard platform. ROI, as opposed to simply perceived need, drives the spread of ECM solutions throughout the company. Senior management are able to deliver value to shareholders making each employee's day-to-day tasks simpler and more effective.

Much of the IT industry in the past 50 years has focused on back-office databases and their management in Enterprise Resource Planning (ERP) systems. ERP has driven exceptional ROI by reducing inventory costs, increasing on-time performance and improving decision making. In the same way, ECM delivers ROI by reducing the time it takes to make decisions because those decision makers are properly equipped.

In addition to increased productivity, which is an indirect saving, ROI can also be realized through more direct savings measurements. Immediate, real-time access to up-to-date and accurate electronic file folders with critical business information reduces the need to physically store documents, reducing document costs, storage space and the need for copiers. Of all missing and lost documents, 7.5 percent of paper documents are lost completely; 3 percent of the remainder are misfiled, and approximately $20.00 US in labor is spent filing or retrieving a single document. Just think about the time it takes to find an email from last month!

Faster response times through more efficient operations will noticeably improve customer satisfaction. Whether it is an improved invoicing system or an organized knowledge base for customer self service, ECM ROI can also be measured in terms of overall customer satisfaction. This means happier customers and a well-protected brand image for the company itself.

The financial worksheet on the following page illustrates the annual impact that implementing a software solution has on profitability, cash flows, ROI and payback period.

FINANCIAL WORKSHEET FOR:				
Pharmaceutical Company A*				

Annual Savings	Base	Year 1	Year 2	Year 3
Savings In Printing Costs	$0	$6,075	$6,075	$6,075
Additional Work Productivity	$0	$47,957	$47,957	$47,957
Total Savings Per Period	**$0**	**$54,032**	**$54,032**	**$54,032**

Depreciation Schedule**	Initial	Year 1	Year 2	Year 3
Software	$100,000	$20,000	$20,000	$20,000
Hardware	$0	$0	$0	$0
Total Per Period	**$100,000**	**$20,000**	**$20,000**	**$20,000**

Expensed Costs	Initial	Year 1	Year 2	Year 3
Software	$50,000	$0	$0	$0
Hardware	$0	$0	$0	$0
Batteries	$0	$208	$208	$208
Personnel	$0	$600	$600	$600
Consulting	$0	$0	$0	$0
Training	$0	$202	$0	$0
Total Per Period	**$50,000**	**$1,010**	**$808**	**$808**

Basic Financial Assumptions				
All Federal and State Taxes	50%			
Discount Rate	15%			
Depreciation - Straight Line (Years)	5			

Net Cash Flows	Initial	Year 1	Year 2	Year 3
Total Benefits		$54,032	$54,032	$54,032
Less: Total Costs		$1,010	$808	$808
Less: Depreciation		$20,000	$20,000	$20,000
Net Profit Before Tax		$33,022	$33,224	$33,224
Net Profit After Tax		$16,511	$16,612	$16,612
Add: Depreciation		$20,000	$20,000	$20,000
Net Cash Flow After Taxes	**($115,000)**	**$36,511**	**$36,612**	**$36,612**

Financial Analysis	Results	Year 1	Year 2	Year 3
Annual ROI		28%	52%	73%
3-Year ROI	**73%**			
Discounted cash flows	($115,000)	$31,749	$27,684	$24,073
Cumulative cash flow		($83,251)	($55,568)	($31,495)
Payback (Years)	**3+**	**NA**	**NA**	**NA**
3-Year IRR	-2%			
3-Year NPV	($31,495)			

Figure 3.3: The Annual Impact of Implementing a Software Solution

ROI by Department

Consider group-level applications that are closely aligned to the way people work to achieve ROI. Figure 3.4 represents a typical organizational chart for a company.

Companies consist of many separate departments—Accounting and Finance, Legal, Administration, Marketing, Sales, IT, Research and Development, and so on. Each department has its own productivity requirements, and solutions must be designed to meet many of these requirements and solve problems specific to a particular department. Typically, these solutions are driven by the need to improve efficiency or save money. Examples include: Purchase Order Processing, Invoicing, Project Management, Claims Processing, FDA Compliance, Product Lifecycle Management (PLM), and Sales Readiness, just to mention a few.

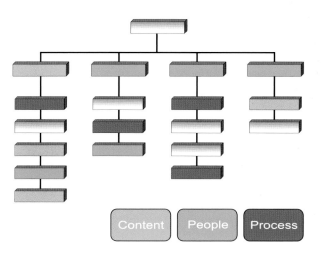

Figure 3.4: Typical Organization

Increasing Productivity

ECM has been increasing productivity within organizations since the early 1980s. Document management systems dramatically reduced paper and storage cost, but perhaps more importantly, increased productivity within the departments that embraced these systems. Now, ECM solutions are a blend of technologies that have come together to create an enterprise infrastructure able to extract ROI in many ways.

One of the underlying principles of ECM is the realization that collaboration has an important role in lending context to content. Capturing the how, when and why content was generated provides an excellent picture as to how relevant the information is to

> Sinclair Knight Merz

Dispersed across geographic boundaries, time zones and companies, Sinclair Knight Merz relies heavily on the effective performance of its virtual teams. The ability to manage, retrieve and re-use documents across all projects and offices is essential, but the high bandwidth cost of a decentralised document management system on a global basis was a major constraint for SKM.

As the company continues to grow, a dedicated wide area network (WAN) represents an increasingly significant component of the IT expenditure and the ability to use leading-edge technology to provide best price performance. A document management system based on a distributed model with partial replication and a single server proved to hold the solution, by optimizing bandwidth and maximizing performance, while curbing associated costs.

A cost-benefit analysis performed on the ECM implementation estimates a 167 percent internal rate of return on investment over a five-year period. The benefits were observed to be predominantly derived from re-use of work and the promotion of virtual teams, which allows the world-wide community of SKM to use best practices while enabling greater team collaboration.

Business Case Benefits and Savings

Internal rate of return 167%

	Year 1	Year 2	Year 3	Year 4	Year 5
Cost	$1.9M	$1.7M	$1.3M	$1.2M	$1.2M
Benefits	$1.5M	$3.1M	$4.6M	$5.2M	$5.5M
Profit/(Loss)	($0.4M)	$1.4M	$3.3M	$4.0M	$4.3M

Re-use of work	Best Practice
Virtual Teams	Document Tracking
Project Focus	Revision Control
Extranets	

Figure 3.5: SKM's Business Benefits and ROI

future undertakings. Being able to easily access accurate information leads to better decisions. Better decisions save time and money. The graph in Figure 3.6 shows the value of making a better decision faster. The area represented by the savings of time shows the true return on investment for an ECM system.

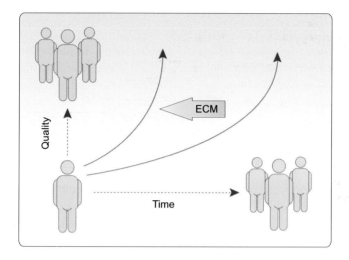

Figure 3.6: The ROI Impact of ECM

The diagram shows that a group normally makes a better decision than a single person, but that they also take a much longer time to do it. The trade-off between the time and the quality of a decision is the basis for managing individuals and groups in many industries. The impact of ECM on changing this equation is shown by the shifting of the trade-off arrows over to the left. The area saved in time by the quality of decisions is the ROI achieved for any given ECM solution.

Today, content and collaboration management is still largely being adopted on a departmental or group level. As infrastructure such as the Internet develops and becomes more transparent and less technically driven, it will become easier to deploy across entire organizations and beyond. Collaborating through ECM solutions will become as simple as clicking on a hyperlink. Simple, effective technology will lead the way to increased ROI.

A new market is emerging to address the needs of knowledge-intensive organizations. Increasing overall organizational effectiveness in a turbulent business world has become a great challenge that ECM can play a role in solving. To achieve ROI while adhering to strict new regulations and legislation, ECM developers will offer applications specific to individual industries. These customized solutions will be of the greatest value if they can deploy across multiple departments, support new technologies and scale to meet the growing needs within the enterprise. The unique ability of ECM to support additional content such as email and rich media files will also increase the solution's value.

Measuring Results

There are many ways to achieve ROI with ECM solutions. To justify the original invest-ment and any further expansion into ECM, organizations must quantify their results. They must capture a baseline measurement of the processes that are to be improved as well as any others that might be affected before adopting an ECM solution. Specific goals must be set and results must be carefully measured. While most organizations will have some type of measurement before the deployment of a solution as a justification for the investment, many will not continue to measure after the deployment. This typically occurs when the savings have become so apparent to all involved that they do not feel it is necessary to measure the obvious. Sometimes, the value of the ECM solution is generated in ways not anticipated by the original justification and there is no easy reference point. This is unfortunate since most ECM solutions result in benefits that far exceed the initial estimate and in ways that were not originally intended. Measuring productivity gains from ECM will normally lead to greater adoption in the future.

Saving Time

Corporate reorganization as well as mergers often create opportunities for ECM solutions to generate ROI. Bringing together disparate accounting systems and managing the paper documents involved can be a difficult task. There is a constant need to refer to paper-based documents under these circumstances. ECM solutions can help with process.

An easy area to measure ROI is document retrieval. It can take anywhere from 10 to 15 minutes to retrieve a paper document, assuming that it is stored on site. To retrieve a document that has been scanned and archived within an ECM solution can take as little as 10 seconds. This resulted in working hours savings of 97 percent in the case of a global leader in the life sciences industry, generating ROI rapidly and creating payback within nine months.

Reebok is always looking for ways to streamline operations, reduce costs and provide employees with an efficient work environment. To automate business application processes and gain a greater return on investment, the company decided to implement an integrated ECM and SAP solution.

Used for document imaging and archiving, the system eliminates the need for manual handling or filing of paper documents. Payment of invoices is processed in conjunction with purchase requisitions, and invoices are scanned and handled digitally. As a result, Reebok's business enterprise is now more automated, productive, and cost-efficient.

"Our experience to date has been a 30 percent increase in productivity in the A/P department. We have reduced costs in many ways, and we have not had to increase staff …We are ultimately held accountable to our end users and to auditors, so it is important that our records are available and in order. The system makes us look good," says Reebok's Accounts Payable Manager.

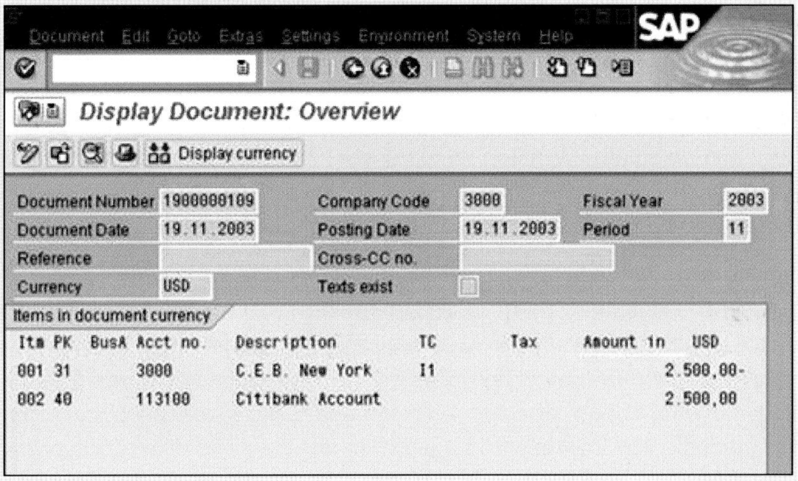

Figure 3.7: An Example of Instant Document Access in Accounts Payable

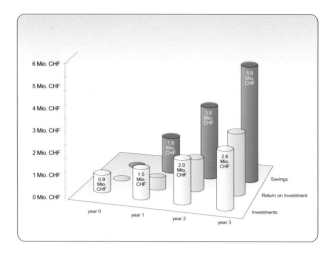

Figure 3.8: Cumulative Investments and Savings

Lowering Distribution Costs

Federations and cooperatives need to report to their members in great detail. The cost to print and courier these reports adds up quickly. Time is lost as paper documents are manufactured and distributed. Waiting an extra week to make an important decision can be costly. Finding information within these reports can be time consuming. Storing these reports for the legislated period of time requires expensive physical space.

One such cooperative in the Financial Services Industry was called upon to generate 15 monthly reports and distribute them to 243 members—over 8 million pages annually. Today, an ECM solution relieves their database by storing their reports in an electronic archive. The information is now closer at hand, and it requires only seconds to find a particular piece of information, whereas it sometimes took several days in the past. The reports are distributed electronically in seconds, saving time and eliminating printing and courier costs.

Increasing Efficiency in Manufacturing

While the time to retrieve documents and the cost to produce and distribute them are tangible savings that are easily measured, they are just the tip of the iceberg. In both Manufacturing and Construction, the savings to be had by improving change management can far exceed these initially obvious areas.

By using an electronic repository with versioning functionality for improved drawing management, engineers are no longer plagued by the circulation of outdated plans. Workflow improves task management. Project status is visible through the solution's accountability and tracking functions. Perhaps harder to measure given that these tools are used to avoid mistakes as opposed to reducing tangible costs, they are certainly major generators of ROI.

A major European bank engaged in two construction projects but only used ECM to manage one of them. This created a unique opportunity to benchmark traditional versus ECM tools and workflows. Contractor management improved, since changes made during the ECM-based project were immediately communicated to all concerned parties. The changes were fully traceable, which reduced the risk of claims and overspending by an estimated 30 percent. Improved change management enabled more efficient planning, resulting in approximate savings of 50 percent. Over five years, a cumulative ROI of 437 percent was realized. The ECM system provided the project team with an efficient tool for information management and dissemination as well as collaboration.

Eliminating Duplication of Effort

In many enterprises, the Marketing Department develops, distributes and archives brand assets that are used for a variety of mediums, including print and the Web. Increasing productivity, controlling distribution and improving market share are all key goals for the Marketing Department—a group that often works within tight budgets. Each day, hours can be wasted by manually searching for files on CDs, desktop systems and servers. Content is often in the wrong file format for its intended use. Marketing content is typically both structured and unstructured data, including desktop publishing files, vector images, bitmap images and rich media files. ECM systems that manage digital assets can dramatically reduce the time it takes to find the right marketing images and collateral. They also eliminate the costly, often error-prone practice of re-creating content. ROI is easily calculated in this case if Marketing staff track their time.

Decreasing Labor Costs

In the Manufacturing sector, the salaries and benefits of employees manufacturing and/or assembling the product are typically the highest single cost. ECM solutions that support efficient methodologies (e.g., Lean Manufacturing, Product Compliance) generate excellent ROI when they can shorten the process and reduce the "human expense." Faster product development and higher responsiveness to change are also outcomes that are typically derived by using ECM solutions effectively. Another source of ECM solution ROI is the reduction of waste, rework and warranty claims by assuring compliance to corporate, customer and government standards at the design and manufacturing stages.

Retaining Staff Reduces Hiring Expenses

Leading edge technology organizations evolve quickly. This can mean long hours, extended travel and high stress situations for employees. Keeping staff happy is often difficult, but the knowledge and experience that they bring to the organization is key to its success. ECM solutions can help retain both employees as well as the knowledge assets that they have either developed or brought with them.

Ensuring that employees are provided with all the tools necessary to do their jobs is important in keeping them happy. Creating an environment in which it is easy to find and share information was the major focus of technology spending after a leading North American telecommunications company conducted an employee satisfaction survey in 1997. A 1.2 million-page intranet was transitioned into a system that pulled all support services information together in one place.

In addition to the benefits of reduced network hardware and software costs, network management savings, HR and incoming personnel productivity savings, this organization recognized a number of qualitative benefits from deployment of the ECM solution. Providing rapid access to information and resources enabled the company to improve the work experience and reduce frustration for new and existing staff thereby improving employee satisfaction. Organized information resources and applications along with integrated search tools reduced the time required for employees to complete standard tasks, such as ordering a mobile phone or reserving facilities, thus increasing productivity and ROI.

Complying Efficiently

To comply with various government regulations throughout the world, organizations are called upon to collect, manage and archive critical business information. Records of all types must be easy to find and easy to present when called upon to do so. ECM solutions can create ROI by managing this process efficiently. Solutions that play a proactive role by securely storing records for a designated period of time as well as cross referencing records to related information and facilitating audit history create additional value. Implementation of best practices for compliance protects the organization from risk while typically streamlining administrative and operational costs. Integrated ECM solutions allow organizations to be proactive in preparing for new or evolving compliance regulations.

Achieving ROI in Government Solutions

The storage and exchange of information is a core business function of government. These same organizations are often called upon to collaborate across the globe. ECM solutions are able to do both efficiently. Perhaps more important for government organizations is the ability to perform these securely.

> HP Singapore

A technology solutions provider, HP Singapore was experiencing rapid growth and an increase in knowledge needs. To establish itself more strongly as an R&D enterprise and increase its leading role in product development, HP Singapore employed ECM technology to facilitate its knowledge strategy and support effective knowledge sharing.

The Web-based solution, named Konnect for 'connecting people with people for knowledge,' supports project and program management and departmental workspaces. Deployed in less than six months, the enterprise-wide implementation allows for capturing, sharing and re-using information and knowledge through workspaces and communities of practice.

Centralizing knowledge has significantly improved project management and collaboration, as access time to information and knowledge has been dramatically reduced from one hour to five minutes. The improvements directly contribute to the organization's goal of operational excellence. Within the first year of implementing the solution, HP Singapore has realized a return on investment (ROI) of approximately 375 percent.

Figure 3.9: HP Singapore's Knowledge Management Vision

Security breaches by white collar criminals, or worse, terrorists, could have a severe impact in terms of financial loss, privacy violations or loss of life. Manually assessing the security of IT systems, networks and applications can take up to 18 months. ECM solutions that manage documents and workflow can cut this by 90 percent based on side-by-side comparisons. Improving this certification process alone creates ROI. Allowing new technologies to deploy up to 16 months faster extends the value of this ECM solution greatly.

Governments also achieve ROI by using ECM solutions for Facilities Management, Case Management, Correspondence Tracking, Program Management, Proposal Management, etc.

Maximizing Education

ECM solutions facilitated communication and collaboration within educational organizations for up to 90 percent less than typical large-scale business groupware systems. These organizations often have over 20,000 users. At an estimated savings of $90 U.S. per user, ROI adds up quickly. These same organizations benefit from being able to function with significantly less IT staff as well. The resulting efficiencies ensure that education dollars are spent on core educational processes as opposed to IT infrastructure.

Spending Healthcare Funds Wisely

Not unlike education, healthcare organizations are often on tight budgets. Patient care is under close scrutiny from the general public, regulators and the media. Patient records must be secure and easily accessed by medical professionals.

This type of collaboration is difficult in the healthcare industry today. Managing the security of information and the disparate nature of industry research and technologies presents a perfect opportunity for ECM solutions. Simplifying the complex processes and communication problems associated with streamlining and advancing healthcare organizations' service levels can not only lead to ROI, but can enhance all aspects of the patient care lifecycle as well.

Extending Applications to Improve Efficiency

Human Resource Departments can often take advantage of Enterprise Application Extensions. HR Departments typically spend up to 70 percent of their time on routine tasks such as address changes or approving travel or vacation, all requiring data re-entry and a search to validate employees with their records. ECM solutions can scan, store, and link email and employee information. Using a workflow, ECM then forwards it to the appropriate entity as an activity request with all employee-related HR records

> Nortel

Nortel is a recognized leader in communications. To be a leader in such a rapidly evolving industry requires great ideas, efficient processes, and retention of great employees. To manage its hiring and departure processes and to provide existing employees with rapid, organized access to the information they need, Nortel looked to enterprise content management.

Employees use their Web browser to access solutions that contain information and processes, such as human resources, facilities, IS, purchasing, travel, business cards, and maps. Organized information and integrated search tools enable users to rapidly access relevant information and act on it. For arriving and departing employees, separate folder areas provide them with relevant information to ensure that their arrival or departure is a positive experience.

Nortel experienced a number of qualitative and quantifiable benefits from deploying an enterprise content management solution. The benefits of reduced network hardware and software costs, network management savings, and HR and incoming personnel productivity savings, resulted in a return on investment of 635 percent over 3 years.

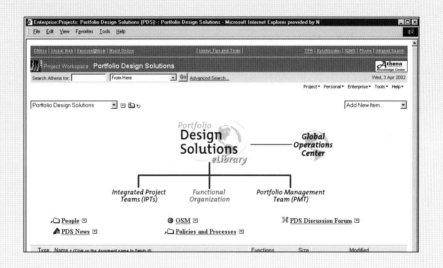

Figure 3.10: Project Workspace at Nortel

being captured in a single, centralized, secure repository. Significant ROI results from eliminating paper-based processes, improved response time to employees, reduced operational costs and increased productivity. Other areas to look for ROI include lowering hardware and maintenance costs.

ECM Will Continue to Provide Excellent ROI

ECM solutions generate excellent ROI. The bottom-line improvements that organizations are attaining from deploying ECM solutions are creating solid payback results. These two factors are driving growth in the ECM sector.

ECM continues to evolve. It all started as a search engine meant to retrieve structured information. Today, ECM encompasses content and collaboration solutions that easily take advantage of both structured as well as unstructured information. Knowledge management has solved many intellectual property and training issues. Document Management has evolved to into Lifecycle Management, Web Content Management, and Digital Asset Management – the list of innovations goes on and on. This constant evolution in the ECM marketplace promises continual ROI for years to come as ECM developers and vendors add value to existing deployments by extending their capabilities.

CHAPTER 4

COMPLIANCE AND CORPORATE GOVERNANCE

Compliance and Corporate Governance is delivered across all departments within an ECM-driven organization. This chapter outlines how ECM solutions are helping many of the world's leading companies address compliance and governance issues. Innovator stories in this chapter demonstrate how organizations are using ECM solutions to comply with legislation, including the U.S. Government Paperwork Elimination Act (GPEA). In these stories, ECM enables organizations to not only achieve compliance but improve business operations. Additional Innovator stories are presented that address email management in the context of corporate governance and overall business improvement.

ECM solutions are playing a major role in helping many of the world's leading companies streamline and accelerate compliance and corporate governance globally.

Corporations in every industry and in all countries face countless government regulations, industry standards and company procedures. How a company manages itself and its compliance efforts has a direct impact on shareholder value. Poor management and/or non-compliance can lead to lost business, financial penalties and even criminal charges. In some industries, failing an auditor's inspection can ultimately lead to a company being closed down until corrective action is taken.

It is critical for any organization to be well managed and compliant, but there is more to compliance than simply following rules. At the heart of each set of industry regulations and standards are basic principles for doing good business—principles derived from the experience of best practices, policies and procedures for each industry. They are often designed to prevent mistakes from being repeated. To understand how ECM helps organizations manage compliance and governance, it is important to differentiate between the two concepts.

Compliance and Corporate Governance Defined

Today's business environment is more complex and regulated than ever, and for good reason. Corporate issues involving fraudulent accounting, malfeasance and data quality issues frequently dominate news headlines. CEOs and Boards of Directors (BoD) are under public scrutiny and, as a result, regulatory requirements have emerged to address these issues using commonly accepted principals of corporate governance.

Figure 4.1: Compliance and Corporate Governance

Each company has unique corporate governance activities. A company's business units, departments, operations, industry and geographic locations all define the environment in which it operates. These variables combine in a very specific way to determine how the company can and, in the case of regulations, must operate.

Formally, corporate governance has been defined as "...the structure that is intended to make sure that the right questions get asked and that checks and balances are in place to make sure that the answers reflect what is best for the creation of long-term, sustainable value." (Robert A. Monks and Nell Minnow, Corporate Governance, Third Edition, 2004, Blackwell Publishing Ltd.). Informally, corporate governance may be defined as how a company manages itself. A company's environment influences and determines governance activities, which include methods to direct, manage and control the company. These methods need to be communicated company-wide and improved over time to drive efficiency and cost savings or to respond to the changing needs of the business.

Compliance may then be defined as conforming to a rule. Types of compliance 'rules' include:

• Government Legislation and Regulation;

• Industry Standards;

• Internal Company Policy and Procedures.

'Rule' implies a consequence for being non-compliant. Government agencies created to enforce legislation, industry standard bodies and corporate directives are examples of such typical regulatory bodies. Furthermore, compliance with the rules can be required or voluntary. Figure 4.2 depicts compliance types and typical corresponding consequences for being non-compliant.

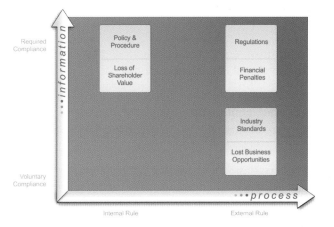

Figure 4.2: Compliance Continuum

In summary, it is important to identify that compliance needs to happen according to a defined rule (regulation, standard or policy) to have meaning, and that compliance is only one component of corporate governance.

The Sarbanes-Oxley Act

One of the regulations that has garnered much attention is the Sarbanes-Oxley Act (SOX). The Sarbanes-Oxley Act, administered in 2002 by the Securities and Exchange Commission (SEC), was enacted to prevent scandals (such as the high-profiled ones in the recent past) from reoccurring.

At its highest level, the Sarbanes-Oxley Act is about restoring investor confidence in the integrity of financial reporting. It is a piece of legislation which has caused some confusion with respect to Corporate Governance. SOX is a regulation which requires compliance; the activities required by the company to be compliant affect a company's procedures and systems.

In summary, SOX regulates a component of corporate governance—the procedures and systems regarding internal controls over financial reporting.

The Sarbanes-Oxley legislation impacts the following four main areas:

- Corporate Accountability and Responsibility
- Internal Controls & Procedures
- Audit and Accounting
- Enhanced Disclosure and Reporting Requirements

While Sarbanes-Oxley is complex and broad in its scope, there are only three specific sections which are having significant impact on corporations:

- Section 302: Corporate Responsibility for Financial Reports – The CEO and CFO must prepare a quarterly statement certifying financial statements and disclosures. This has been in effect since August 2002 – certifications can found in the 10k and 10q filed with the SEC.
- Section 404: Management Assessment of Internal Controls – An "internal control report" must accompany an annual report taking responsibility for and assessing the effectiveness of internal controls. Compliance dates are described in the following section, the earliest being for calendar years ending on or after November 15th, 2004.
- Section 409: Real-Time Issuer Disclosures – Material changes affecting financial disclosures must be reported on a "rapid and current basis." Compliance is effective beginning in August 2004.

Companies are in great need of technology solutions that can organize, automate and make efficient the effort involved in complying with these sections. ECM solutions are designed to enable organizations to operate in accordance with SOX and other regulations.

Why Organizations Need Corporate Governance

Two key objectives contribute to why organizations need to address governance: mitigating risk and optimizing operations. The primary goal is to maintain and increase shareholder value. Poor governance exposes a company to unacceptable risks and the threat of disastrous consequences.

In a growing number of industries, organizations are required to not only achieve regulatory compliance but to prove compliance as well—and penalties for non-compliance are severe.

But improved governance goes far beyond simply mitigating risk and avoiding penalties. Regulations are based on demands that inherently describe optimal business operations. By meeting regulations, organizations ensure that their business processes adhere to industry-established best practices and procedures.

Corporations across the globe are wisely striving to learn from—rather than react to— the enormous governance failures of companies such as Enron and Parmalat. Each industry has its own regulators and regulations but much can be learned and applied to organizations in any industry.

ECM allows a systemizing of these processes and their underlying data, so that organizations ensure nothing important is omitted, and everyone is aware of who is responsible for doing what, when, how, why and where. This helps ensure that everyone is not just "doing his or her thing," and that time, money and other resources are used efficiently.

Governance is changing business on a global level. A representative sample of the various global regulations and regulatory bodies is shown in Figure 4.3:

	USA and Canada	Europe and Rest of the World
Telecommunications	CRTC	CCITT, OfCom, OFTEL
Financial Services	CFTC, FDIC, FRB, FSA NAIC, NASD, OSFI, SEC	Basel 2, BaFin, CCA, FSA FSAP, GICS, IMF
Engineering	APQP, QS	ISO9000, ISO14000
Government	DoD, PIPEDA, RDIMS	DOMEA, EMEA, PRO, SAGA, MoReq, VERS
Pharmaceuticals	FDA, Health Canada, TPD	CPMP, EMEA, MHLW
Healthcare	HIPAA	
Cross-Industry	Bill 198, COCO, OSHA SEC, SOX	King II, KonTraG, Legge 321, LSF, Turnbull,

Figure 4.3: Who Sets the Regulations for Your Business?

A Platform for Compliance and Corporate Governance

Enterprise Content Management platforms play a key role in allowing organizations to provide compliance and corporate governance in a cost effective and efficient manner. Figure 4.4 provides a framework for how the components of ECM support business requirements to ensure governance and compliance with appropriate laws, regulations and court orders that form part of the environment in which an organization operates.

Although technology alone cannot satisfy compliance requirements, it can play a critical role when integrated into the proper processes and organizational structure.

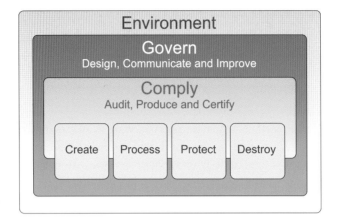

Figure 4.4: DLM Functionality is the Core to Efficient Information Compliance

ECM platforms assist in defining and supporting governance policies by providing capabilities to specify the policies and by allowing the organization to enforce and audit compliance with these policies. The following ECM technologies are key to helping organizations achieve compliance and manage corporate governance:

• Document Lifecycle Management

• Archiving and Records Management

• Enterprise Application Extensions

• Email Management

• Rich Media and Digital Asset Management

• Web Content Management

• Search

Document Lifecycle Management (DLM)

Pertinent corporate information must be identified, captured and communicated in a manner and timeframe that enables people to carry out their responsibilities. Effective communication must also occur in a broader sense, flowing down and across an organization, as well as to customers, suppliers, regulators and shareholders. Compliance

The Fluor Corporation has more than 2,000 engineering, construction, procurement and maintenance projects. Operating unit Fluor Hanford is a prime contractor to the Department of Energy (DOE) at the Hanford Site in Washington State. Hanford is one of the world's largest environmental cleanup projects. Correspondence between Fluor Hanford and DOE averages more than 2,000 letters per year, including attachments. Overall, the Hanford project involves millions of pages of records, including emails, documents, and various media such as photos, videos, and engineering drawings.

Fluor Hanford needed a solution to improve a labor-intensive, paper-based correspondence process. In addition to ease-of-use concerns, new regulations governing electronic records were also key drivers for moving to a new system.

By upgrading its Enterprise Content Management (ECM) system to include correspondence workflow and records management, Fluor Hanford has been able to meet the new regulatory requirements.

The system also provides simple and secure records management tools, and a streamlined correspondence process. The Livelink ECM solution provides easy access to all project information, including records databases, schedules, and engineering drawings. With good access to project information, Fluor Hanford employees and project managers are better equipped to meet or beat cleanup milestones at the Hanford site.

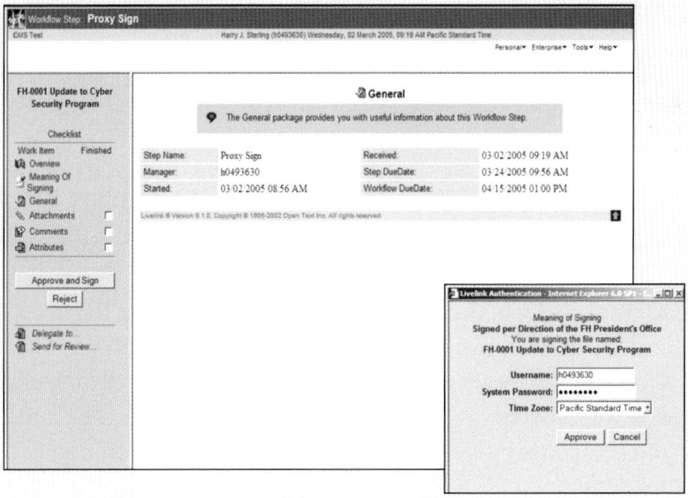

Figure 4.5: Digital Signatures are Used in a Correspondence Workflow at Fluor Hanford

and governance necessitates the effective capture and dissemination of information. As part of an ECM solution, document lifecycle management plays a crucial role in helping organizations to achieve compliance cost effectively. DLM delivers the ability to capture any type of electronic information and apply retention schedules to it, ensuring that it is archived or deleted and physically destroyed. This capability is essential to organizations pursuing compliance. Permissions and auditing capabilities provide controlled access to critical information. An audit trail capture ensures that all access and actions are recorded so as to prevent unnecessary access to information that is subject to privacy regulations. Chapter 8 provides an in-depth discussion of DLM.

Archiving and Records Management (RM)

Maintaining impeccable records throughout their lifecycle can be difficult, especially in globally dispersed organizations whose files need to be stored for decades. Companies are increasingly seeking new ways to effectively preserve valuable data and ensure destruction of obsolete records. In order to meet stringent regulatory standards, tracking of records throughout their lifecycle is becoming an increasingly complex activity that requires the integration of records management practices and procedures with collaboration and content management.

ECM platforms provide technology that allows organizations to specify types of information and the retention schedules associated with these types of information. A records management system enables an auditor or interested party to identify underlying reasons for a chosen policy. When policies change, the system keeps track of old policies, allowing interested parties to see the sequence and justifications for all policy changes over time.

Every jurisdiction in the world has legislation on what types of information must be retained by organizations and for what period of time. The Food and Drug Administration (FDA) specifies that clinical trials data must be retained for 100 years, while SEC rule 17a specifies that all electronic communication between the client and traders within a brokerage firm must be retained for three years. Many jurisdictions have standards that dictate what functionality records management systems provide. Examples of these include the Department of Defense's DoD 5015.2 specification, the Public Records Office (PRO) specification from the United Kingdom of Great Britain, and the VERS standard from the government of Victoria, Australia. Agencies and organizations that fall under the influence or jurisdiction of one of these standards are advised—even required—to acquire a records management system which has been certified according to the appropriate standard.

Accounting and Records Retention

Following recent corporate scandals, financial records in accounting practices have become a core compliance requirement. Traditionally, organizations relied on the original paper files, invoices, receipts, order forms and more to validate finance practices and respond to litigation. While paper files may help organizations comply with mandates, they also increase the possibility of error, inefficiency and corporate expense. In addition to requiring time and resources to find critical documents, storing paper files often creates enormous administrative overhead.

Though organizations generally store financial documents for extended periods, they fail to fulfill many current regulations on long-term storage. Compliance necessitates that companies present requested financial records upon request, demonstrate how each record was used, or show other records that contributed to a designated process.

ECM solutions can help organizations meet transaction-related requirements and satisfy storage requirements by archiving all documents in a central repository. By enabling organizations to produce images of original documents and linking these scanned records to related financial records, ECM helps organizations prove the accuracy of their financial records.

Enterprise Application Extensions (EAE)

An ECM system supports the scanning and storing of all accounting documents in their original state and in a format that cannot be altered. When integrated with an enterprise resource planning (ERP) system, ECM can link scanned financial records (such as invoices) and ERP-generated documents to the respective booking section in the ERP system. If an auditor asks for a particular invoice, employees can access supporting documents to confirm the invoice's accuracy and justify its use. An audit trail traces the activity path for each requested document. When critical information is destroyed in compliance with corporate policy or regulations, an audit entry for the object in question can be presented as proof, in some instances allowing an organization to avoid spoliation penalties or summary judgments.

Email Management

Records management legislation governs the content of information in question but not the format in which it is stored, communicated or conveyed. Records management legislation covers all forms of electronic communication, such as email and instant messaging. However, due to the unprecedented rate at which email has been adopted by organizations and the sheer volume of communication that occurs through this medium, email represents one of the largest information and risk management problems today. Many organizations have faced large losses because they lacked an effective email management system. A major tobacco manufacturer was fined $2.75 million U.S. in August, 2004, because key executives failed to comply with a court order to retain emails relevant to pending litigation. ECM platforms reduce risks and maintain compliance with regulations that apply specifically to email.

Regulations such as SEC Rule 17 a 4 and NASD 3010 define strict rules on how long emails must be retained. Indexes on emails and attachments allow for auditing and recovery of all content upon request. ECM solutions provide both the technical and logistical functionality needed to fulfill these requirements.

Rich Media and Digital Asset Management (DAM)

Compliance and corporate governance necessitates the communication of appropriate policies, obligations and standard operating procedures to all employees responsible for the implementation of these policies. An ECM platform delivers rich-media training formats including synchronized voice, video, text and presentations. As well as supporting these formats, the system automatically captures all necessary data required as proof that employees have been trained and certified. This is essential to organizations in industries like financial services and pharmaceuticals, where non-compliance can mean the collapse of the entire organization.

The Investment Dealers Association of Canada's Policy Number 6 lays out guidelines for the ongoing training and certification of employees. Under these guidelines, firms are required to develop compliance training and maintain proof of successful completion of training in employee records. ECM platforms can be used to automate both the process and the documentation for certification, enabling organizations to lower the costs of compliance.

Web Content Management (WCM)

Web content management functionality allows organizations to effectively distribute compliance or governance-related information to large numbers of employees. As part of an ECM solution, WCM reduces the cost of communicating standard operating procedures, quality control documentation and policies to a global audience. The ISO 9000 standard is an example of an international best practice that has been widely adopted by manufacturing organizations worldwide. The standard is so prevalent that certification has become a requirement for doing business in the manufacturing sector. ECM platforms have proven themselves essential to cost effective implementation of ISO 9000 quality documentation.

Search

Although the technologies outlined above help organizations comply with standards and regulations, they do not prevent litigation or audits. U.S. Freedom of Information Act (FOIA) legislation can force organizations to produce information within very short periods of time. Search technology, as part of an integrated ECM solution, can help auditors or legal discovery staff locate all relevant or required information. A records management system can be used to group this information into a consolidated list, where "holds" can be applied to suspend the lifecycle of the information. Holds can be applied to entire categories of information using classifications and taxonomies. A workflow can be implemented to automate the review of all collected information.

On completion of the review, export and packaging capabilities allow the information to be produced for delivery to the requesting party.

Financial Services: Accreditation and Certification Management

In the financial industry, employees dealing in the sale of financial products (mutual funds, stocks and other investment products) must be registered with one or more regulatory authorities. Employees are registered with authorities based on where the employee operates and which products they wish to sell. These registrations are term-based (usually annual or multi-year) and are renewed based on criteria established by each authority.

To provide highly effective corporate management and training solutions for the Financial Services sector, ECM gives users the ability to provide corporate learning and training programs that meet regulatory objectives.

ECM was designed to address a number of needs: growth in regulatory reporting requirements; leveraging existing investments in training content and programs; maintaining detailed registration and licensing records for compliance management; and the need to manage all detailed records necessary for regulatory compliance.

Financial Services: Anti-Money Laundering

In the wake of the September 11 terrorist attacks in the United States, the focus on money laundering prevention and detection has intensified. Governments around the world have enacted laws requiring banks and other financial institutions to take an active role in preventing and detecting money laundering. Money laundering is a risk that must be managed at the highest levels of any organization.

Financial institutions in particular are vulnerable to money laundering due to the range of customer relationships they manage and the array of products, services and transaction types they offer. Weaknesses in policies and procedures, regulatory and internal audit compliance functions, and transaction and information systems all compound the financial institution's exposure to money laundering risks.

ECM provides a secure environment for managing customer information, including multi-lingual forms and workflow, that is used to capture, track and verify information required to authenticate customers.

Sasol North America (SNA) employs approximately 700 people in five major locations in the United States. SNA is fully owned by Sasol Limited, an international producer of coals, fuels, gases and lubricants. An ECM repository provides support for secure document management and ensures ISO and regulatory compliance.

Workflow is the key tool for supporting the regulatory requirements for controlled documents: check-in/approval workflows were created at SNA to support ISO/PSM (Process Safety Management) change control audit requirements necessary to meet compliance and maintain the ISO certification process. Document control is also supported by the ability to receive email notifications whenever a document is updated.

The controlled document environment enables the organization to keep accurate and current process-safety information in accordance with OSHA (Occupational Safety and Health Administration) 1910.110 PSM policies. The ability to set attributes and advanced search functionality support tracking procedure certification. "We cannot remain in business if we don't remain in compliance with the law," says the ISO Coordinator at SNA.

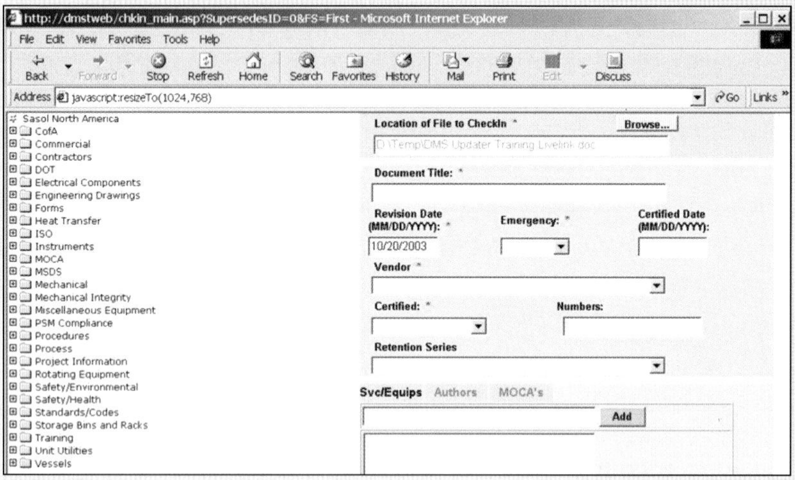

Figure 4.6: Check-in/Approval Workflow at Sasol

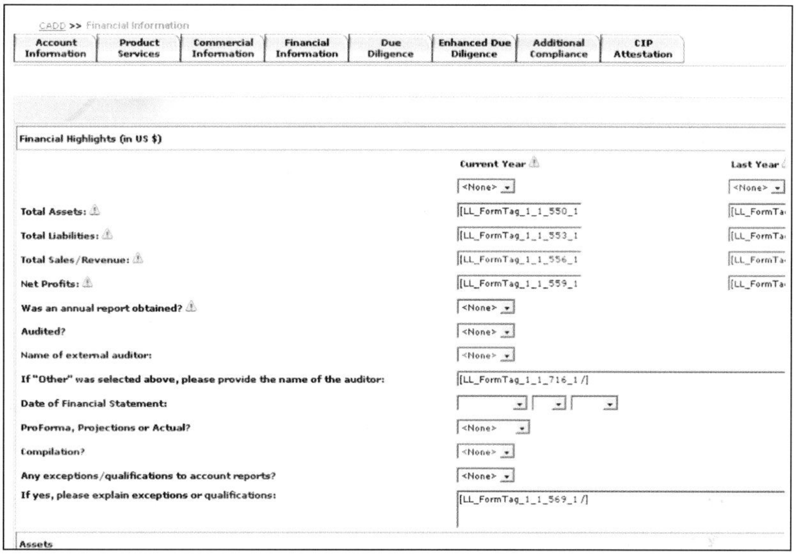

Figure 4.7: Anti-Money Laundering

Compliance Applications

As part of an integrated system, ECM can provide a powerful and targeted tool for delivering information and training on anti-money laundering policies and procedures to all employees. The system ensures compliance with Sections 312 and 326 of the U.S. Patriot Act by automating the generation and escalation of notifications for account renewals, as well as enabling effective management of archived records when closing accounts. With this solution, ECM reduces the risk associated with non-compliance by making control of the customer acquisition process more efficient and compliant.

Pharmaceutical: Clinical Trials

ECM provides the infrastructure, knowledge management and real-time collaborative workspaces that pharmaceutical employees need in order to share, manage and analyze clinical trial data throughout the entire clinical trial process. ECM's combined content management and collaboration functionality helps to reduce costs and improve quality by providing instant access to CRFs, SAEs, queries, patient diaries and inventory reports. ECM extends an organization's ability to manage and share clinical data across organizations and with partnering companies, such as Contract Research Organizations (CROs) and sponsor companies, by providing a secure extranet environment in which researchers can work together.

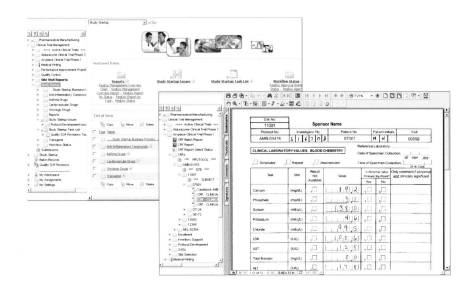

Figure 4.8: Clinical Trials Applications

Government: Email Management

Email messages and attachments represent business records that must be retained and managed securely to support regulatory compliance, avoid legal fines or litigation costs, and satisfy auditing requirements. Regulations like SEC 17-a4, NASD 3010 or DoD 5015.2 define strict rules as to how and for how long emails must be retained. Indexes on emails and attachments allow for auditing and recovery of all content when requested. ECM solutions provide both the technical and logistical functionality to fulfill these requirements completely and efficiently.

ECM: Bringing it All Together

All companies today face the difficult challenge of maintaining performance while operating in an increasingly risky and regulated environment. The key to successful compliance with high corporate governance standards is to ensure that consistent processes are rapidly deployed throughout an organization, that all critical information is managed, and that people are fully trained and able to work together within the compliance framework.

ECM provides organizations with an enterprise-wide platform that delivers compliance and governance solutions. ECM solutions were designed to address a number of governance needs: growth in regulatory reporting requirements; levering existing investments in training content and programs; maintaining detailed registration and licensing records for compliance

> Vintage Petroleum

Vintage Petroleum, Inc. is a rapidly growing independent oil and gas company. A large organization with facilities across the globe, Vintage operates its satellite offices as independent smaller businesses, while processes such as invoicing remain centralized at the corporate headquarters. As a result, the company's U.S. accounting office processes approximately 10,000 invoices per month.

The company selected ECM as a platform for business process improvements to increase productivity, control information and meet compliance requirements associated with the Sarbanes-Oxley Act. In addition, the solution manages the invoicing process, maintains corporate content and enables employees to access information in a central repository.

Invoicing cycle times at Vintage have been shortened thanks to a more controlled process. All invoices are stored in a central location and can be reviewed and processed from various locations. As well, using reporting capabilities, Vintage has improved its forecasting process and its audit and revision controls to ensure compliance with regulations such as Sarbanes-Oxley.

		NORTH		WEST		EAST	
		PAID	UNPAID	PAID	UNPAID	PAID	UNPAID
2001	2001 Q 1	$849.00	$6,314.00	$408.00	$.00	$.00	$.00
	2001 Q 2	$2,975.00	$.00	$478.00	$.00	$.00	$.00
	2001 Q 3	$28,490.00	$.00	$4,668.00	$.00	$.00	$.00
	2001 Q 4	$323,870.00	$1,293.00	$75,241.00	$.00	$3,609.00	$.00
	2001	$356,184.00	$7,607.00	$80,795.00	$.00	$3,609.00	$.00
2002	2002 Q 1	$7,964,921.00	$.00	$1,798,193.00	$.00	$254,781.00	$.00
	2002 Q 2	$13,937,544.00	$410,066.00	$2,360,406.00	$1,863.00	$1,057,428.00	$577.00
	2002 Q 3	$4,871,260.00	$1,726,000.00	$1,328,274.00	$363,216.00	$294,349.00	$190,182.00
	2002 Q 4	$12,055.00	$19,915.00	$.00	$108.00	$.00	$.00
	2002	$26,785,780.00	$2,155,981.00	$5,486,873.00	$365,187.00	$1,606,558.00	$190,759.00
		$27,144,029.00	$2,172,990.00	$5,567,668.00	$365,187.00	$1,610,193.00	$190,759.00

Figure 4.9: A Data Mart at Vintage Petroleum

management; and the need to manage all detailed records necessary for regulatory compliance.

With a proven history for implementing compliant records management solutions, including ISO 9000, the U.S. Patriot Act, SEC, DOE, and OSHA, ECM delivers the document and process management functionality required, for example, by the Sarbanes-Oxley act in the U.S. ECM provides a secure environment for managing customer information, including multilingual form and workflow, to capture, track and authenticate customer information. As part of an integrated system, ECM can provide a powerful and targeted tool for delivering information and training on anti-money laundering policies. The system ensures compliance by automating the generation and escalation of notifications for account renewals, as well as effective management of archived records when closing accounts. ECM reduces the risks associated with non-compliance by making the control of information and process more efficient, transparent and compliant.

In the chapters that follow, we'll take a closer look at all of the solutions that are inherent to effective enterprise content management deployments. The application of ECM to implementing governance solutions within specific departments of an organization or across various industries have many similarities.

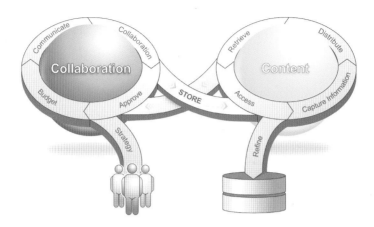

Figure 5.1: Creating an Annual Budget

One of the critical tasks of the Enterprise is the creation and monitoring of the annual budget for the organization. There is a need to co-ordinate all of the resources that will be used by the organization to produce the goods and services that keeps that group in business. This lifecycle begins with a **strategy** developed by the executive. The Accounting team will then take this strategy and develop a corporate **budget** which is **communicated** to the middle management team. Then the department (or division) budgets are developed by the management team.

Collaboration is at the heart of the budget process during the development of plans and implementation objectives. Typically, there are several stages, including multiple reviews and **approvals**. Once the new budgets have final approval and are tagged with relevant metadata for reference during the course of the year, the budget and all its components are integrated with the ERP system of the organization.

With the budget securely **stored in** a repository, the departments, regardless of location, can **access** these materials in a self-service manner through secure Web publishing and can compare their progress throughout the year. The materials can now be **retrieved** and also transform each desired budget module that best suits their **distribution** needs by department or division.

It is critical to the success of an organization and to the executives to **capture information** about the effectiveness of operations and any underlying issues. This information can be leveraged so that the original budget and future budgets can be **refined** based on real-world feedback and results. This information can be stored in an archive along with budgets from prior years to create a knowledge repository that will lead to more effective operations and increased accuracy of budgeting.

CHAPTER 5

THE ENTERPRISE

Effectively and securely managing content is good for business. When information is properly managed, it is highly accessible and easy to use. The right information at the fingertips of the right person can make the difference in completing a timely response to the opportunity of a lifetime for an organization. When an entire enterprise can provide effective and timely responses to changing market situations; that is the ultimate in competitive advantage and flexibility.

By improving business processes across the enterprise, organizations stand to recover their investment, decrease time to market and increase overall productivity.

At this very moment, the critical breakthrough or business practice improvement that could sharpen competitive edge exists somewhere in an organization—in the engineer's notepad, in the product manager's briefcase or embedded in an email. Such seeds of innovation, an organization's intellectual capital, too often go untapped.

Enterprise Content Management (ECM) represents a critical new stage in the advancement of the Information Age. ECM is more than just a product or a solution. It describes both a philosophical approach and the underlying technologies used to help businesses transform content into competitive advantage.

The critical value of ECM solutions at the Enterprise level lies in the fact that they transcend departmental and organizational boundaries, leading to value creation that is greater than the sum of its parts. This is an evolution of ECM that is not easily achieved at the beginning but instead requires a carefully planned process of adoption.

For an organization to effectively take advantage of ECM solutions at the enterprise level, it must have the leadership of the executive team. Any inter-departmental use of knowledge will almost always require intervention and direction from the executive team.

Executive Department

The Executive Department is the critical source of information that the organization requires to manage itself. Therefore, this department needs timely management of knowledge and intellectual property (IP). A particular mandate of the executive group is to achieve close co-ordination among departments.

ECM solutions for Executive Departments provide a context in which management practices can be treated as intellectual property that can be created and inventoried for current and future use. Executive Departments have high content challenges that require a variety of ECM solutions. The Executives must share knowledge with colleagues from other departments, customers, partners and suppliers to manage new programs and proposals as well as develop effective new products and services. Effective use of ECM will make an executive team more productive. This is critical to achieving competitive advantage.

In many industries, the Executive Department is the most important in the company. In fast-changing environments, co-ordination with just one or two departments such as Marketing or Research and Development can mean the difference between success and failure. The role of ECM with executives covers both collaboration and content requirements. For the purpose of this discussion, we will define the Executive Department as the Board of Directors, Senior Management and Officers of the company.

The executive group has many operational and strategic duties. Some of these include governance and regulatory obligations. As we discussed in Chapter 4, most major regulations involve at least an overseeing function by the executive group. Legislation such as the Sarbanes-Oxley Act (SOX) is promising to make this involvement even more direct for members of the Executive Department.

Balancing Governance and Productivity

The biggest challenge of an Executive Department is improving the productivity of the organization while meeting quality and governance goals. This is a delicate balancing act for executives, since an over emphasis on one area could cause problems in the other. For example, being overly efficient in the short term can create profits that are then offset by long-term regulatory problems that restrict operations and severely damage the long-term value of the organization. The reverse is also true. Too much adherence to regulatory or litigious concerns can create too much overhead and hurt the bottom line. Achieving and maintaining a balance between these two requirements is the responsibility of the executive team.

Board Management

One of the most common executive management tasks is reporting financial results to the board. The board has a duty to represent shareholders by proper review and discussion of performance and results. This is a critical function of the board and, for public companies, is an area governed by the Sarbanes-Oxley legislation. ECM delivers this information via secure Web access and permits discussion and deliberation over the Internet. This proves to be advantageous for board members entrusted with governance of the organization. Not only is electronic transition of information beneficial (because of its immediacy), but the information is also recorded and archived for future retrieval. Another benefit is the elimination of travel costs and logistical delays. Using online collaboration tools also permits the capture of decision-making for future reference, a critical aspect of Sarbanes-Oxley.

Establishing Company-wide Goals

The most important task of a management team is to create a budget. Without one, organizations lack company-wide goals. Therefore, effective organizations create budget documents that are a result of bottom-up collaboration to achieve "buy in." It is critical that this collaboration can be captured for future reference.

In today's business environment, maintaining a competitive edge while satisfying the increased scrutiny of industry regulators is the critical balance that the executive team must achieve.

Regulatory compliance is a primary concern of global organizations today. Both financial regulations such as Sarbanes-Oxley and Basel Capital Accord II, as well as industry-specific regulations such as New Drug Approvals (NDAs) for the FDA, are creating new challenges for firms. It is now more important that ever to ensure that all employees understand regulatory requirements, and that the company can prove their compliance.

Capabilities associated with Employee Accreditations provide the infrastructure to support effective employee compliance initiatives by:

- Ensuring that training courses, product information and corporate information are delivered to the right employees at the right time;

- Effectively distributing tests, surveys, questionnaires, courseware and other corporate content;

- Automatically tracking employee progress, accurately analyzing the effectiveness of courses and comparing the performance of individuals taking the same courses;

> Johnson Controls

The dig permit process at Johnson Controls, a global market leader in automotive systems and facility management, was a manual, paper-driven process. Every time a project required a new excavation to be initiated, a single sheet of paper gathered all of the requisite details and signatures. This process resulted in lengthy approval processes and untraceable documents and links, consequently delaying the organization's services to its clients.

The solution was a parallel, automated process, and ECM was identified as the vehicle to implement it. Moving to an automated, workflow-based approval process provides Web-based, real-time reporting, allowing managers to check the workflow status at any time. In addition, customers have gained visibility of the process through direct access to the dig permits in progress.

Prioritization and process definition have been enabled by the change management process, which allows for improved user organization and clearer form structures. Every account worldwide at Johnson Controls has a project portal page which leads to controlled documents stored in the system, granting easy access to vital documents, that are never lost.

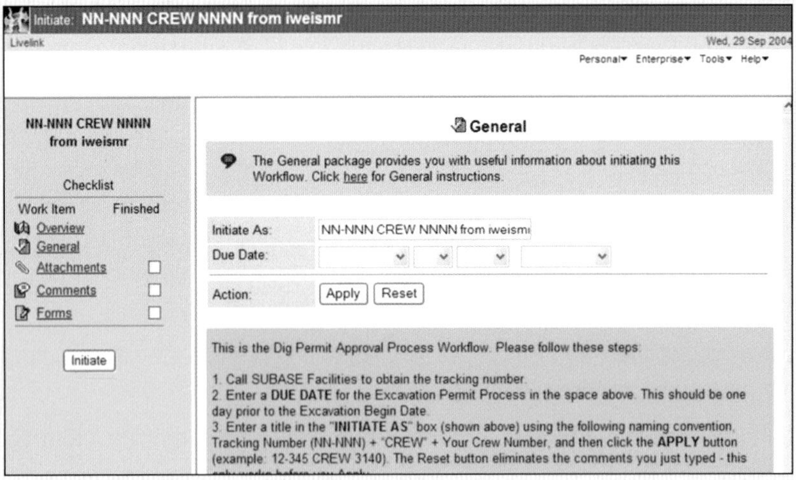

Figure 5.2: Dig Permit Approval Process at Johnson Controls

- Building a full suite of exams and questionnaires in a variety of formats, including multiple choice, single answer and short essay;

- Incorporating standard multimedia types, including HTML, Word, PDF, Flash and more;

- Ensuring that these learning initiatives map correctly to employee licensing and certification requirements as they apply to corporate regulations such as Sarbanes-Oxley, Basel II and the U.S. Patriot Act.

Committee Management

A committee can be any group of people working together for a particular task. Typically, committee members work across organizations and geographic boundaries. Most often, their assignment to a committee is in addition to regular duties. The challenge for organizations is to enable disparate committee members to collaborate effectively and efficiently, minimizing time and costs spent on achieving objectives:

- By the time committee initiatives reach consensus, have the results of decisions lost their impact because the issues at hand are not as critical as they were when the committee was founded?

- Do geographic boundaries impair the ability of committee members to collaborate effectively?

- Have the actual costs of committee initiatives surpassed projected costs?

- Does the impact of committee decisions fall short of its potential scope because committees lack an effective means of publicly communicating their decisions?

With an ECM solution for online committees, organizations can facilitate informal decision-making with quick polls and more structured voting requirements with a comprehensive forthcoming eBalloting system—ensuring that consensus is reached according to the organization's rules. With ECM, organizations can implement tools for managing committees, their structures and their members.

ECM Adoption Stages

At the Enterprise level, it is important to understand the process by which the organization adopts ECM solutions. Understanding the stages of adoption will lead to more effective results achieved in a more efficient manner. As with other forms of learning and technology adoption, ECM is normally adopted within organizations in a very distinctive, staged manner. While the definition of stages can be arbitrary, the concept of set stages is con-

In response to the new compliance requirements posed by Sections 302 and 906 of the Sarbanes-Oxley Act, UBS, one of the world's leading financial institutions, implemented an internal certification process for financial reports, in which the senior executives of the individual business areas formally certify their financial figures and processes via a 'sub-confirmation' process.

During the internal certification process, appropriate persons are notified via email when their input is required and are then granted personalized access to the relevant documents on the UBS intranet. All relevant processes are archived and tracked in a log file. The CEO and Group Controller—generally the CFO—issue a final certification for the Security Exchange Commission only when all internal processes have been completed.

The UBS corporate governance portal enables the company's business managers worldwide to collaborate on developing internal and external business reports. Relevant departments have access to a complete overview and status of the certification processes at all times. All related processes have been automated and simplified, expediting the entire certification process.

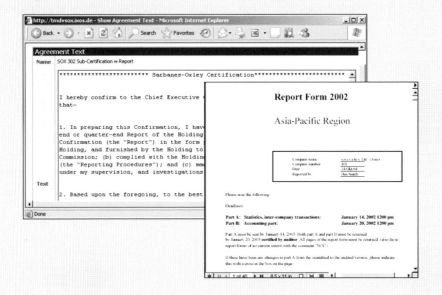

Figure 5.3: Examples of Documents for the SOX Certification Process

stant. This discussion provides one set of stage definitions. These can be adapted to suit the needs of your organization. Stage identification is critical to deployment success. Knowing what stage you are at is a key factor in the readiness identification of the organization to accept change and move on to the next stage. While it is possible to jump stages, this is typically only done by going through a stage in an accelerated manner.

ECM adoption can be defined in seven stages that range from the simple adoption of a single solution in a department to the most complex adoption involving an entire marketplace. The difference between the two is substantial, and it is unwise to jump from a solution for 50 users directly to a solution for 1 million users. There are very distinct phases that an organization must go through to evolve from a single departmental deploy to a marketplace deployment.

The table below lists the basic attributes of each stage:

Stage	Description	Organization Level	Users	Applications
1	Application	Department	<1,000	Single solution
2	Multi-Department	Division	2,000+	Single to many departments
3	Multi-Application	Department/Division	2,000+	Multiple applications to one department
4	Application Standard	Enterprise	5,000+	Single application for company
5	Multi-Application	Enterprise	10,000+	Multi-App For company
6	Extended Applications	Extranet to named users inside the firewall	20,000+	Single external App for a department
7	Multiple Extended Applications	Online Marketplace	100,000	Multiple applications with guest access in a non-secure market

Figure 5.4: This table shows the gradual learning curve that is followed as applications are first delivered as a single solution and scaled up to a full marketplace.

A typical ECM deployment begins with Stage 1, which is a simple adoption of an application that solves a particular departmental problem. This is shown in Figure 5.5. Typically, the deployment is made to less than 1,000 people, and it is normally sought and deployed by a small department manager who is the business owner of the problem.

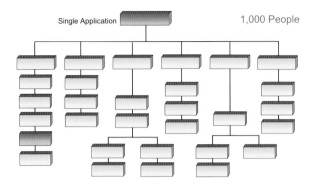

Figure 5.5: Stage 1 – Department Application

Stage 1 is followed by Stage 2, the adoption of the same solution in other departments.

Normally, the IT Department takes an existing and proven ECM solution to other departments that have similar problems. Typically, 2,000 or so people are involved.

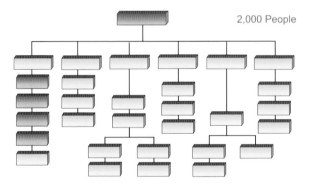

Figure 5.6: Stage 2 – Multiple Departments deploying the same Application

Stage 3 is the adoption of additional solutions within the same department, as shown in Figure 5.8. Here, the original ECM solution is extended by other ECM components within the same department, typically by the same business owner and possibly by IT.

> bioMérieux

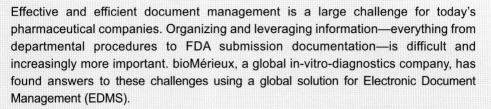

Effective and efficient document management is a large challenge for today's pharmaceutical companies. Organizing and leveraging information—everything from departmental procedures to FDA submission documentation—is difficult and increasingly more important. bioMérieux, a global in-vitro-diagnostics company, has found answers to these challenges using a global solution for Electronic Document Management (EDMS).

The corporate EDMS platform ensures that right information is delivered to the right people at the right time. The entire document lifecycle is regulated from creation and editing to approval, publication and record management. A workflow manager enables employees to set milestones and dates, and sends out alerts and email notification regarding documents that require action.

Integration with the existing ERP system has enabled direct printing, reprinting and error report generation upon failure. Benefits are being derived from the audit functionality that workflow technology brings. No correspondence between the manufacturing site and subsidiary needs to take place, which brings consistency and conformity to the process and falls in line with the FDA's recommendations.

Remote Print Category Id:	796072	Enter Remote Print Category Id
Item Number Id:	2	Enter Item Number Attribute Id
Batch Size Lower Id:	6	Enter The Batch Size Lower Limit Attribute Id
Batch Size Upper Id:	7	Enter The Batch Size Upper Limit Attribute Id
Document Type Id:	5	Enter The Document Type Attribute Id
Valid Server IPs:	10.155.1.162 10.155.1.8 127.0.0.1 10.155.1.9 Enter The Server IPs Allowed To Request	
Print Wait Time:	20	Enter The Number Of Seconds To Wait On The Print Process
Login Id:	remoteprint	Enter The Remote Print Login Id
Password:	••••••••••	
Admin Server Name:	livelink	Enter The Livelink Admin Server Name To Perform The Remote Print
Temporary Directory:	c:\RemotePrintLogs	Enter The Remote Print Shared Temporary Path Directory
MD PDF Document Password:	••••••••••	
Action:	Save Settings Reset	

Figure 5.7: Configuration of a Custom Printing Module at bioMérieux

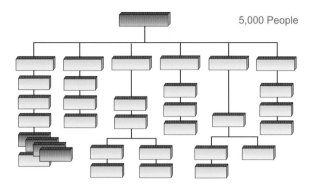

Figure 5.8: Stage 3 – Multiple Applications

The next and most critical stage is Stage 4, which represents the first time that an organization decides on an ECM solution as an enterprise standard. This stage involves not only the IT Department but also the senior-level management team, since the implementation will occur across all departments within the organization, be highly visible, and have a direct impact on operations. Stage 4 typically involves 10,000 or more people in a large organization (shown in the figure below.)

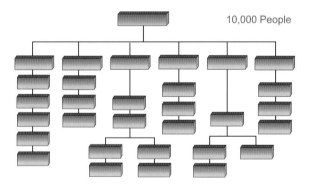

Figure 5.9: Stage 4 – Adoption at the Enterprise level.

It is possible to evolve to Stage 4 quickly, establishing a standard for the organization; however, the jump must be accomplished by going through Stages 1 and 2 at an accelerated rate! In other words, even in attempting to go straight to Stage 4, the organization must pilot a Stage 1 adoption, if only for a short period of time.

Stage 5 represents the proliferation of the standard into multiple different applications throughout the enterprise.

> Cable & Wireless

Cable & Wireless, a global telecommunications enterprise, deployed ECM technology in 2001. It quickly became the cornerstone of the company's knowledge management program and is today viewed as a mission-critical system.

When the Law Department at Cable & Wireless embarked on a complete review of all material contracts, it discovered that the company's ECM technology could be leveraged to set up a database of all the contracts for the entire enterprise. The database captures all key information about each contract and provides a link to a scanned copy of the actual contract. An advanced search mechanism is combined with automatic emailed reminders of contracts due for review or expiry. The result is a powerful resource available to any employee who needs to manage contracts or assess risks.

Using its existing ECM platform, Cable & Wireless deployed a highly tailored solution and has saved up to 90 percent of the major initial and on-going expense of purchasing a standalone contract management system. "Because the interface is familiar, user adoption has been rapid and training costs reduced by 95 percent. Productivity enhancements alone are forecasted to deliver a 100 percent return on investment within a year."

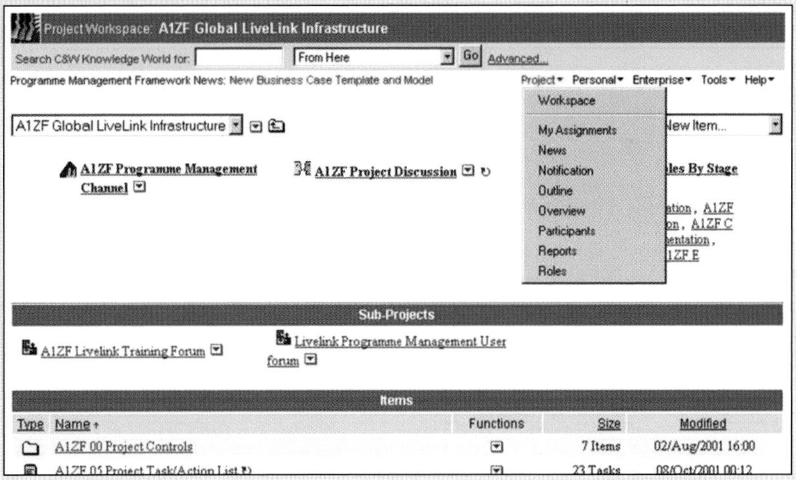

Figure 5.10: Cable & Wireless' Contract Management Solution

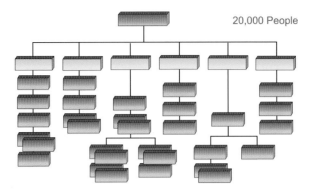

Figure 5.11: Stage 5 – Multi-Application Enterprise

The Extranet stage shown as Stage 6, is a natural evolution from an internal collaboration group that wants to extend the definition of a team member to outside the organization. This is typically done in limited cases in which the users are named users and well known to the organization. These groups are typically built around an existing internal application with a limited number of external users granted permission within the firewall.

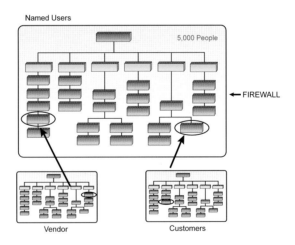

Figure 5.12: Stage 6 - Extranet

The seventh and final stage is the Online Marketplace, as shown in Figure 5.14. In this stage, a series of extranets are extended to include a broad range of market participants, including competitors. An online marketplace functions as the main clearing house for all of the issues of a particular industry. When a marketplace is created around a major organ-

> Motorola

The Telecommunications Industry is fast-paced and Motorola understands that to maintain its market lead, it must leverage its intellectual capital. A consolidated ECM solution serves as the foundation for Motorola's COMPASS system, a global collaboration and knowledge sharing environment that also acts as a central repository for a wide range of information.

Business-critical documents need to be available 24x7 to users dispersed around the globe—downtime is not an option at Motorola. Continuous system improvements and performance monitoring result in a system availability rate of 99.9 percent 24 hours, 7 days a week. Even during peak load periods, users expect a high quality of service that can support high traffic: COMPASS supports over a million transactions per day.

The system has currently 60,000 active users in addition to supporting a guest mode. 10 million documents have already been stored—this roughly amounts to an uncompressed 7.9 terabytes—and this amount is growing by some 400 gigabytes per month. The provision of a common toolset across Motorola has lowered training and increased accessibility, while the use of discussion groups and online meetings has improved collaboration.

Figure 5.13: Motorola's Collaboration Environment

ization, that organization then acts as a "hub" and typically is responsible for the administration of that marketplace. Chapter 20 reviews the different kinds of marketplaces and extranets that exist today.

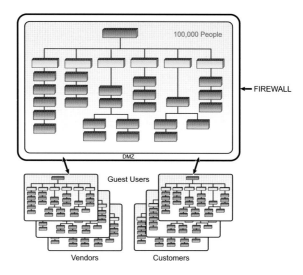

Figure 5.14: Stage 7 – Online Marketplace

It is important to realize that each stage of ECM deployment is built on the shoulders of the previous stages.

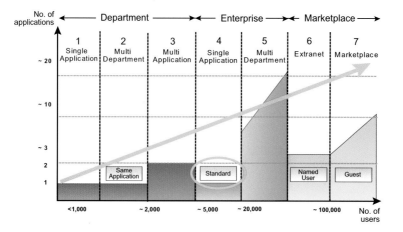

Figure 5.15: The Complete Adoption Cycle of ECM in the Enterprise

Siemens AG, headquartered in Munich, Germany, has more than 400,000 employees and a presence in more than 190 countries. The organization has one of the most geographically complex and comprehensive ECM deployments in the world. This global solution extends to partners and customers, while providing streamlined processes, collaborative workspaces and shared content across the enterprise.

The IT Department introduced various ECM technologies to different business areas at Siemens in a step-wise fashion. As the departments began realizing significant benefits, including time and resource savings, and improved team efficiency and productivity, the final step in the ECM implementation was to create a corporate-wide knowledge strategy led by C-level management. Cost reductions could be realized by organizing various ECM technologies into common standards across the enterprise.

"As a global company with employees all over the world, it is critical to provide our teams with tools for virtual collaboration and knowledge sharing across geographical and organizational boundaries. This system will serve as the backbone of the company-wide Siemens ShareNet. Complementary divisional solutions deliver these capabilities and support our ability to work faster, smarter and more efficiently," says Siemens' Corporate Knowledge Officer.

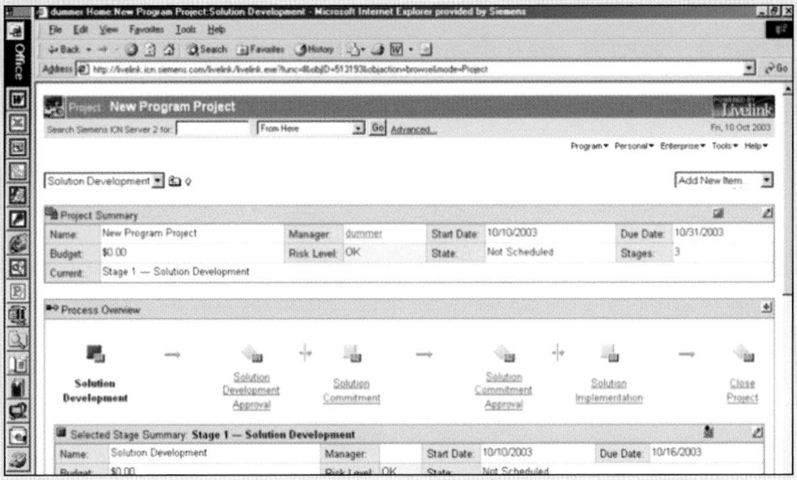

Figure 5.16: New Project Workspace at Siemens

From Stage 1 to Stage 7 at Siemens

In the mid 1990s, Siemens began experimenting with ECM technologies within months of the public availability of a Web browser. Initial deployments of basic search and document management technologies managed growing amounts of information in Web-based reposi- tories. At the time, Siemens was experimenting and adopting Web-based search engine technology well before these tools were on the market. With this base of experience, Siemens' IT Department introduced Web-based ECM technologies to various departments throughout the corporation. The following excerpts illustrate the evolution of departmental installs into the enterprise-wide deployment of ECM that occurred at Siemens.

Stage 1: Sales and Marketing

One of the most important early applications of ECM took place in departments related to customers in Sales and Marketing, as illustrated in the example below.

Siemens Industrial Solutions & Services (I&S) is a leading global supplier of electrotechnical equipment, drive systems, automation and IT solutions for the metals, mining and paper industries, for oil and gas, infrastructure, marine engineering, airports and traffic control. To support the lifecycle of offer preparation and tendering, Siemens I&S created a customized workflow and project template. When users initiate a new offer tendering process, the sys- tem automatically creates a project and populates it with the framework for an offer in the form of a compound document. The workflow uses process steps and a dynamically gener- ated address to send email notification to key people throughout the process.

Stage 2: Additional Department Applications

Working on cross-divisional projects, Siemens Netherlands sells, manages and exe- cutes building projects, adding professional services and consulting value for cus- tomers. To reduce the amount of time spent setting up new projects and to ensure that consultants and engineers were all working from the most current version of a docu- ment, Siemens Netherlands implemented technology to facilitate collaboration at the departmental level, within user communities and among cross-divisional project teams. Capturing knowledge gleaned through collaboration means that customers benefit from best practices, project time savings and improved productivity.

Siemens Enterprise Networks has developed an application called EZA, which is an acronym for easy access to contracts and customer engagement information for solu- tions and services. EZA pulls together all Siemens activities for a single engagement with a customer, from the time a prospect becomes a lead, through installation and final confirmation of the arrangement. As a unique approach to sales and customer engage- ments, the solution helps the sales force interact with customers, business partners and internal people.

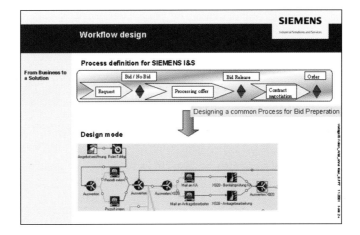

Figure 5.17: Workflow Design Drives the Bid Process at Siemens

Stage 3: Multiple Applications in different departments

After sales and marketing, ECM was adopted at the production level within Siemens, specifically in areas where employees required quick and easy access to technical information to improve efficiency and effectiveness, both within and outside of the organization. By this time, the sophistication of ECM deployments had increased and applications began to include workflow and business process management elements, closely integrated with document management. Collaboration began to take on a more important role in the deployments, and early versions of knowledge management repositories with advanced search techniques were implemented.

OSRAM, a subsidiary of Siemens AG, is one of the leading lamp manufacturers in the world. As customers grew highly knowledgeable about the sophisticated materials and technology they were using to develop lighting solutions, access to technical information became increasingly important. Using content management technology, OSRAM's Marketing Department developed a solution to support its sales force with detailed technical information on thousands of lighting products. Today, when a customer asks a technical question, the sales representative has immediate access to product-related documentation that provides the answer.

Research and Development

As the need to produce technical information in electronic format increased within Siemens, the next logical step was the deployment of ECM to Research and Development Departments. As this happened, the use of more creative forms of collaboration, like notification messaging and online meetings, became more widespread increasing the effectiveness of teams as they worked in common document repositories.

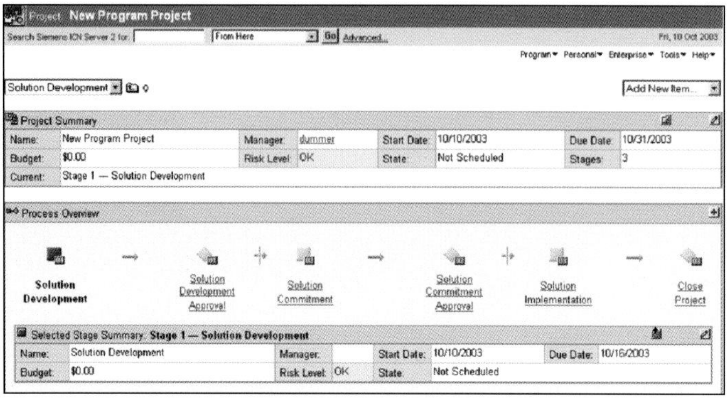

Figure 5.18: Program Management in Research and Development at Siemens

Stage 4: Enterprise Standards begin at Administration

Administration was the last departmental area at Siemens to adopt an ECM solution. As more divisions and departments came to rely on the Internet for communications, the administration department followed suit and deployed an ECM solution to maximize their reliance on Web-based technology and the Internet. Company wide, the need for compliance-driven documentation extended ECM applications to include records management and document lifecycle management technologies.

Stage 5: Enterprise Collaboration across departments and business units

Sharenet is the global intranet, project and knowledge management solution for **Siemens Financial Services (SFS)**. Based on ECM technology, Sharenet provides extensive business process support, from selling products and solutions to quickly responding to customer requests and finding experts across the organization. Building efficient processes across business units and regions based on best practices, SFS can set up new projects using predefined templates in minutes.

Replacing 26 document management systems, **Siemens Enterprise Networks** developed a single, integrated knowledge management and Web publishing application for all of its product documentation, process and procedure materials—essentially all critical business documents. Keeping its internal people knowledgeable about the products and about changes in processes and procedures in the organization, this solution for finding and disseminating key documentation is a critical part of Siemens' Web-based efforts for ongoing collaborative communication with partners and customers.

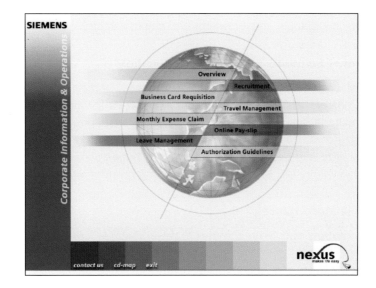

Figure 5.19: Siemens' Screen Capture

Using ECM technology, **Siemens Singapore** hosts a centralized standard solution, called Nexus, for the entire Siemens Asia and Australia region. Nexus is a completely Web-based, employee self-service solution that automates administrative approval processes, such as signature authority, travel booking, expense claims, leave management, training management, asset management, recruitment, separation, purchase requisition, business card ordering, timesheets and more. Tightly integrated with its ERP system, Nexus helps ensure adherence to business rules and policies.

Stage 5: A Multi-Department Enterprise-Wide Platform at Siemens

Stage 5 in the ECM deployment cycle at Siemens began with a corporate-wide inventory and evaluation of ECM technologies and applications, as well as other applications that could be made more efficient by the use of ECM. This resulted in the creation of a corporate-wide knowledge strategy at Siemens which was lead by C-Level Management. By this time, virtually all elements of an ECM system were in use at Siemens at various department and division levels. Cost reductions could be achieved by organizing these technologies into common standards across the enterprise.

Motivated by the desire to gain better returns on investment, the achievement of an enterprise-wide ECM system is key to achieving corporate memory. This is a concept that describes a corporation's ability to maintain a "memory" of all the documents and processes it relies on to function. ECM increases the stability of organizations that rely on intangible assets (people and knowledge) to create value.

Stage 6: Extranet Solutions by Division Application

As the systems engineer for total solutions, **Siemens Building Technologies (SBT)** needed to collaborate and share information with seven locations and six divisions. Turning to an extranet solution, the organization today manages all information related to building and construction projects online. ECM technology has enabled SBT to address productivity and customer satisfaction challenges caused by time-consuming searches for documentation, data and images during building projects.

Stage 7: Online Marketplaces

Siemens Automation and Drives knows that world-class customer care is a critical part of the sales process—the winning and keeping of customers. To that end, the division built a knowledge management system that relieved its Customer Support Hotline staff of supplying daily routine answers to Frequently Asked Questions (FAQ), leaving them free to aid customers with critical issues. The intranet was further designed to host answers in five languages for problem-solving, downloadable software updates and technical documentation, such as end-user or service manuals.

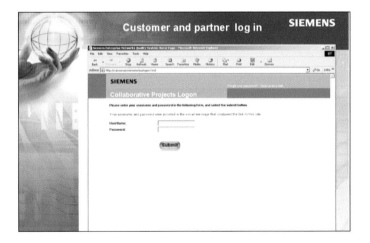

Figure 5.20: Collaboration with Customers and Partners at Siemens

Using the 10 years of online experience at Siemens with ECM, we have illustrated how an initial ECM deployment occurs at the department level and expands to other departments and divisions after six to nine months. After consolidating several applications on a common infrastructure, organizations begin to consider a full enterprise-wide implementation of an ECM solution.

Inter-departmental Benefits

The primary focus of enterprise-level deployments of ECM beyond simply setting a standard in Stage 4 for common applications is the benefits of implementing inter-departmental ECM solutions that create competitive advantage. An ECM solution works on existing infrastructure, is accessible from anywhere in the world and leverages peoples' knowledge of common Web technology. Because it is easy to use and improves the way people work together, it significantly increases overall productivity, employee satisfaction and the workplace environment.

The inter-departmental benefits of deploying an ECM Solution include but are not limited to harnessing enterprise collective knowledge, making a distributed organization effective and breaking down geographical and organizational obstacles.

Today's organizations are changing. Traditional management hierarchies have been broken down by the necessity to move further and faster than ever before to stay ahead of the competition.

Communities form across all levels of the hierarchy. Some are traditional - such as the management team that puts the heads of department together once a month to debate corporate policy and direction.

'Project' communities cross departmental boundaries on many levels. For instance, imagine a project to install a new computer network in your office. Information Technology will be involved with engineering, logistics, administration and finance. In fact, just about every department in the enterprise will be effected in some way and will need to play a role in the project community.

And even a simple business process such as raising a purchase order will touch a 'virtual' community of employees within the business.

Internet technology enabled companies to overcome the geographical barriers that prevented collaboration between different office locations. In a hyperlinked enterprise, individuals can collaborate with peers and work in virtual communities that span the globe.

Combining People, Processes and Information

Organizations generate vast amounts of information that they need to control, from invoices, records and contracts to emails, spreadsheets, design specifications, marketing materials and Web pages. For global organizations, productivity can suffer without a system that helps people find information and work together to deliver results. To succeed, individuals need to work as teams that can cross geographical and departmental boundaries. They need to be able to access best practices and information from previous projects, share documents and collaborate throughout the development process to rapidly supply team members with the information they need to get their jobs done. An effective ECM solution needs to bring together people, process and information. The software must seamlessly combine collaboration with content management, transforming information into knowledge, providing the foundation for innovation, compliance and accelerated growth.

Measuring Productivity at the Enterprise Level

Measuring ECM productivity at the enterprise level is not unlike measuring any other process change within a business at the department level. The scale and scope of an enterprise ROI calculation is much larger since it involves longer time periods and several inter-related activities in different departments. To determine ROI, organizations must benchmark enterprise-level performance before and after implementing an ECM solution. In many cases, this is tangible and easy to calculate. The reduction of costs associated with the physical storage of records can be easily seen on a comparative statement of expenses. Improvement in time to market can often be easily benchmarked and measured as well.

The effectiveness of an ECM solution can be measured by assessing the difference between value created by the business with the ECM Solution in place versus value without it. The traditional metrics include return visits, referrals, cycle times, retention rate, and satisfaction. Overall profitability, profits as a percentage of revenue, and sales generated per employee are other metrics.

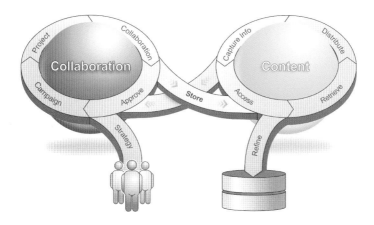

Figure 6.1: Marketing Strategy Lifecycle

For Marketing and Sales, the ECM lifecycle begins with a sales and marketing **strategy**. The Marketing team will then take this strategy and develop **campaigns** made of one component (direct mail piece) or multiple components (billboards, print ad, and TV commercial). Once the components of the campaign have been identified, a collaborative **project** can begin involving the details around the execution, including project plans, resources, budget and the creative components that will be used to create the campaign piece(s).

Collaboration during the development of campaign materials is at the heart of this creative process. Typically, there are several stages, including multiple reviews and **approvals**. Once the new materials receive final approval and are tagged with relevant metadata for reference during future projects, the campaign and all its components are **stored**.

With new materials securely stored in a repository, the sales force, distributors, channel partners and other sales oriented groups, regardless of location, can gain **access** to these materials in a self-service manner. Because the marketing assets are well organized and include important metadata information, sales can readily determine which assets are the most relevant. They can now **retrieve** these materials and also transform each desired asset into a file format that best suits their **distribution** needs.

It is critical for the success of the Sales and Marketing Department to **capture information** about the effectiveness of marketing campaigns and the underlying component materials. This information can be leveraged so that the original campaign and future campaigns can be **refined** based on real-world feedback and results.

SALES AND MARKETING

The relationship between sales and marketing is highly intertwined. Both share the same goals of capturing new prospects, increasing sales and market share and retaining customers.

Marketing is the group that collects information about the collective customer being served and develops competitive sales strategies, campaigns, and materials to best raise awareness and demand for the company's offerings in the marketplace. Marketing must establish and maintain the company's brand so that the market perceives a clear, consistent and differentiated identity for the company. The Sales team is the group that carries out the strategy, leveraging the materials and brand that have been created to close sales.

The Marketing Department relies on Sales to provide information about the market it serves, as well as real-world feedback about the effectiveness of Marketing's various campaigns. The Sales Department then relies on Marketing to transform what is learned about its constituencies' buying habits into increasingly effective materials and messaging.

All of this coordination must be accomplished within increasingly compressed time frames and budgets, and by teams that are often distributed globally. This process can benefit greatly from ECM solutions that leverage both content and collaboration in context.

Compounding the challenges faced by Sales and Marketing is the requirement to comply with numerous recent industry regulations such as the U.S. Patriot and Bank Secrecy Acts. These Acts demand that companies have well-defined identification processes and procedures for such tasks as opening an account for a new customer or in the review of existing accounts. Other regulatory acts mandate that companies maintain a detailed record of all promotional claims made about the company's products or services, including elements as diverse as commercials, fact sheets or promos run in newspaper circulations.

Ensuring that a company's Sales and Marketing functions meet compliance regulations protects it from penalties, and maintains the character of a company's brand.

Today's consumers have unprecedented access to information and are therefore a more savvy and demanding audience for Sales and Marketing to influence. With the costs of new customer capture increasing, the importance of keeping existing customers happy rises significantly. A significant portion of a company's revenue is directly associated with the support and service to its customer base. Customer satisfaction requires organizations to know how and when they have interacted with customers to build upon those interactions to remain competitive.

All of these demands ultimately call for technology and processes that effectively handle marketing and sales content in the broadest sense of the word – documents, records, audio, video, graphics, photographs, Web content and more. Those responsible for sales and marketing must be able to quickly access content in a timely and cost-effective way, understand its history and use and synthesize information into powerful, timely sales strategies and materials.

Time to Market

Time to market is one of the most fundamental challenges for any company and its sales force. The Sales Department is constantly coping with new trends, the competition and the fickle nature of buyers. When a salesperson meets with a prospect, they want to be sure that they are delivering the most competitive and compelling message, products and services possible. For the organization, this is a costly endeavor as it often means incurring significant expenses to create, re-create, update and distribute materials.

The ability to solve this "distribution" asset management challenge can mean the difference between being ahead of the sales curve, instead of behind the competition. Distribution asset management in this context allows direct, field, and channel sales to automatically receive the most current finished marketing materials and information. It also permits an automated process whereby authorized field personnel or affiliates engaged in selling or promotion can retrieve materials from a secure fulfillment system in a self-service model. This eliminates historically costly people and material-intensive workflows. Large sales teams, dealer networks, distributors and franchisees can all have real-time cost effective access to the marketing and sales materials they require.

This type of system not only ensures that Sales is armed with the most up-to-date materials, but allows Marketing to quickly and cost effectively refine and amend materials as new information comes to light. Product changes, new regulations and strategy refinement can readily be uploaded and distributed into the hands of the sales force.

Within the context of a Marketing Department, the primary challenges involve the ability to quickly respond to market demands with new, fresh and meaningful materials regardless of the required medium (print, TV, radio, Web, etc.). New material development must also be done with an eye on the company's brand as a marketer must ask, "does this campaign support the brand image?"

In developing new campaigns and materials, one of the more costly areas is development of new creative content (video, audio, photography, graphics, artwork, layouts, etc.) Costs include paying for creative services (agencies, freelancers, etc.), intellectual property usage rights, and the time/cost of multiple iterations to get to a final product. Often, several directions will be developed and presented during the creative process. Valuable creative elements not used in the final selection historically get discarded, left as it is on the cutting room floor.

Companies that understand the inherent value of these materials are storing their marketing "assets" in an ECM system. By doing so, the creative professionals within Marketing can readily access a repository of previously used and unused materials. Entire campaigns and projects can be stored in the system with valuable historic information such as how the materials and their components were used and ideally data describing the success of these materials in the marketplace. With this wealth of content at their disposal, the creative process can be more creative and far less expensive.

Key considerations that often drive the introduction of an ECM system within Marketing include:

- Do I have control over creative and marketing content?

- Am I re-creating creative content instead of reusing existing content?

- Can my sales team quickly and easily access current marketing materials?

- Am I unnecessarily paying shipping fees instead of using a digital distribution system?

- How am I dealing with and paying for amending marketing materials that have errors or quickly go out of date?

- Do I know what I have the legal right to use in my marketing materials?

- Do all materials support and maintain the integrity of the company's brand?

By addressing some of these fundamental questions, a company can quickly bring efficiencies and realize ROI.

For the Marketing Department, imperatives include increasing productivity, gaining control over development and distribution of marketing content and gaining visibility with buyers. Being able to do "more with less" is becoming a common theme. For instance, an ECM system dramatically reduces the time it takes to locate marketing assets. Without an ECM system, designers could spend hours or days looking for CDs that may or may not include appropriate content. Even if they were fortunate enough to locate desired content, it could take several more days to determine usage rights, and there is a likelihood that content is not in the right file format for their needs. As a result, it is often easier to re-create marketing elements that may already exist— a costly and time-consuming activity.

With an ECM system, marketing and creative professionals can search across their organization for assets. Once identified, they can quickly ascertain where and how the marketing asset was used and if they have the necessary usage rights. In addition, file formats can easily be transformed, allowing the value of that digital content to be further increased.

With assets securely stored and appropriately catalogued, a company's ECM system can effectively serve as the hub supporting varied distribution channels such as print, TV and the Web.

In the case of the Web, speed-to-market and ability to engage and captivate is unprecedented. The Web project team typically has a short timeframe to design and implement sites. International and global companies need to provide multilingual sites for worldwide publication of information and access to broad ranges of services. Corporate identity enforcement is also key to a successful Web presence. Because most companies have a large number of existing homegrown Web sites, consolidation and reduction of overall cost is crucial.

An ECM solution lets organizations create and manage content once and re-use it as many times as necessary in a variety of publication types, including intranet, extranet and Internet sites. Not only does it provide the ability to effectively manage increasing volumes of content, it makes it easy for business users to author content and participate in the Web content management process, balancing the need for content control with the need for corporate agility and individual empowerment.

Real-Time Web Applications

Web sites that publish content internally and externally are crucial to doing business. To ensure accuracy, avoid duplication and reduce the total cost of ownership a comprehensive Web content management strategy is vital.

The emphasis in developing a Web site lies in communicating the corporate identity and associated values of the corporation. In addition, sales and marketing sites have the difficult task of gaining customers' attention and meeting their needs.

INNOVATOR STORY

> **Swiss Air**

The Web Content Management (WCM) platform at Swiss Air enables the Sales & Marketing department to maintain a direct channel to the Web. The corresponding Web site offers a set of services including online-bookings, information, frequent flyer management, reservations, and journey planning to the Web community.

One of the major concerns of today's airlines is to keep aircrafts at the highest possible seat load factor. While destination networks, schedules, pricing, and soft factors such as service and image are essential to succeed, clever management of vacant seats also results in a better load factor.

Swiss Air's WCM platform combined with a booking engine empowers Sales & Marketing to release specials offers to vertical markets. The offers can be placed short term, but are integrated with the booking engine and corresponding information management. With this platform, Sales & Marketing not only has a solution to increase seat load, but also an instrument to challenge new markets with almost immediate feedback (for example, terms of booked seats). The gained intelligence from special offers is used to optimize Swiss Air's destination network and pricing strategy.

Figure 6.2: Web Content Management at Swiss Air

Today, it is not enough to use basic systems that let Sales and Marketing services manage documents and Web pages. Content needs to be put into the context of applications. Therefore, it is not only a challenge for Webmasters, but also for application developers. Basic best-of-breed Web Content Management systems will fail, because they don't provide real-time capabilities that enable Webmasters and application developers to jointly engage in Web initiatives.

Web Publication Challenges

To address all needs around Web publication, the ideal system includes components to facilitate management and publication of Web pages and documents, integration with existing and new applications and portals and development of applications to bring everything into one coherent context.

Sophisticated yet easy to use functionality of an ECM system ensures that each task is on schedule. For the management and publication, the system provides the application of languages, personalization, access rights and auditing beyond documents and pages to granular elements such as text paragraphs, lists, tables and images.

Special features may include ways in which vertical markets are taken into consideration and the obligatory integration of interaction with business data and processes. Online sales capability is a prime example of how these requirements are fulfilled.

The successful cushioning of peak times – those moments with the highest cluster of user interaction – is critical for contributors as well as visitors. To achieve this, the system must be robust and scalable and fit into an environment that can be optimized with respect to the operating system, runtime environment, data storage and Web delivery.

The most important aspect of the ideal Web Content Management system is its ability to integrate with other ECM solutions. Different best-of-breed solutions can be assembled with common standards to cover many aspects of ECM but it will require immense effort to get close to the benefit of an integrated ECM platform.

> Columbia Sportswear

As one of the largest outerwear manufacturers in the world and the leading seller of skiwear in the United States, Columbia Sportswear is passionate about its brand. The organization develops a vast majority of its marketing materials in-house, and it is critical that current, approved and brand-wise materials are delivered into the hands of both internal and external users in a timely and cost-effective manner.

In order to better serve its vendors, provide a full array of product content quickly and cost-effectively, get materials out into the market, and be assured that brand integrity is maintained, Columbia Sportswear introduced a digital asset management system. Before the implementation, external vendors would have to call the marketing department to request images—a process which required the manual location of the image, formatting and billing.

Now, when the time comes to produce a new season's catalog and vendors are requesting new product images, Columbia Sportswear can provide access to the digital asset management system and a Web-based, user-driven selection of product materials. As a result, the organization is not only able to provide an added service, but has also reduced the time the marketing group needs to spend servicing vendors.

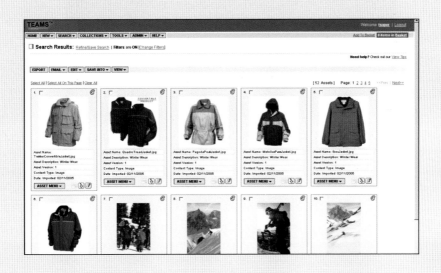

Figure 6.3: Columbia Sportswear's Digital Asset Management System

Increase The Value of Human Capital through Corporate Training

In today's business climate, Sales Departments need to remain competitive and innovative while using fewer resources. Organizations must efficiently and effectively train employees from globally dispersed locations without incurring the high cost of travel and related expenses. Typical challenges include:

• A training budget that is continually being reduced while more employees are hired;

• Corporate training initiatives grounded by high travel costs;

• An inability to effectively track course content, usage and understanding, which skews training initiatives' ROI and weakens corporate sponsorship.

Figure 6.4: Online Training and Certification

A Web-based online training solution provides the infrastructure needed to support effective learning initiatives. It offers recorded training materials that replicate the essential characteristics of a live speaker. The benefits are:

• Minimizing and even eliminating the need to travel to other locations to transfer knowledge – significantly reducing the cost of training and travel;

• Enabling the company to measure the effectiveness of materials, identify gaps in comprehension and ensure that materials are up-to-date and accurate;

> Meredith Corporation

Meredith Corporation is a leading media and marketing company with businesses centering on magazine and book publishing, television broadcasting, integrated marketing, and interactive media. Meredith has an extensive Internet presence, including 25 Web sites, and 17 magazine brands, including Better Homes and Gardens and the Ladies' Home Journal. Meredith's consumer database, which contains more than 75 million names, enables magazine and television advertisers to precisely target marketing campaigns.

Prior to introducing a Digital Asset Management (DAM) system, the process for identifying and tracking down assets for reuse was extremely manual and time consuming. Having performed extensive analysis to identify areas where meaningful ROI could quickly be realized, Meredith focused on leveraging the DAM system to reduce external labor costs, primarily the time spent on searching and repurposing content; reduce scanning fees and process duplications; and reduce photo production costs by eliminating new photography and/or stock image licensing.

Providing support for processes and procedures, the DAM system has enabled Meredith to use its vast inventory of existing digital assets to develop new products more effectively and efficiently.

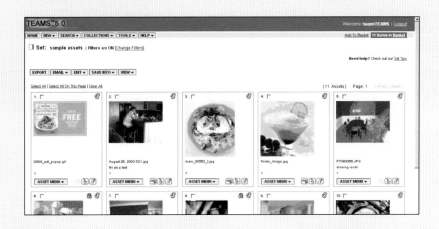

Figure 6.5: Digital Asset Management at Meredith Corporation

• Tracking facilities for course content and usage provide reporting required to meet a broad range of compliance requirements. This ensures that the information is being pointedly delivered to the appropriate audience and that certification reports can prove it.

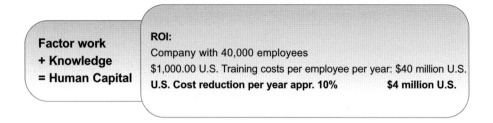

Factor work + Knowledge = Human Capital

ROI:
Company with 40,000 employees
$1,000.00 U.S. Training costs per employee per year: $40 million U.S.
U.S. Cost reduction per year appr. 10% $4 million U.S.

Figure 6.6: Online Training and Certification Result in ROI

Reducing Risk with Due Diligence

Depending on the region, the economy and the corporate culture, Sales and Marketing Departments employ different kinds of organizations and have diverse priorities.

The regulations implementing SEC 326 of the U.S. Patriot Act require screening for a much broader population of accounts and business relationships with a more extensive and time-consuming enhanced due diligence process.

Organizations that implement effective due diligence solutions reduce risk and gain competitive advantage through quicker response to market and customer needs.

ECM in Sales and Marketing

ECM solutions for Sales and Marketing Departments are about providing a context within which intellectual property can be created and inventoried for current and future use. Sales and Marketing Departments have significant content challenges that require a variety of ECM solutions which permit sales and marketers to share knowledge with colleagues from other departments and through them to customers, partners and suppliers to manage new programs and proposals, and develop effective new products and services.

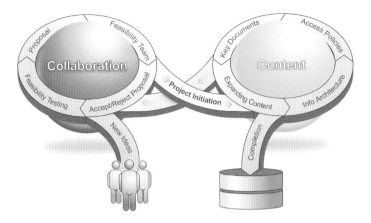

Figure 7.1: Clinical Trials Lifecycle

In Research and Development, it is critical to effectively involve teams of scientists and engineers in projects, but most often **new ideas** are initially proposed by individuals. They may work to **test the feasibility** of these ideas with a small group, usually from the same department. Before presenting a **formal proposal** to senior management, a cross-departmental **feasibility team** is established to ensure that the proposal has broad support based on a detailed understanding of market needs, the opportunity to develop unique intellectual property (IP), freedom from infringement of the IP of other parties, and the ability to acquire necessary licenses and regulatory approval, budget, etc. If **management rejects** the proposal it is beneficial to pass on the reasons for that rejection to people that are considering other new ideas. With approval however, a **project initiation** process is commenced. As projects advance they accumulate extensive documentation that may range from the very informal, such as emails, to formal reports and process documentation. It is necessary to devise an **information architecture** to accommodate the project content in a consistent fashion between projects so as to ease user navigation and enable formal records management processes. It is also necessary to develop appropriate user **access policies**. In some companies the policy is to encourage and facilitate knowledge exchange between all project teams, while in others, it may be necessary to limit access on a "need to know" basis. Team members add **key documents** to the content repository. As projects advance these elements need to be revised and extended to accommodate **expanding content** until projects are terminated or archived on **completion**.

RESEARCH AND DEVELOPMENT

The Research and Development (R&D) Department provides a critical function in most organizations by generating new products and services that can create and sustain competitive advantage in the marketplace. Research requires the assessment and internalization of external information in the context of internal ideas and discoveries. This repository of knowledge is then directed to the development of superior products and services. Research information is often particularly diverse compared to content found in other departments, and must be used and maintained for proprietary advantage. The scientists, engineers and technicians involved typically have unique cultural perspectives and work habits, necessitating a careful approach to the design and implementation of collaborative processes that facilitate and support efficient research. Ensuring that product requirements remain valid requires effective knowledge exchange with colleagues from other departments and through them to customers, partners and suppliers. Finally, successful decisions on project directions require access to comprehensive and timely knowledge.

In most industries, investments in Research and Development endeavors are critical to long-term corporate growth because they can create competitive advantages that will sustain financial success. Innovative new products and services can displace competitors' offerings in an existing market or create a completely new market.

In some companies, R&D investments are primarily tactical and intended to adapt products to a customer's requirements to secure a given sale or contract. Other companies strategically fund planned R&D programs to build sustainable advantages. In such cases, the first step in an R&D program is to identify the intellectual property (IP) that could be generated and whether it would then be satisfactorily protected through patents, copyrights, trademarks or as confidential trade secrets. Innovative products that are properly protected will have an enduring market presence.

The development and defense of IP absolutely depends on precise and complete records containing accurate, relevant dates. As business processes become increasingly electronic, this requires that electronic content and collaborative processes be amenable to IP capture and defense.

Whether product lifecycles are as short as a few months, as in the software and food industries, or longer than a decade, as in the pharmaceutical and aerospace industries, nurturing an efficient and productive collaborative R&D environment is an essential corporate objective. But R&D processes can present unique challenges to the design and implementation of effective ECM support systems. R&D staff, such as scientists and engineers, often shun controls and hoard information. At the same time, R&D processes are extremely variable and content is highly diverse – ranging from very large structured datasets to masses of dissimilar documents.

Innovation as a Key Driver

Innovation drives corporate growth. While short-term growth is driven by small innovations, long-term growth depends on successful sustained innovation. But R&D resources are always finite, and there is no certainty that any project will lead to a successful product. Balancing and selecting among R&D opportunities is a management imperative that depends on access to comprehensive information at every stage of every project and the application of clear decision making criteria.

R&D is typically a multistage process. In the early stages of research, projects are fluid and staff pursue many different paths. As projects advance toward development stages, corporate investments typically increase and processes become more formalized. The progress of a project from one stage to another may require passing a defined "decision gate." Management demands a clearer idea of the likely return on their investment, plus defined objectives and milestones including a likely product launch date. A common strategy to maximize return on R&D investments is to identify projects less likely to succeed and to terminate them before the investment in time and money becomes significant. This also reduces opportunity costs and maximizes staff availability for more promising projects. On the other hand, it is often the most innovative projects that have the greatest uncertainties associated with them. If companies focus primarily on reducing uncertainty, they may also reduce innovation and focus on "me too" products that seldom achieve desired market success.

> Fraunhofer OIC

Made up of five geographically dispersed institutes, Fraunhofer Office Innovation Center (OIC) develops and tests concepts for the office of the future. The research is characterized by a dynamic and interdisciplinary approach. To ensure that such complexities would not affect project completion, OIC introduced an IT platform to enable efficient collaboration among the different institutes.

A Web-based content management system enables direct intranet access to expertise from earlier or current projects, preventing "reinvention of the wheel." Research materials can be managed, stored and disseminated, ensuring better visibility across all disciplines. An extranet portal for online collaboration enables improved cooperative work with clients.

Virtual project spaces enable team members to work together regardless of location or what IT platform they use. "We are able to disseminate crucial information from our existing data inventory much faster than before. In addition, our project teams can now create their organizational structures at the click of a mouse," said an IT Management representative at Fraunhofer OIC.

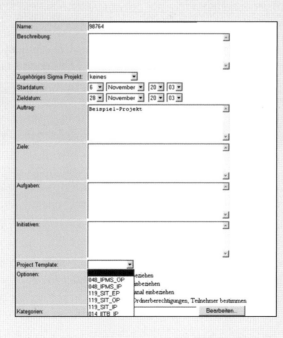

Figure 7.2: Project Template at Fraunhofer OIC

Project Selection and Management

Successful companies nurture good ideas and the processes that generate them. The best ideas often arise from encounters between staff with diverse backgrounds, whether they meet at the classic "water-cooler" or in an online community of practice (CoP). Posting challenging problems can lead to effective suggestions from staff or people outside the company as a number of pharmaceutical and chemical companies have shown. A more deliberate approach to finding professional advice is to search a corporate skills repository, where expertise is catalogued based on deliberate entries by staff or the Human Resources Department, or by automated profiling of the documents viewed by each staff member and the projects in which they have participated.

Companies usually have a process by which good ideas may be translated into sponsored, exploratory projects. Once an idea has been translated into a project proposal, the phased approach to product development begins; projects then advance, are reviewed and proceed to the next phase or are terminated. In long R&D cycles, many people may participate in a project at different stages, but few people are involved throughout an entire project lifecycle. Knowledge transfer is therefore critical. This transfer may simply depend on ensuring adequate documentation is kept at each stage or it may be more complex.

In some industries, research generates large quantities of data, much of it in original electronic form with the balance entered manually or by scanning of paper records. IT Departments can dedicate considerable effort to ensuring that this corporate data is captured in central databases. However, as we have seen elsewhere, structured data is only a part of the picture, and even in research, much data is unstructured. More importantly, often the context in which the data was gathered is not saved in with the data, making it much less useful in the future. We need to know why an experiment was done, why the experimental conditions were chosen, the conclusions derived from the experiment, their implications for future experiments, and the progress of the project as a whole. Even if experimental context is recorded, other researchers typically do not have the time or the necessary expertise to reanalyze the data again; they can benefit most from summarized results in document form.

ECM systems recognize that data is used to create information and that knowledge is based on actionable information. But too often, companies focus on raw data, rather than making information more widely available to support informed decision making. For example, there may be a database of experimental data but no strategy to capture, save and effectively distribute project reports. Yet it is these reports that are the most useful in informing other staff of project progress and to enable senior management to make critical decisions. They are also critical to supporting IP positions.

> U.S. Army Aberdeen Test Center

In these times of drastic global change, the United States Army Aberdeen Test Center has utilized ECM to revolutionize the Test and Evaluation process for Army material. A collaborative system connects disparate groups and improves the T&E process by transforming data into knowledge and greatly reducing the time, by years, from concept to combat.

The implementation has over 5,000 users nation wide, several users in Canada and a few international users for NATO work. VISION — a knowledge management Web-based library for information fusion based on ECM — embodies a comprehensive, holistic, top-down approach to data/information collection, management, and eventual transformation into knowledge.

Thanks to VISION, the U.S. Army can provide timely, high quality test information and knowledge. Custom enhancements to workflow technology have replaced lengthy email or paper-based approval processes, ensuring request and order tracking and saving the U.S. Army valuable time. The solution has also helped revolutionize the T&E processes: Stryker Tank and Slat Armor are two examples of successful programs.

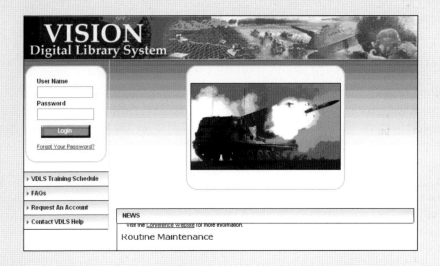

Figure 7.3: Digital Library System at Aberdeen Test Center

From time to time in some companies, Research Departments are disconnected from changes being experienced by the other parts of the organization (e.g. Sales). Sometimes, this can result in a fatal problem, as when products are developed for a market that no longer exists or never existed. Ensuring that Sales and Research are talking to each other is normally the task of the Marketing Department and in most organizations, the Product Management and Product Marketing groups. As organizations are often geographically dispersed and staff travel frequently, direct contact between key players may be infrequent. In an ideal world, these groups should be connected in a constant and detailed dialogue on the right directions to take without sacrificing development efficiency. ECM can go a long way to achieving these ideals in large and dispersed organizations.

The integrity of any research project can be compromised when researchers do not have access to all of the information relevant to their investigation. After they review prior research by the organization, they must integrate that experience with published information resources such as professional journals, conference proceedings and increasingly, online journals and repositories including databases of patents. This content integration challenge is often facilitated by an enterprise research library. It is also necessary to review this information to determine whether work in the project is truly innovative and might be used as the basis for patent claims.

Patent Applications and Intellectual Property

Supporting patent applications requires demanding processes, especially in the U.S. In many countries, priority of invention is determined based on the date that an application is received by a patent office ('first-to-file'), but the U.S. uses the 'first-to-invent' system. This means that accurate and legally defensible records of the exact date of invention are required, which can be especially challenging in electronic systems. Traditionally, signed and dated paper records and secure microfilm images were sufficient. Electronic equivalents employing digital signatures or external electronic notarization are being developed, but acceptance may take time and will depend on emerging case law. Most companies will not risk defending IP by purely electronic means, often printing or microfilming key records and documents and passing these to third parties for review and archiving. Tracking both electronic and physical records and the association between them is very effectively facilitated by ECM systems.

Adding Value to Information across Departments

We have seen how researchers need to understand information that is available inside a company as well as the latest published findings. How can they expect to innovate if they are not current with the research and literature in the field? Research libraries play

> U.S. Office of Naval Research

The Office of Naval Research (ONR) coordinates, executes, and promotes the science and technology programs of the United States Navy and Marine Corps through schools, universities, government laboratories, and other organizations. ONR has adopted ECM technology to improve collaboration and to better manage documents and data for research projects.

At any time, there may be dozens of active research programs underway, with each project requiring close collaboration between ONR staff, the Navy and Marines, and research organizations. ONR must manage the large volumes of research documents and data that are created with each project. ECM provides document control, reduces the handling of physical documents, and improves cycle time.

Custom applications automate the submission of research proposals via the Web to ONR, so that they can be processed and managed in ECM. The collaborative work-space makes it easy for researchers to work together online, providing task lists, threaded discussions, news channels and access to a wider range of similar research information in ONR's ECM system.

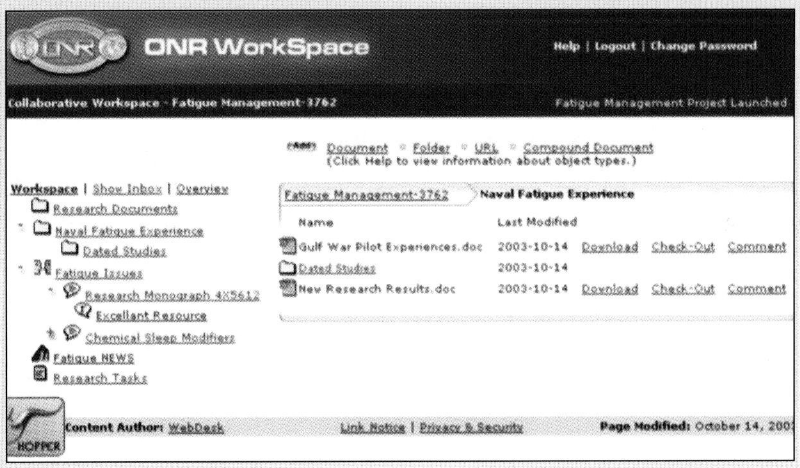

Figure 7.4: Collaborative Research Workspace at ONR

a critical role in supporting R&D staff. Even researchers who remain current need integrated information retrieval tools to find an article relevant to a new project. The research library can coordinate subscriptions and the purchase of published content to facilitate circulation and organize distributions so that expensive research materials can be shared, optimizing the return on investment. As part of an ECM solution, the research library helps to improve the quality and efficiency of a research project by providing a single point of access for all of the authenticated content from the field. Organizations with a legacy of research face a unique content management challenge to maintain formal collections of technical research reports and documentation for 20, 40, 80 years or more.

To effectively manage intellectual property, information professionals or subject-matter experts often add value to asset collections by applying detailed descriptive analysis, complex metadata, or controlled vocabulary in order to leverage maximum contribution to subsequent research.

Research and Development Departments must ensure that they are working on the right objective and certainly a close liaison with Sales and Marketing will ensure that research is current with the marketplace. Another objective is the smooth and efficient transfer of completed research. The Manufacturing Department must have this information to produce the new product on time and with good quality. The Marketing Department needs to know about the performance of the product so that the Sales Team can be trained in advance of its release and so that marketing promotional materials and documentation can be created to herald the new or improved product. It would not be wise for an automotive company to develop and produce a great new automobile and not tell anyone about it.

ECM in Research and Development

Many players in the R&D process are trained in different cultures. Supporting systems must be designed to help them do their jobs more effectively, reducing rather than increasing workloads. Optimal user interfaces may differ according to roles, while support for collaborative processes must range from ad hoc collaborations such as Journal Clubs to highly structured, repetitive workflows to manage critical events in product testing. By the same token, the types and volumes of business content that are generated vary tremendously. This creates challenges in effective information organization, storage and retrieval which must meet immediate process needs while at the same time supporting long-term regulatory audit and tracking requirements as well as defense against patent and legal challenges.

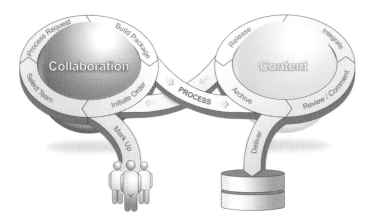

Figure 8.1: New Product Launch Lifecycle

A major process that manufacturing departments conduct daily is a Change Request. Change Requests start when a customer **"marks up"** a copy of a product specification and/or Computer Assisted Design (CAD) documents and submits the changes as a Change Request to the Manufacturing Department. The Change Request is logged and the key decision makers as well as those affected are **selected as participants**. The Change Request is **processed**, then package then **built** and the Change Request workflow is **initiated**.

The workflow delivers the appropriate information to the selected people in the correct order. Each individual involved in the process will be delivered a task notification, either to **review**, **comment upon** or **approve** the Change Request. If necessary, the workflow reroutes the request to a previous step for more information or approvals. Once the change is approved, the workflow sends **integrated** change request information to other legacy systems. Once the changes are made to the affected documents and CAD masters, new renditions are created and **released** into the ECM system. Other departments have immediate access to the latest product information. Once completed, Full audit trails are captured and retained throughout each workflow. When the Change Request is **archived** in the ECM system, it can be analyzed for lessons learned, best practices and process improvements. Throughout the active workflow, detailed change notifications are **delivered** real-time to concerned parties. Additional ECM features such as electronic signatures, electronic forms and secure document and content management capabilities can solve product review and approval problems quickly and cost effectively.

CHAPTER 8

MANUFACTURING

A Manufacturing Department is the business unit of a company responsible for the design, manufacture, assembly and shipment of a company's products.

Products are often made up of parts made by the company itself (e.g. assemblies), parts from a sub-contractor (e.g. castings) and parts bought wholesale (e.g. nuts and bolts). A company's manufacturing plants can be divided into plants that make parts and plants that assemble parts into final products.

All manufactured products start with a design owned by the engineering side of a manufacturing department. These designs also specify how the assemblies and sub-assemblies work together to make a product. The engineering and manufacturing teams must continuously work closely with each other and with their suppliers to minimize duplication and waste. Manufacturing is also responsible for developing and publishing a product's specifications and procedures (e.g. product performance ranges, acceptable assembly and maintenance procedures, standard operating procedures).

Manufacturing's Quality Assurance (QA) Department is responsible for overall product compliance. QA oversees production, ensures that product quality meets or exceeds design specifications and that proper procedures are in use across a company's manufacturing and assembly plants. The QA department even influences a supplier's product.

Common results or measurements of a successful manufacturing department are:

• High inventory turns;

• Continuous control or reduction of costs;

- Increased manufacturing velocity, flexibility and responsiveness towards market demands (new product innovations);
- High product quality with few or no returns, repairs or warranty claims.

Compliance Requirements

Manufacturing enterprises are under increasing pressure to improve quality, reduce product lifecycles, implement and enforce standards compliance and minimize costs. Product proliferation, new environmental and regulatory requirements, globalization and international competition are forcing companies to better manage product compliance not only between departments but throughout the entire company, even to where it involves suppliers. Manufacturers are now confronted with product compliance requirements in three major areas: Environmental (e.g. CAFE, WEEE), Regulatory (e.g. IEEE, ISO, FDA, OSHA, TREAD and SOX), and Operational (e.g. Six Sigma and TQM).

Reducing Cost

Shorter cycle times make processes more flexible and responsive to change. The highest single cost in manufacturing a product is the "human expense" (the salaries and benefits of employees assembling or manufacturing the product). A shorter process results in higher worker productivity (lower human expense), faster development and production and higher responsiveness to change. Assuring product compliance to corporate and customer standards at the design and manufacturing stages reduces or eliminates waste, re-work and future warranty problems. ECM used in support of efficient methodologies (e.g. Lean Manufacturing, Product Compliance) will significantly increase Return on Investment (ROI), reduce Total Cost of Ownership (TCO) and improve the bottom line.

Reducing Time to Market

Ensuring compliance reduces time to market by making the management and control of key documents in heavily regulated industries secure, efficient and compliant with relevant regulations. There are many manufacturing standards organizations including OSHA, NHSTA, NIST, SEC, APQP, QS9000 and ISO 9000/ISO 14000.

ECM solutions ensure that product specifications, manufacturing and operational procedures are fully developed, tested and distributed company-wide in a compliant manner. Compliance information that comes from different sources can be gathered, organized and archived or developed into workflows in a very efficient manner. This can dramatically reduce timelines internally as well as those involving interaction with external organizations.

BMW Manufacturing Corp., based in Spartanburg, SC, U.S.A., manufactures Z3 roadsters. The facility is designed to focus on quality and create an easy exchange of information by placing all manufacturing processes under one roof. The organization looked for a solution that would streamline the materials document response time, while adhering to the high standards set by BMW.

ECM was chosen as an imaging and archiving solution for the facility's SAP system because of its seamless integration and breadth of functionality. The system is utilized to image and store each of the six-page inspection cards that follow every Z3 roadster throughout the production process. If a particular card needs to be viewed, it can be instantly retrieved from the system.

BMW has been able to cut down on paper processing and filing storage, and enjoy faster data access and optimum system performance. "We've seen dramatic improvements in our materials documents' response time since we started data archiving with ECM," said the SAP System Administrator at BMW Manufacturing Corp.

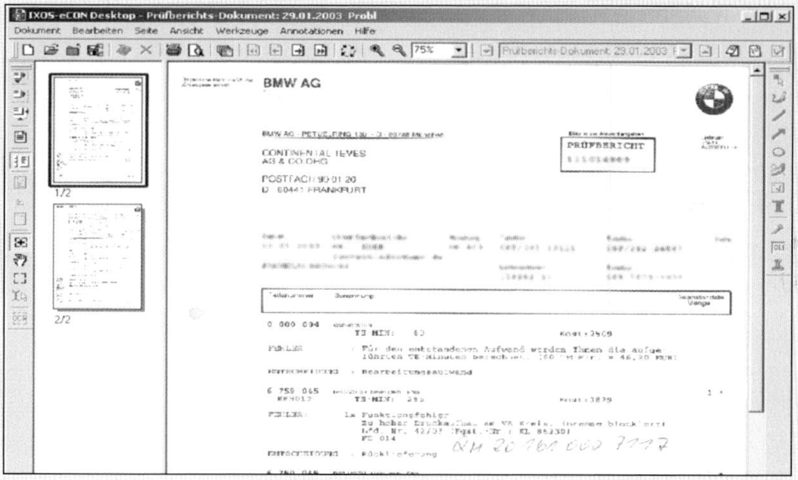

Figure 8.2: Test Report at BMW

Collaboration across Departments

Important collaborative issues manufacturing companies are trying to solve today include:

• Achieving scaleable, permissioned synchronous and asynchronous collaboration;

• Protection and retention of collaborative results between departments, divisions, teams, projects, customers, consultants, contractors and suppliers;

• Implementation of company-wide records retention policies;

• Achieving and maintaining regulatory compliance;

• Consolidation of all enterprise content and the reduction of the overhead to maintain it;

• Implementation and enforcement of Business Process Management.

Examples:

Engineering:

The Manufacturing department must work closely together with engineering. New product development must be brought to production. The overhead and delays in managing changes to existing products must be reduced as they are published by the engineering department and transferred into the manufacturing process.

Logistics and Purchasing:

Collaboration between with logistics and purchasing is crucial for just-in-time production. Supply chain management for production must ensure that the right amount of material is in the right place at the right time.

Quality Assurance:

Quality Assurance is critical to the manufacturing process. The company's quality programs must be certified to industry standards in order for a company's product to be sold in global markets. Quality must be monitored constantly during the production process. Test reports and other documents must be made available throughout the company and its supplier to fulfill compliance issues. Once ISO certified, companies must be able to maintain that certification without little or no overhead increase.

Part of the Volvo Group, Volvo Aero was founded in Sweden as a provider of engines for the Swedish air force. The company produces airplane engines for commercial and military airplanes, as well as racket engines.

For many years, Volvo Aero's technical drawings were managed in a free-standing system, which functioned with a number of separate components: one to scan the drawings; another to archive; and yet another specially developed program to print the drawings. As the organization could no longer receive the necessary support from the old system, they instead seamlessly integrated an Enterprise Content Management solution into their strategic ERP system.

"Today, the combined products supply all functions, which provide greater user-friendliness, transparency and functionality. Hundreds of people use the technical drawings, and with the new system the drawings are much easier to manage. Previously, users were forced to exit the ERP system to gain access to the drawings. Now everything is integrated in the same user-interface," says Volvo Aero's Project Manager.

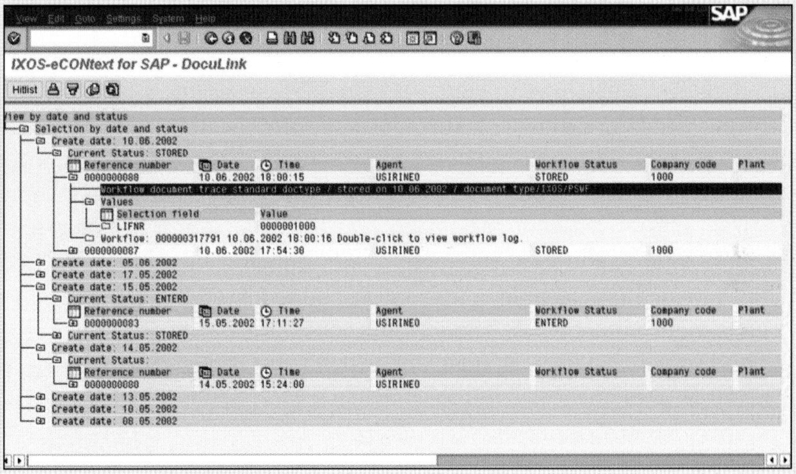

Figure 8.3: An Example of Integrated Workflow Monitoring

Manufacturing Processes

Manufacturers are finding that the amount of work needed to complete their tasks is rising or, in a best case scenario, static instead of declining. Manufacturers are on a never-ending quest to reduce the number of steps required to run the business each day (Lean Manufacturing). Increasing product complexity affects the quality processes, programs and product compliance (Six Sigma/TQM) while customers demand higher quality and value. Change management within a department is complex, difficult and time consuming. Required inter-departmental, inter-divisional, inter-company and inter-supplier cooperation and compliance adds new dimensions of difficulty to process complexity.

Manufacturing Facilities

Manufacturing companies geographically disperse their manufacturing, engineering and headquarter facilities when skilled labor can be found at relatively low cost. These geographically dispersed communities continuously face difficult communication and collaboration challenges.

Product Development and Planning

Managing and distributing product specifications and procedures is complicated and expensive. Automated design and data management systems such as Computer Assisted Design (CAD), Product Data Management (PDM), Product Lifecycle Management (PLM) and Enterprise Resource Planning (ERP) store data in proprietary structured database systems. Product-related unstructured data that is increasing exponentially is spread across different silos. Typically, there is little or no integration with structured product information (e.g. product related, papered information and physical items are difficult to locate and retrieve when warehoused in off-site buildings). Product design and planning information is "siloed" and collaborative sharing is limited. Each system is proprietary and exists in its own realm (PDM and PLM in Engineering, ERP in Finance). Limited information discovery and collaboration abilities result in expensive duplication of development and production efforts.

ECM solutions best control the complete process including design and development phases, prototyping, testing, quality assurance, production, service, maintenance and warranty. Important ECM components are process management, project planning and content management. Within the product lifecycle, the manufacturing department needs access to the information generated from each of these processes. This means correct support of the manufacturing process is centrally located information stored in the ECM solution since very different sources must be combined. Some information sources would be:

Miele is a European manufacturer of high-end domestic appliances, machines for commercial applications and built-in kitchens. The organization believes that its success in new product development depends on sharing information with all departments involved in the entire product lifecycle.

For Miele, the product lifecycle involves all aspects of construction, design, and production, through to service and maintenance. All content produced during the steps of each lifecycle, including engineering drawings, is provided to all departments through a single point of access to the company's Product Documentation Management System.

"The Product Documentation Management System provides all product details within seconds to each employee during the entire product lifecycle. The fact that the information is shared across different locations pays off in production, as well as in maintenance and service," says the Project Manager at Miele.

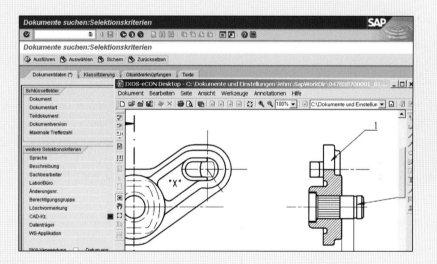

Figure 8.4: Document Management at Miele

- Design systems that produce engineering drawings (CAD), product specifications (for both the company and the customer) and testing requirements;

- The ERP system that manages information involving any production and non-production material requirements, logistics, ordering and supply processes necessary to the manufacturing process;

- The Program Management Office that supports the overall lifecycle management of the company's products;

- The Quality Assurance Department that generates and enforces operational procedures throughout design and manufacturing processes.

Cross-Departmental and Global Collaboration

Globalized manufacturing places facilities around the planet, so that access to product design, specifications and compliance information must be made available to different locations. Each employee requires access to the information at any point of time.

"Just-in-time" production works far better when all information is on a single platform that links supply chain control with the production lines to provide continuous production while reducing production downtimes.

An ECM solution for a manufacturing department involves sharing the right amount of information and content across all departments throughout a product's lifecycle.

From an IT perspective, various IT systems must openly share information across departments, e.g. CAD systems for engineering, ERP for production planning, logistics, material management and portals for the online integration of suppliers.

An ECM platform supporting product compliance and lifecycle management connects all these systems and makes the information and the content available to all departments. The content is provided in a way that each task can be performed quickly and efficiently.

ECM in Manufacturing

Although manufacturing productivity has been greatly improved by ERP systems which reduced inventory times and increased quality, there is still a great deal more to be done by integrating ERP with ECM and achieving higher standards of production in terms of quality and flexibility of response to new variables. Manufacturing departments can also benefit from adherence to regulatory requirements by adopting ECM solutions to document the various steps in the manufacturing process efficiently.

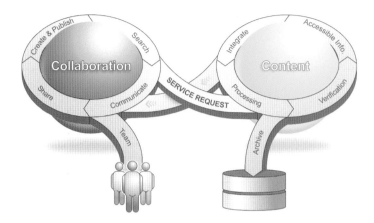

Figure 9.1: Customer Services Request Process

In the Customer Services Department there are two key processes that are based on ECM applications.

The first process is providing customers with easy online access to complete information. In all industries, a cross-functional **team** from Sales, Research, Production and Services Departments need to **share** a common platform, where as much information as possible is **created and published** online. Customers can easily **search** for information and can **communicate** with internal staff and among one another in communities of practice (CoP) Web sites to exchange information. CoPs break down the geographical and hierarchical barriers in an organization, enabling groups of people with common interests to create an online community where they can easily find one another to create and share the information that matters to them.

The second process starts when a customer places a service request or asks for complaint resolution. This typically starts a structured process where existing content is used to **verify** the validity of the request or complaint. Complaint resolution becomes effective and can create a positive image for the company if all structured and unstructured information about the customer is immediately accessible to the call center agent in one integrated application.

Processing a service request requires creating work orders for the field staff. These may include detailed operating procedures or drawings, a workflow component to assign tasks to individuals and an **archiving** system to store all processed work orders to document the fulfillment of the request. Other key processes can include supporting contract renewal and management, customer data management and fulfillment.

CHAPTER 9

SERVICES

The Services Department functions play an important role in creating competitive advantage and are an essential element for any organization.

ECM solutions for different types of Service functions are as varied as the functions themselves. Portal solutions to define self-service applications for customers provide the latest information (product manuals, discussion groups) created by many other departments. ECM solutions for Call Center applications need integrated access to customer data in structured (ERP systems) and unstructured forms (contracts, documentation, scanned images, email, technical information, and correspondence). When a Customer Service Department manages a large number of incoming orders (e.g., in the Utilities Industry) the creation, processing and archiving of the respective documents is a key business process – based on the ECM backbone of the company.

Transforming the Customer Services Department from a cost center into a profit center and using excellent customer service as a key differentiator to improve customer loyalty are today's drivers for change.

One element of this strategy is to change the customer's behaviors to adopt the use of self-service. Each phone call replaced by an online self-service inquiry, each letter transformed into an online form filled out by the customer saves money immediately. Online response centers can increase accuracy and service levels resulting in a "win-win" situation for both the customer and the organization. To achieve this transformation, the quality and wealth of the information presented in such portals is key. This requires integrating structured and unstructured information from many sources in the company such as financial statements, product information, marketing collateral, etc.

Another element is the efficient processing of service requests. Product and customer information must be compiled into a work order for the field staff, ideally propagated to a mobile device via a workflow and processed there. The service request together with an audit trail of the workflow trigger the billing process and are stored in the electronic customer record for legal purposes and to answer subsequent customer requests.

Compliance Requirements

There are many ways in which compliance influences the way a Customer Services Department operates.

In regulated industries such as Aerospace or Pharmaceutical, documentation is required for all steps in processing a service order. Each step must adhere to strict Standard Operating Procedures (SOPs). ECM solutions are used to guarantee that the latest version of SOPs are used. They control the workflow of multi-step processes and archive all documents used and created to perform the service request. For an airplane that is flying in the United States, these modification documents must be stored for up to 99 years.

Compliance with public regulations is also very important in the Utilities Industry. Major gas distributors must ensure that all installations that deliver gas to households have been properly set up by maintenance staff and are approved by local authorities. Storing the proof of such documents is very important in case of accidents and subsequent litigation.

ECM in a Services Department

Services Departments are multi-faceted. Each may have interaction with vendors/suppliers, internal customers (other departments) and external customers.

In today's customer-centric business environment, there are many faces of Services, such as:

• External Service departments (Customer Service or Customer Support);

• Internal Service departments (Legal);

• External Service providers (Advertising agencies);

• Professional Service providers who provide on-site project management and specialized skills.

Let's review each of these environments in the context of what the customer wants, the business challenges to provide these services, and how ECM Solutions can improve the overall level of service and deliver savings/ROI.

> EcoRecycle

EcoRecycle Victoria is an Australian government agency founded to deliver strategy, programs, infrastructure, advice and support for Victorians in the area of waste reduction. A small agency with approximately 40 staff members, EcoRecycle had ambitious plans that reached beyond the budget scope: in order to maximize existing resources, the agency turned to ECM technology.

Coco, or Channel of Organizational Cooperation & Openness, is EcoRecycle's Intranet portal to content management functionalities, with a custom-made look and feel. The solution also provides support for stakeholder management, records management and project management. Two extranets have been developed as successful tools for communication and collaboration between EcoRecycle and its strategic partners.

EcoRecycle Victoria is currently delivering way beyond size of resources as a result of improved business process management and significant time savings. Collaboration and project management tools have increased productivity and efficiency as staff can search for and instantly access all vital documents. Organizational performance has improved as progress and understanding can be shared throughout the organization.

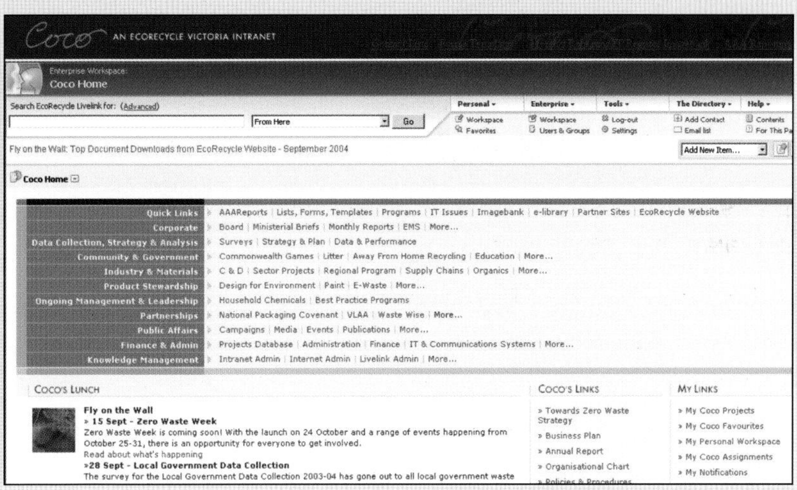

Figure 9.2: EcoRecycle's COCO Home Page

What Customers Want from their Online Service Experience

Today's time-challenged customer expects fast resolution of their service requirements and a degree of quality that is consistent with the brand. If there is a problem, feedback must be captured so that resolution may be tracked and reported as part of overall service delivery performance metrics.

Customers also must have easy access to information about the company's products and services. Given the cost of providing one-to-one phone support, online help and product/company information is an expected part of the overall service offering.

Managing content effectively within a services environment enables staff of varying experience levels to develop a set of content-rich service offerings. Challenges within Services departments include a higher number of entry-level positions, higher turnover, and minimal time/limited budget for training compared to other parts of the organization.

What Services Staff Need to do Their Job

Services staff rely on published information that they may refer the customer to, such as Frequently Asked Questions (FAQs) and online queries for follow up. They also need access to the customer's contract terms and conditions. As well, they must be able to correspond with the customer independently and understand what needs to be escalated. All of this combines to deliver a positive customer experience.

Tracking customer interactions, along with having access to customer history, while interacting with the customer in the method they choose (email, phone, messaging) all combine as essential ingredients to successfully service a customer.

Call Centers

The service expectation of today's customer is higher than ever before. Extended hours mean that staff must work evenings and weekends. The higher the perceived value of the product offering, the greater the services expectations will be.

Mega Call Centers represent one of the fastest growing segments of the Services Industry. By centralizing the call center function in low-cost areas, companies can dramatically decrease their overall costs. Many companies are outsourcing this function to call center service providers, who specialize in providing the processes, training, technology and low cost for a flexible service offering. The success of these Call Centers depends on their people, access to information, and business processes. If the right people do not have access to the information they need to service the customer, there is immediate dissatisfaction. ECM plays a critical role in the consolidation and fast delivery of critical information to support a particular service offering.

> E.ON Energie

As Europe's largest public energy provider, E.ON Energie serves more than 14 million customers with electricity and gas. A question about an invoice, a move to a new home, or a switch to a different pricing scheme—regardless of customer need—they expect a quick and accurate response.

E.ON Energie uses customer relationship management software to manage the vast number of documents that must be processed every day: new contracts, rate changes, meter cards and invoices. Each incoming document is scanned in the mailroom, automatically creating an activity which can be processed immediately.

The solution provides all call center agents with access to every piece of information that has been exchanged between the company and its customers. The result has been a dramatic reduction in call center response time, requiring less service agents to complete the same amount of work.

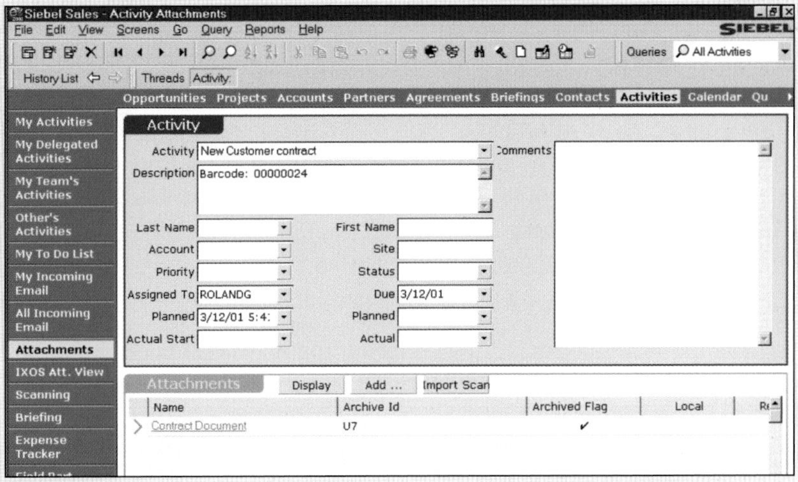

Figure 9.3: Customer Care at E.ON Energie

Traditionally, Customer Service has depended on Customer Relationship Management (CRM) systems to provide the customer data needed to do their jobs. Limitations arise when access to unstructured content is non-existent or incomplete. Unstructured content such as emails related to specific customers, or messaging between customer service representatives and their managers in the dispute resolution process are key to effective service delivery. CRM is a well-known structured data process of the IT industry (for a complete discussion of the difference between structured and unstructured data, please see Chapter 1 of this book). CRM does not provide the ability to collaborate with the customer, nor does it provide the business processes that enable that collaboration, or the capture of the output. This can only be achieved by integrating an ECM solution that has a knowledge repository of the key unstructured data.

Internal Service Departments

Legal

A Legal Department must be able to manage contracts throughout the organization. Each department has its own set of contracts (vendor agreements, customer purchase agreements, etc.) which are typically administered by the Legal Department. Each contract goes through a series of changes as part of the negotiation process. Each change needs to be tracked, along with the author of the change, and the final version needs to be archived. Without the history of the contract revisions, there is no knowledge of what the requirements from each party negotiating for the service were. Capturing the changes allows for a deeper understanding of the contract value, and a better transfer of knowledge to the lawyer involved in the re-negotiation process.

With easy access to these contracts Service Departments who support vendor relationships have a greater understanding of the terms and conditions that were negotiated as part of the contract, which could ultimately save the company money.

ECM provides the ability to capture, track changes, store and ultimately archive contracts throughout their lifecycle. Behind an effective ECM Solution are the business processes that manage the lifecycle and ensure that all regulatory requirements are being met.

External Service Provider

Advertising Agency

Advertising agencies collect a large number of media files for their clients. Many of these files need to be accessed regularly, so filing and retrieving is a critical need. The size of these files may become unmanageable, which can lead to increased storage costs.

> Booz Allen Hamilton

Booz | Allen | Hamilton

An international strategic management and technology consulting firm, Booz Allen Hamilton needed a tool to manage documents, projects, and client engagements. An unfriendly user interface and difficult-to-manage group structures, accounts management processes, and security were resulting in rising costs and absorbed resources.

A company-wide, global collaborative tool, ECM provided a basis for business process automation to protect, organize, and categorize information. The capture and dissemination of knowledge assets across organizational and regional boundaries were streamlined, while security modeling helped differentiate between users and protected intellectual capital.

Improved collaboration among over 15,000 employees and approximately 3,000 external contractors and clients across 18 time zones has enabled a performance increase of 50%. The ECM solution maximized and leveraged technical and business resources to deliver a world-class service and business process integration solution to Booz Allen Hamilton's clients, resulting in significant direct and indirect cost savings.

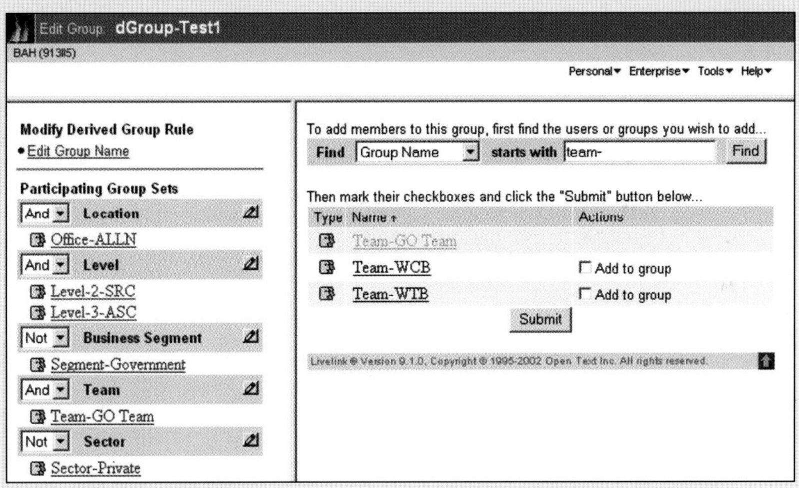

Figure 9.4: Managing Group Structures at Booz Allen Hamilton

Too much of designers' valuable time can be spent searching for the right graphics or media files. This can affect the productivity of the entire team and slow the time to market for critical design projects. Many ideas could be reused if the designers could file, store and retrieve this creative work. In addition, designers must understand the legal rights regarding the use of creative materials.

Ad agencies need control over their inventory of creative and marketing content. This inventory represents their "Digital Assets." Digital Asset Management (DAM) dramatically reduces the time it takes to locate marketing assets. Once located, file formats can easily be transformed, which increases the value of that asset over time.

By managing digital assets on behalf of the client, there is increased value added to the customer for the overall design service. This also allows agencies to provide branding standards packages for their customers, which can be easily accessed globally (templates, logos etc).

Professional Services Project Management

A customer engagement for a Professional Services provider generally involves a complex sale and service model. The service itself is high value and people centric versus product centric. The assessment of the project scope, pricing and assumptions made are critical to the successful project delivery. Part of this assessment is captured in structured data, however much unstructured data is involved.

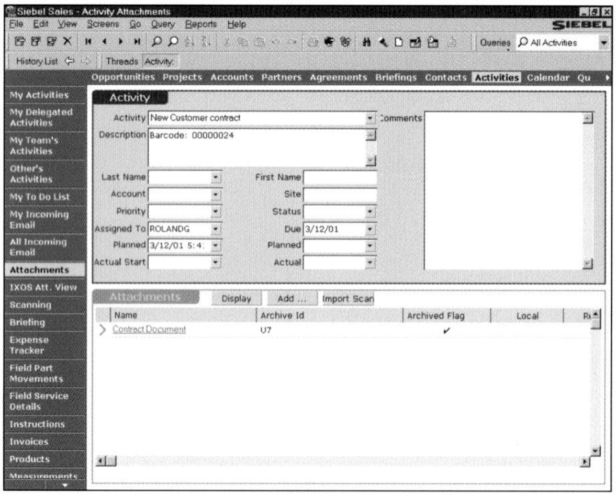

Figure 9.5: An Example of Customer Contract Management

> International Tracing Service

Since 1943, the International Tracing Service (ITS) has been searching for civilians missing or displaced during World War II. In the year 2000 alone, the institution received more than 300,000 such requests. To process them in a timely manner, ITS decided to expand its database systems to include a process management solution.

At the heart of the new system lies electronic processing. All requests and vital documents, whether in paper or digital form, are imported into the workflow system, enabling significant time savings. Because of the integration of the process management system with ITS' existing database, complete workflow processing of paperless requests is possible.

Workflow automation enables data to be captured and read locally—a tremendous advantage for the various ITS locations. The shortened access time to files allows for more timely and effective processing of requests, setting another milestone in ITS' objective of continuing to improve the provision and security of information.

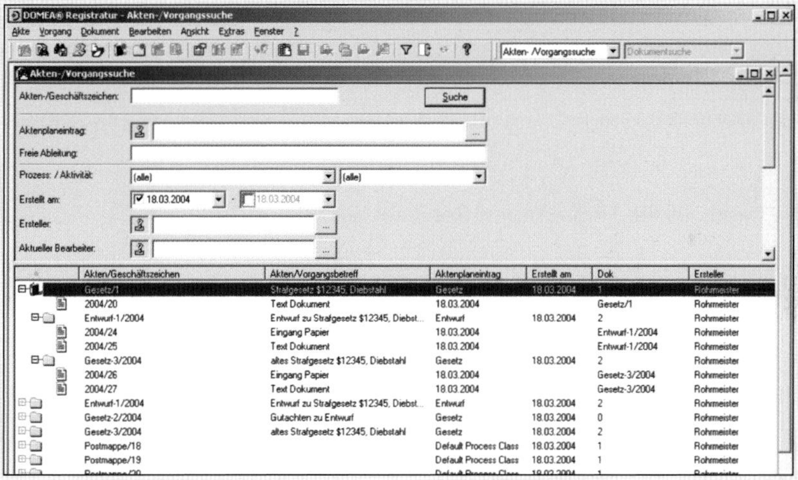

Figure 9.6: An Example of a Process Search

In addition, once the project is approved, there is the overall project management which may include:

Detailed definition of the project milestones/tasks and deliverables: At the initial project planning stage, the project plan sets out the details behind the project scope in order to effectively execute the plan. This may include the task details, along with resources responsible, and the timelines requested for completion. The management of this plan is of paramount importance to demonstrating the value of provided, and proof of overall resourcing.

Business Process Improvement: The improvement of business processes may sometimes deliver the highest ROI in a project plan, with savings from streamlining human engagement and interaction.

Training/Organization structure changes to accommodate the changes: Change Management as part of a business improvement project will often require training for staff to accommodate changes, along with new roles and responsibility definitions for access to the entire organization.

Integrity and continuous improvement: The changes implemented must have integrity throughout the entire business process. Especially in light of regulatory requirements, business processes must provide transparency in order to isolate where information is captured, along with areas where the ability is available to change/update corporate data.

Some of the needs of the Professional Services provider include:

• a method to track and document all customer interactions in relation to the project

• the ability to define and document business processes to recommend improvements

• the ability to collaborate with all team members (both clients and consultants),
  and include the collaboration within the project documentation

ECM Solutions provide full case management so that individual projects can be managed within an environment of multiple projects.

ECM in Services

ECM Solutions can be an integral part of a company's overall Services offering. The ability to access and control customer information, along with the publishing of company information helps to improve overall service levels, which are critical in today's battle for customer loyalty. Increasing efficiency and productivity by reducing file retrieval time and exceeding customer expectations are but a few ways in which implementing ECM can benefit the not only the Customer Services providers, but the customers as well.

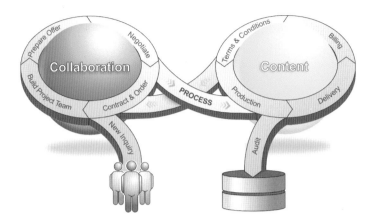

Figure 10.1: Purchasing Process Lifecycle

Companies of all sizes face challenges in increasing the efficiency of order management processes. Fundamentally, order management processes enable organizations to reduce the number of lost deals by effectively qualifying, managing and processing incoming **inquiries** and prospects.

In service-oriented industries, single projects require an extensive project **negotiation**, planning and **preparation** phase. Large **project teams** that span Sales, Service and Legal Departments need to collaborate and cooperate to manage project-related tasks such as **offer preparation**, technical specifications, resource planning, contract creation and **negotiation** with customers. Existing orders, **pricing and payment conditions**, all managed within a back-bone Enterprise Resource Planning (ERP) system, must be considered before a **contract** gets signed and an **order** is submitted in the system. Teams in Manufacturing, Service and Accounting take over the responsibility to **produce**, **deliver**, and **bill** goods and services.

All data and documents created within this process remain securely stored and accessible as a template for sales or service in other projects, or for fiscal authorities in case of **audit**.

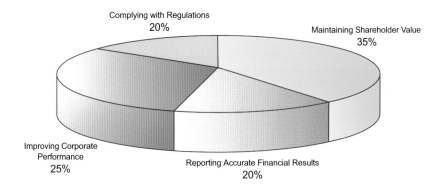

CHAPTER 10
ADMINISTRATION DEPARTMENT

In many organizations, the Administration Department is one of the biggest consumers and distributors of content. It typically serves a vital role by measuring, recording, and documenting a vast array of activities across the company. Administration is involved in the development and execution of key strategies including the budget, cash flow and procurement. This group also plays a role in decision making regarding pursuing new directions and developing new products. The accurate preparation of financial reports and the protection of shareholder value are critical goals. In today's business environment, it is also of utmost importance that the Administration Department carefully manages compliance throughout the organization.

Complying with Regulations
20%

Maintaining Shareholder Value
35%

Improving Corporate
Performance
25%

Reporting Accurate Financial Results
20%

Figure 10.2: Breakdown of Administrative Activities

Administration Departments require a complete Enterprise Content Management (ECM) solution suite that enables administrators to share knowledge with colleagues from other departments and external partners such as customers and suppliers. By leveraging ECM to collaborate effectively and manage content of all types efficiently, the Administration Department is able to achieve its goals consistently and reliably.

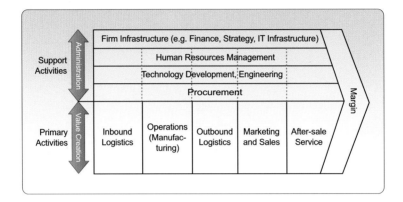

Figure 10.3: Components of the Administration Department

Business Challenges

Administration Departments face similar challenges across the globe. Reducing costs, dealing with awkward paper based workflows, responding to changes in the organization's structure and managing evolving compliance regulations are all core administrative functions.

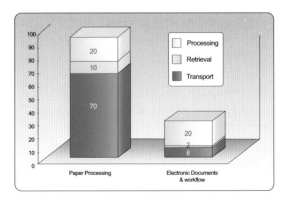

*Figure 10.4: Typical Savings Incurred When an Integrated
ECM Solution Enhances Processes*

With the introduction of computers, networks and ERP systems, organizations have cobbled together a variety of solutions to cope with these challenges. These approaches were selectively successful; companies benefited from increased business transparency and higher productivity but continued to develop an increasingly costly and unmanageable wealth of content. Microfiche and optical archives provided a temporary but cumbersome solution; information was accounted for but locked away. Only by giving content a business context can organizations extract real value. Further cost-cutting, resulting in the need for more productivity per employee, plus globalization and stronger legal regulations force companies to set up appropriate infrastructure. With an ECM solution, companies can address all of these problems.

ECM systems allows the creation of shared service centers to cope with the requirements of decentralized offices. At the same time, ECM eliminates manual paper processing. Process steps are transparent and auditors can determine if the process is compliant.

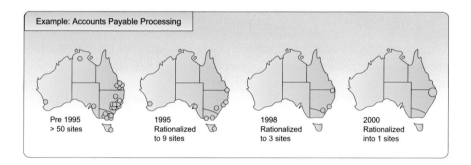

*Figure 10.5: Ongoing Cost Reduction through introduction
of Shared Service Centers and usage of ECM*

Productivity in the Accounting Department

For most Accounting Departments, core business operations revolve around optimizing working capital—handling receivables and managing payables—and dealing with the inevitable volume of related paper work. But Accounting Department operations use resource-intensive and error-prone manual processes that increase costs, create employee inaccuracies and decrease efficiency.

In Accounts Payable (AP), inefficiency leads to missed due dates, late fees and missed cash discounts on invoices. In the Accounts Receivable (AR) world, every day that a payment due remains outstanding (known as Daily Sales Outstanding or DSO), the less likely the customer is to pay. Inefficient collection processes prolong collection time, increase bad debt and erode bottom line revenue.

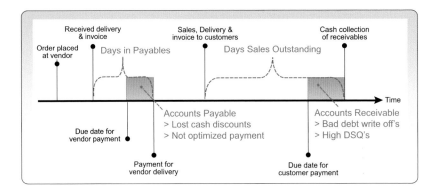

Figure 10.6: Accounts Payable Timeline

Accounts Payable: Cash Discounts and Reducing Cost per Transaction

If an organization has to process large volumes of supplier invoices, cumbersome paper-based invoice verification often results in early payment discounts being missed. Studies have shown that invoice processing costs can be as high as $25.00 U.S. per invoice. ECM systems that move this information digitally can save as much as 50 percent or about $12.50 U.S. per invoice in processing costs and speed up verification to ensure early payment discounts.

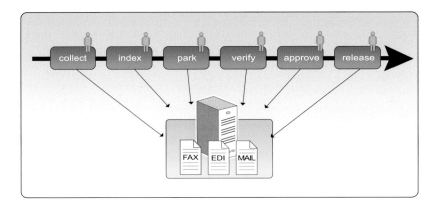

Figure 10.7: Automated Accounts Payable Process

> Dow Corning

A global leader in silicon-based technology and innovation, Dow Corning provides performance-enhancing solutions to serve the diverse needs of more than 25,000 customers worldwide. When Dow Corning needed an archiving solution for financial documents, customer data, and SAP reports and transactions, they turned to ECM technology.

Financial documents have been consolidated from 23 sites across 12 countries into one Financial Shared Services Center that processes about 6,000 documents per month, including expense reports, invoices and customer payment information. In the Accounts Payable department, approximately 9,500 invoices are processed every month. Invoices are scanned upon receipt, linked to the appropriate SAP transaction and archived.

Dow Corning employees have direct and immediate access to archived documents and SAP reports and transactions can be easily stored and automatically generated. This streamlined approach saves hundreds of thousands of dollars per year. Increased productivity and efficiency have also been realized as a result of simplified processes, and the solution has streamlined customer service and accounts payable operations.

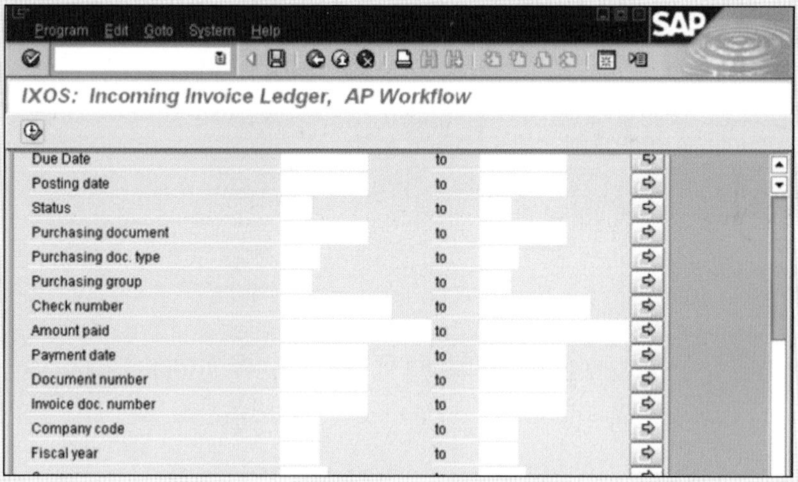

Figure 10.8: An Example of an Incoming Invoice Ledger
for an Accounts Payable Workflow

Invoice exceptions break the flow of the accounts payable process. These exceptions can take hours or days to clear, increasing both the likelihood of missing discount terms and the cost per transaction. ECM systems can route an exception to the individual or group that can clear it the fastest. Data gathered during the exception-handling process can be used to help understand the causes, establish trends and initiate internal or external behavior modification to reduce or eliminate exceptions. Of a similar nature, approval of invoices without a purchase order is one of the largest contributors to high AP cost per transaction and lost discount terms.

ECM solutions address the issues that drive up AP cost per transaction. Rapid data entry as well as invoice digitization through Optical Character Recognition (OCR) dramatically reduce data entry costs. Tight integration with ERP systems ensures that data captured in the AP process is automatically and accurately posted in the ERP system without violating ERP's built-in checks and balances. In fact, ECM solutions can greatly enhance governance over the AP process by providing a more extensive audit trail of the process beginning at the corporate mailroom.

Shared Service Center for Accounts Payable Processing

Organizations consolidating to Financial Shared Service Centers (SSC) have seen dramatic processing improvements while reducing staff. The ability to have all financial staff in one location allows for standardization and consolidation of processes. This tends to streamline certain parts of the process but creates the need for collaboration with those outside of the SSC. A key component of a successful SSC is the utilization of workflow technology and other collaboration tools. Workflow ensures that a standard process is used for invoices; it maintains overall control and gives supervisors and managers visibility into the entire process.

SSCs can achieve best practices by having all invoices arrive at the SSC and then utilizing workflow to push invoices out based on business rules. If properly configured, the workflow system can "age" the invoices based on due dates and proactively escalate work items or notify supervisors or managers of possible late payment scenarios.

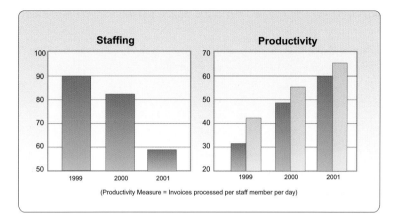

Figure 10.9: Increasing Productivity Measures while Reducing Staff

Accounts Receivable: Increasing Profitability by Reducing DSOs

The Accounts Receivable world revolves around payment collection. The longer a payment remains outstanding, the less likely it will be paid in full. An inefficient collection process prolongs collection time, increases bad debt and erodes bottom line revenue.

Employees in Accounts Receivable Departments need supporting information from multiple sources to reconcile differences between customers and invoices. They must review account information generated throughout the organization before they can effectively field customer questions, troubleshoot problems and facilitate timely collection. An integrated ECM solution streamlines the accounts receivable process by integrating disparate accounting, sales and support information into a central repository with a single point of access. The ECM solution captures order information when entered or scanned into the system, links it to corresponding customer information and then archives the information. AR staff simply need to enter basic customer data to access related information, reducing the time spent manually looking for information scattered across various systems.

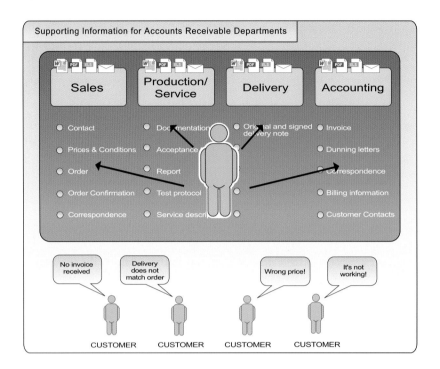

Figure 10.10: Integrated ECM Systems Help Accounts Receivable Staff Reconcile Differences with Customers

In addition, an integrated ECM solution can deploy monitoring and measurement tools to track user activity and deliver an overview of the status of each process. This audit history helps AR agents understand and monitor the progress of each step in the collection process and identify where and why issues arise.

By helping AR personnel identify issues that can delay payments, an integrated ECM solution improves debt collection rates, increases free cash flow to lower the risk of bad debt write-off and reduces a company's credit line.

Optimizing the Human Resources Department

Elimination of Paper-Based Employee Files

Employee records need to be stored for many years for active and retired employees. Paper-based records consume office space and require huge efforts for manual processing. Many employee records are incomplete or faulty. Paper-based storage, access and manual routing result in high costs, long processing times and decisions based on incomplete or faulty information. The average annual cost of manually handling one employee record is $15.00 U.S. to $30.00 U.S. Retrieving a misfiled document costs $120.00 U.S. An integrated ECM solution saves storage costs, relieves the HR Department's administrative work load (e.g. manual paper handling) and improves employee service.

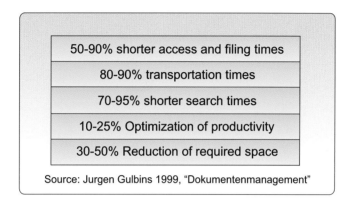

Source: Jurgen Gulbins 1999, "Dokumentenmanagement"

Figure 10.11: The Usage of an Electronic Employee
Folder Facilitates Time and Cost Savings

Employee records need to be safe and secure, and for some employers federal, state, union and other regulations may apply. For instance, in the transportation industry, driver and pilot records must contain competency and medical certifications. Ensuring that such documents are current and on file is critical, and not having these can result in penalties or fines to the company.

ECM solutions can streamline the process and ensure compliance with regulations. New hire workflows can ensure that the correct process and documents are gathered for each new employee, while existing documents can also be seamlessly managed to ensure compliance with regulations.

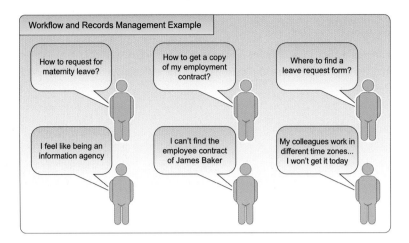

Figure 10.12: Using Workflows to Streamline Processes

Skills Management

Depending on the industry, an average employee spends two percent of his or her time learning new skills and keeping up to date amid rapidly changing conditions. When you consider that, on average, employees change jobs every three years and that labor costs constitute a huge percentage of overall company costs, the motivation behind effectively measuring and managing employee skill levels is obvious. With active skills management, companies can effectively monitor, analyze and develop employees' corporate knowledge and comprehension.

Organizations need to be able to identify the human resources required to achieve corporate objectives and quickly assess whether existing resources are sufficient. Skill deficiencies need to be addressed. Assessing skills in a globally dispersed or restructuring organization presents significant challenges. The hiring process must be focused on effectively addressing skill shortages.

Using an ECM solution to manage skills has many benefits. ECM systems allow for simple identification of skill deficiencies in particular areas and the ability to create an effective plan to address deficiencies in training or recruitment. Targeting skilled employees for particular project teams or for new company process, and redistributing or reorganizing resources in times of restructuring and internal change are significant benefits as well.

> Industrial Technology Research Institute (ITRI)

The Industrial Technology Research Institute (ITRI) played a key role in Taiwan's economic miracle by accelerating the research and development of industrial technologies, eventually becoming both a technical center for industry and an important arm of the government's industrial policies. A largely distributed enterprise, ITRI needed a scalable document management tool integrated with the familiar SAP environment.

Each document at the Accounting Resources Center is now scanned upon receipt and the merged document content and image files are archived in the ECM system and assigned a barcode which is entered into SAP. As a result, users have simultaneous access to both document content and information on related documents with easy document identification.

All dispersed locations are able to directly access, create, organize, store and retrieve documents from within their familiar SAP environment. Scanning and imaging technologies have enabled process automation and time savings have been realized through the elimination of lengthy search and retrieval processes.

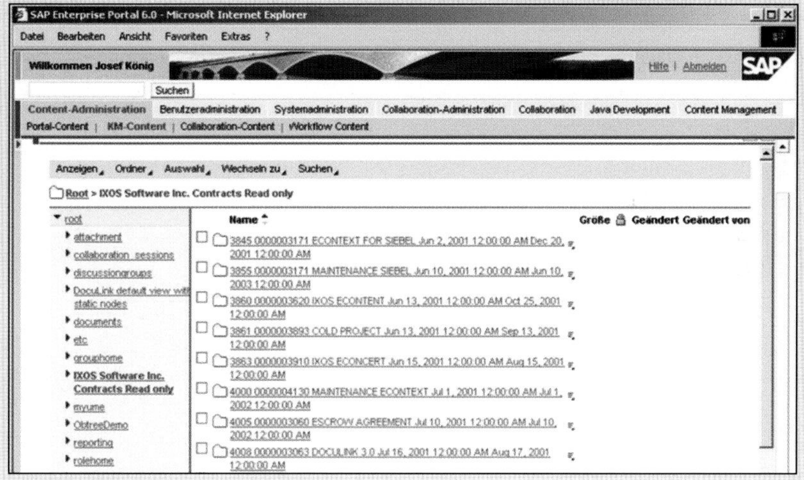

Figure 10.13: An Example of an SAP Enterprise Portal

Standard Processes in Administration Departments

The work in Administration Departments is characterized by tasks that need to be done with precision, along a fixed business process and across functional departments or regional sites. In addition, legal regulations require that many processes within administrative departments are fully traceable and auditable. Working on standardized business processes is characterized by excess paperwork that mirrors inefficiencies, errors caused by processing bottlenecks, media interruptions, delays, duplications and inaccuracies. In fact, many administration employees spend 80 percent of their time retrieving, inputting and sending information, then waiting for follow up information. ECM solutions automate key processes that drive the success of an organization. It shortens cycle times and brings products and services to market quickly, while reducing operational costs, increasing quality and ensuring regulatory compliance.

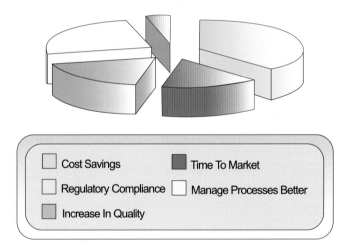

- ☐ Cost Savings
- ☐ Regulatory Compliance
- ■ Increase In Quality
- ■ Time To Market
- ☐ Manage Processes Better

Figure 10.14: The Benefits of BPM

Unifying Numbers and Words

Enterprise applications like ERP and CRM systems presented organizations with a vision of high process transparency, lower costs and excellent customer service. However, for most companies, this vision remained unfulfilled because content (invoices, orders, employee files, etc.) was managed separately from business processes (ERP or CRM processes). Classic document management systems could not seamlessly integrate business processes with corporate content.

> Mercer

MERCER
Human Resource Consulting

Mercer Human Resource Consulting helps clients understand, develop, implement, and quantify the effectiveness of human resource programs and policies. The organization has thousands of consultants around the world who need to create, re-use, and manage intellectual capital. In order to leverage existing knowledge resources and ensure compliance with increasingly pressing regulations, Mercer turned to ECM technology.

Currently, records management allows for storage and retrieval of archived information in a timely manner. A portal to a centralized Web-based knowledge repository ensures that all employees can effectively share and re-use existing resources. Search functionalities and communities of practice support collaboration and information sharing between consultants all over the world.

Workflow technology enables Mercer to manage decentralized sites, thus achieving consistency in support, training and governance, and ensures tracking for audit purposes. The organization can use its flexible storage management to achieve compliance with state and federal regulations such as privacy legislation. In addition, the solution enables multi-national compliance for all of Mercer's geographically dispersed sites.

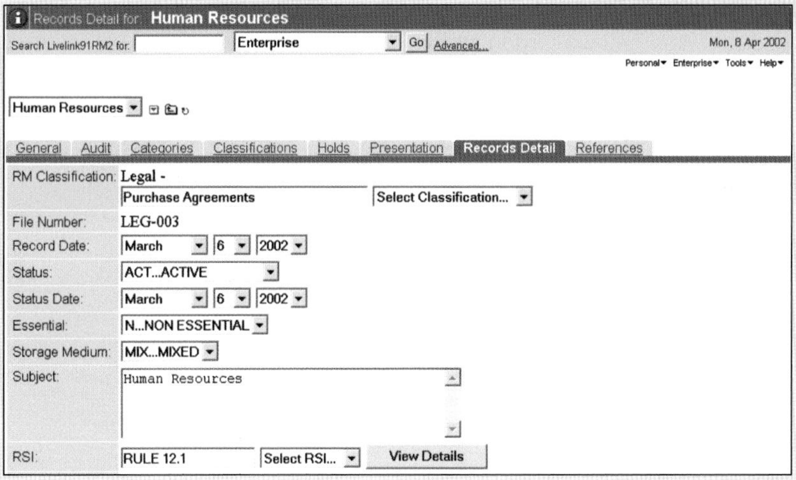

Figure 10.15: An Example of a Records Detail Tab

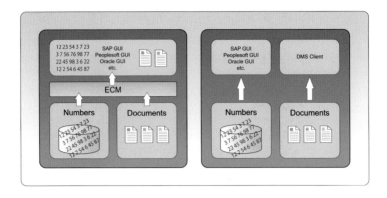

Figure 10.16: ECM Solutions Unify Numbers and Words

Integrated ECM links document content to the business context of enterprise applications, eliminating information silos, the need for resource-intensive postal mail, express delivery services and paper archives. Enterprise applications provide the underlying business structure that supports business processes. Allocating unstructured content to the corresponding business process places information at users' fingertips, without requiring them to search for individual documents.

An integrated solution allows organizations to jointly create, access, manage and securely archive all enterprise application content, addressing stringent requirements for risk reduction, operational efficiency and IT cost savings.

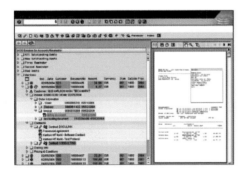
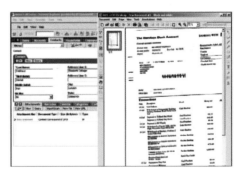

ECM integration into
SAP Business Suite

ECM integration into Siebel CRM

Figure 10.17: ECM Integration

Reducing Costs in the IT Department

Administration Departments, and IT Administration and Planning play a critical role in ensuring the long-term health and success of any company. IT innovations change the positioning of organizations. For example, setting up self-service ticket counters radically alters the IT approach to managing help requests. On the other hand, CIOs today face decreasing budgets and increasing IT operation costs. More efficient IT operations enable organizations to do more with less. Integrated ECM solutions make IT operations more cost effective.

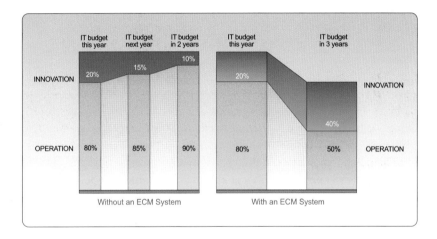

Figure 10.18: Demonstration of ECM's effect on IT Innovation and Operation in Administration

Managing Transactional Data

Every business process generates data and tends to increase the volume of an enterprise application's database. The growing volume of data hampers system performance and slows down access to information. The prolonged backup and restoration of information adds to an administrator's workload and increases costs.

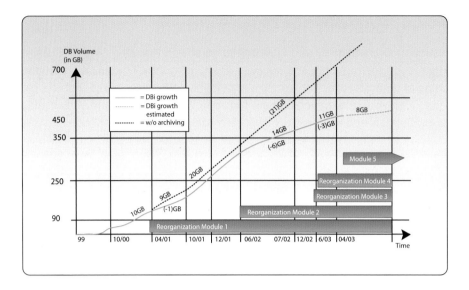

Figure 10.19: An Example of Data Archiving for Enterprise Applications

Integrated ECM solutions offload old data from an enterprise application, providing long-term access to archived information that is stored in a durable, tamper-proof format. This helps companies lower the costs and risks associated with data retention and disposal requirements. In addition, offloading data facilitates faster backup and recovery times, reduces administrative and hardware costs and decreases the time needed for enterprise application upgrades.

Automating the Migration of Legacy Data

When organizations overhaul their IT infrastructure, many business systems once integral to operating efficiency are relegated to "maintenance mode," becoming legacy systems. This forces IT Departments to integrate new applications and systems. Consequently, many decide to maintain legacy systems rather than "decommission" them, believing they can leverage their initial investment to maintain a more cost-effective solution. Maintaining these legacy systems often proves expensive and can hamper future returns on technology investment and introduce operational inefficiencies.

Organizations that need to store data from inherited or outdated IT systems for reference or to comply with regulatory requirements should consider legacy system data archiving. Adopting this strategy makes information and data readily available via various clients of the enterprise application. It avoids complex migration and associated costs, expedites the decommissioning process and ensures that regulatory requirements are met.

ᒑ NOVARTIS

Novartis is one of the world's leading suppliers in the field of public and consumer health. Speed is essential in the pharmaceutical industry when critical medications must be delivered as quickly as possible to patients. Novartis Pharma GmbH guarantees its customers prompt delivery of goods: for orders received before 11:00 am, the medicine is delivered the same day—a significant challenge for the sales staff who receive 500 to 600 orders a day by fax alone.

To provide immediate customer service, a fax server interface is used to integrate the documents rather than relying on print versions. Orders are received by the fax server and then immediately stored in the electronic archive, indexed, and forwarded to the right person in sales—completely automatically.

Since the solution was implemented, employees are able to answer almost every customer question immediately—without tedious searches of filing cabinets—while the customer is still on the phone. It is easy for the sales staff to monitor the status of every order and react quickly to any problems. The solution displays orders and workflow information together in an overview.

According to the Novartis project manager, "Once we get to the point where we are handling all our incoming mail electronically, we'll be able to further reduce the amount of paperwork, and make other processes, such as our invoicing processing, more efficient as well."

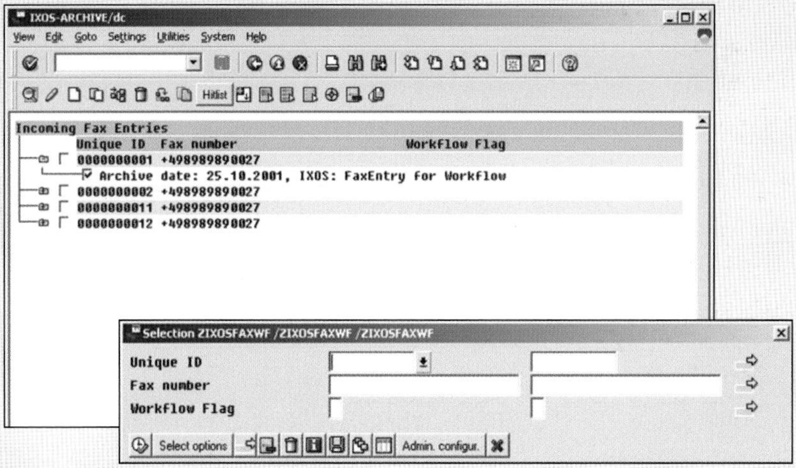

Figure 10.20: An Example of a Fax Entry Interface

How a Single ECM Infrastructure Saves Costs through Standardization

Companies today are asking a lot from their CIOs. They are handed a fixed budget, and are expected to maintain all the systems in place. Administration, upgrades, security, integration—these cost factors are constantly driving up expenses. CEOs are demanding new processes and new systems to support innovation within a budget. The only way out is to reduce the Total Cost of Ownership (TCO) to allow for further innovation. There are three ways to reduce TCO: standardization in software applications, standardization in storage hardware and rationalization.

CIOs face increasing challenges to their storage infrastructure, including increasing data base sizes, diverse platforms and increased demands to meet compliance requirements. An Enterprise Content Repository (ECR)—part of an integrated ECM solution—abstracts the storage infrastructure. It allows the CIO to choose his preferred storage vendor or run a mix of vendors under one abstraction.

An integrated ECM Solution incorporates ECM into all major software applications. Customers benefit when one repository manages all content, whether it is enterprise application content (SAP, Siebel, PSFT, etc.), groupware content or content from records management.

Business processes do not stop at the border of software application. Call center agents need access to every customer interaction document. Invoice verification is bridging ERP users and non-ERP users who prove the invoice. Content solutions on top of the ECM platform give customers a flexible infrastructure to depict content-driven business processes.

The Benefits of Standardization at a Glance:

• Hardware virtualization leads to lower Total Cost of Ownership;

• single platform allows quick addition of new ECM disciplines to existing infrastructure;

• various information islands and silos connect and create true cross-application business processes.

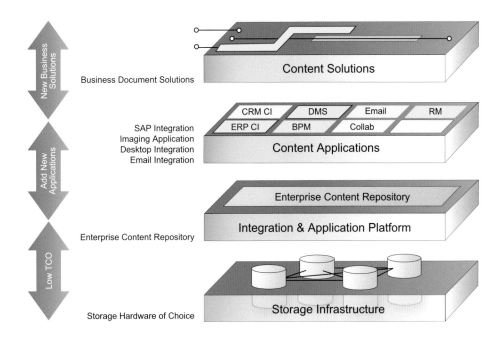

Figure 10.21: The Benefits of Standardization

Compliance in Administration

Although regulations vary from country to country, they consistently require organizations to track, manage and retain critical business information and quickly present that information upon request. Developing and implementing best practices for compliance requirements not only protects organizations from risk but helps them streamline operations, reduce administrative costs and proactively prepare to comply with emerging and changing regulations. An integrated ECM solution plays an integral role in fulfilling evolving legal requirements by securely storing content for designated periods, linking related information, providing an audit history and giving organizations easy access to any document on demand.

Figure 10.22: Implementing Best Practices Protects and Streamlines Organizations

Corporate Governance

Organizations must continue to rapidly develop innovative solutions while ensuring compliance with increasingly stringent industry and government regulations. Transparency and accountability have become crucial to corporate success. A comprehensive framework is required to ensure that each aspect of the regulations is properly addressed. It is not enough to merely be compliant with the Sarbanes-Oxley Act (SOX); demonstrating compliance is crucial.

The organization needs a reliable means of storing and retrieving business-critical and sensitive information. The ability to track regulatory deliverables and certifications must exist. Disclosure and reporting processes must be cost effective and efficient. The organization must have an integrated means of managing records, from creation, to maintenance, to eventual destruction. Employees must be able to effectively communicate and fulfill task requirements. The organization must have an established training certification program and the ability to quickly demonstrate its effectiveness.

The best way to address these challenges is by setting up an ECM framework for corporate governance. Such a framework must provide robust document management, collaboration, training certification and records management functionality in an integrated, secure, single-repository environment. This environment forms the framework for establishing compliance proof points, ensuring employee certification, enabling effective information dissemination and assessing and mitigating corporate risks.

Achieving compliance is an increasingly complex task. Due-process procedures require that organizations recognize a suitable control framework on which to base compliance efforts. The Committee of Sponsoring Organizations of the Treadway Commission (COSO) Internal Controls Framework is the industry standard for improving the quality of financial reporting through business ethics and effective internal controls. Corporations that fulfill its conditions will be SOX-compliant.

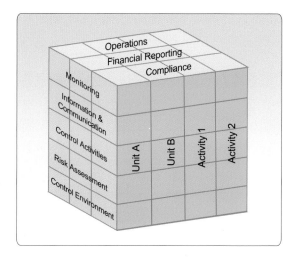

Figure 10.23: Compliance and Corporate Governance in Administration

ECM solutions provide a role-based control environment that encourages collaboration while maintaining discipline and structure. Users can effectively publish, store, share and find all information relating to corporate governance, including board meeting minutes, corporate policies, risk data, corporate control, U.S. Securities and Exchange Commission (SEC) filings and other managed documents in these custom workspaces.

ECM solutions provide a robust content repository for storing and controlling documents that describe organizational charts, policies and Standard Operating Procedures (SOPs). These policies and procedures are a necessary part of compliance, as they ensure that management directives are carried out and corporate objectives are pursued and achieved. Workflow and electronic signature capabilities allow SOX processes (Sections 302 and 404) to be standardized, automated and verifiably followed. Comprehensive auditing and reporting capabilities enable an organization to quickly refer to the details of archived processes such as approvals, authorizations, verifications, reconciliations, reviews of operating performance, security of assets and segregation of duties.

An ECM solution provides rich-media SOP certification systems that ensure that employees are properly trained on the latest SOPs and measures how these processes impact governance. Comprehensive assessment and management reporting enable the company to verifiably demonstrate that all employees have been certified.

ECM solutions for corporate governance risk assessment facilities enable companies to quickly determine the type, severity and probability of each potential risk. They can compare at a glance the odds of occurrence with the level of impact. An ECM solution for corporate governance ensures that high impact risks with a high probability of occurrence are acknowledged and handled accordingly.

Impact Types		Impact Levels	Probabilities				
Financial	Legal		Very Low (1%)	Low (10%)	Medium (25%)	High (40%)	Very High (60%)
< $100k	Complaint Letter	Small Impact	Very Very Low	Very Low	Low	Medium	High
$100k to $1M	Inquiry	Moderate Impact	Very Low	Low	Medium	High	Very High
$1M to $5M	Investigation	Material Impact	Low	Medium	High	Very High	Unacceptable
> $5M	Indictment	Severe Impact	Medium	High	Very High	Unacceptable	Unacceptable

Figure 10.24: An Example of an ECM Risk Matrix

Employee Accreditations

Industry regulators continue to place increasingly strict requirements on organizations, forcing them to take appropriate measures to ensure that employee training programs meet acceptable educational standards. However, not only do organizations need to ensure employee comprehension and compliance, they need to quickly and reliably prove it. Global enterprises have thousands of geographically dispersed employees separated by time zones and language barriers. Organizations need a solution that effectively manages every step of the employee accreditations process reliably, consistently and across the enterprise—from course content and comprehensive reports, to employee progress and license and compliance records—all without compromising productivity.

Business reputations can be irreparably damaged if organizations cannot quickly respond to inquiries or subpoenas. Inability to produce proof-of-compliance documents in a discovery process during arbitration or litigation can create significant legal expense, default judgments, undesirable settlements, or compliance fines. An ECM solution for employee accreditations enables a company to mitigate the risks associated with being unable to retrieve employee certifications information quickly, reliably and transparently. Furthermore, a company can manage, view and report on the organization's accreditations and licensing activities, so that the company is always aware of how the organization measures up to industry standards and demands. The company can quickly analyze various metrics, including the effectiveness of entire classes and the courses themselves.

Inter-Departmental Solutions for Administration

Central Customer Folder

In large organizations, several business units communicate with customers. For example, a car manufacturing company sells the car through the sales organization, organizes financing through their own bank, resells insurance, and provides licensed garages for maintenance. If a call center agent receives a call from the customer asking details about the financing, the call center agent cannot provide effective assistance until he or she can collect all the information distributed in several business units' systems. Retrieving information from several systems is tedious, requires expertise and time, and call centers have high employee turnover, which results in high employee education efforts. Having a central customer folder with all information improves service and creates opportunities for cross-selling. In many cases, a central customer folder enables Internet based self-service scenarios.

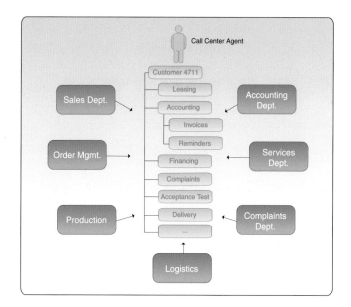

Figure 10.25: Central Customer Folders Decrease Time Costs and Increase Opportunities for Cross-Selling

Getting ROI out of an ECM Investment

Although many problems exist for Administration Departments throughout the world, each one is unique. Depending on the region, the economy and the corporate culture, Administration Departments will have a variety of processes and priorities. ROI out of an ECM solution varies and depends heavily on the amount of paper the industry must handle. To understand how many documents there are in specific industries and what ROI you can expect from an ECM solution see Figure 10.26. At the end of the day—and for all industries—compliance is a real driving factor behind regional variances.

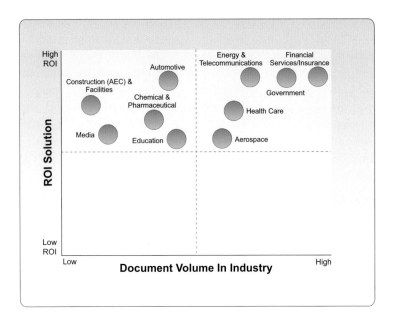

Figure 10.26: What ROI You Can Expect From ECM

There are many ways to get ROI out of your ECM investment and many ways to be more compliant. The matrix in figure 10.28 helps to quantify the solutions implementation effort versus ROI an organization can expect.

> Lufthansa Cargo

⊘ Lufthansa Cargo

Lufthansa Cargo ships about 2 million tons of air cargo and air mail annually and every transport is accompanied by documents generated at trans-shipment centers and reloading points. To ensure optimal business performance, fast document access is needed for tracking reasons as well as for efficient accounting and cost determination. Paper-based processes could no longer meet these requirements and Lufthansa Cargo decided to implement an Electronic Document Management System (EDMS).

The solution—DORA (Document Retrieval and Archive)—delivers the key benefits of an EDMS by providing easy document access and search and retrieval functionalities. In addition, 26 million documents were migrated into the system leaving storage space for many more to come.

"We reduced the effort of retrieving and managing air cargo documents tremendously while decreasing our warehouse capacities. Furthermore we need no client roll-outs and can easily include field organizations and external companies of Lufthansa corporate group," summarizes a representative of Cargo Revenue Accounting, Lufthansa Systems.

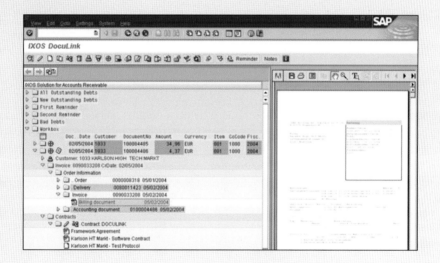

Figure 10.27: An Example of Integration of AR Processes with an ERP System

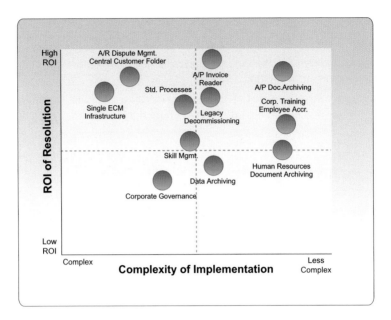

Figure 10.28: Complexity of Implementation and the Resulting ROI

ECM in Administration

ECM solutions for Administration Departments provide a context within which intellectual property can be created and stored for current and future use. Administration Departments face content challenges that require ECM solutions. Solutions that permit administrators to share knowledge with colleagues, customers, partners and suppliers. This facilitates the management of new programs and proposals, and the development of effective new products and services.

The Administration Department is impacted the most by ECM due to its use of paper and processes and its interactions with all people inside and outside the organization.

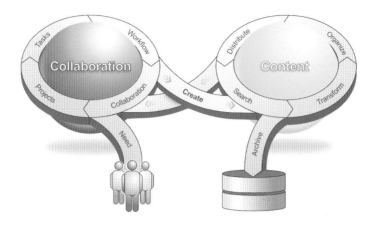

Figure 11.1: Creative Process Lifecycle

In the world of media content, the catalyst for the creative lifecycle is a **need**. This need—whether fulfilled by copy, a photograph, a book or a television program—spawns **projects** that become the basic organizing construct for many creative activities or **tasks**. In more complex media environments, these collections of project-based activities form workflows. **Workflows** in the media community are seldom structured or rigid, given the nature of the creative process. This is especially true where multiple contributors must interact in developing creative content. **Collaboration** becomes a central theme of media-centric workflows.

Once a team has been assembled, relevant creative elements must be identified. For efficiency and cost savings, team members can access an Enterprise Content Management system and perform a **search** to find existing applicable content. How these elements are **organized** plays an important role in determining how quickly the team can identify and decide which creative elements are appropriate for the project.

Selected creative elements may be ideal in content but incorrect in format for the desired use. Team members can **transform** the media element to the appropriate format, such as rendering a photograph from a TIFF to a JPEG for use on a Web. The finished media content, whether the product of new creative efforts, reuse, or some combination, is ready to be **distributed** to the next point in the media value chain. Finally, team members ensure that the creative assets are appropriately organized, categorized and **archived** so that they may easily identify these elements for reuse.

MEDIA

If a picture speaks a thousand words then full motion video positively shouts. In recent years, rich media content, loosely defined as images, audio, video and any other visually oriented unstructured content such as animation and PowerPoint presentations, has exploded on the public Internet, as well as behind the firewall of the corporate enterprise.

Perhaps no other industry has been more revolutionized by the advances and demand for rich media content than the Media Industry. With the mainstreaming of rich media consumption, media organizations are increasingly challenged to deliver their products and messages to the market faster and in more innovative and memorable ways. New compliance regulations, anti-trust issues and the fear of strict penalties have further complicated the technological needs and challenges of these organizations.

Media companies are among the largest and most powerful corporate entities today, as the content they produce reaches unprecedented numbers of consumers in direct and influential ways. The variety of content produced serves a number of audiences and objectives including educating, influencing, entertaining and selling. The mechanisms to distribute are vast and diverse, ranging from enduring media (books and magazines) to up-to-the-minute reporting of news and events.

In today's digital creative world, managing an overwhelming volume of digital assets is only half the challenge. Digital technology allows the creative and production community unparalleled freedom in creating and distributing its message. However, by its very nature, digital creativity is a non-linear process that permits individuals to look at all of their assets at one time. Because of this, companies need a powerful tool that allows them to search, access, share and distribute assets. With an ECM solution, organizations not only address these challenges, but also remedy them and maximize their potential.

Meeting Efficiency Challenges

Media and Entertainment companies are some of the most significant producers, managers and distributors of rich media content, and produce such diverse products as books, magazines, music, radio, television programming and motion pictures. Because of the breadth of content and the multitude of distribution channels (print, Web, broadcast), the initial and most fundamental challenge a company must address is managing the exponential growth of digital content to get the most out of it now and in the future. As a result, the technology market has seen the development and standardization of technical solutions to bring efficiency and cost savings to the management of digital content, and such upstream functions as digital asset production and distribution. This increasingly mainstream category of content-centric computing is broadly defined as the ability to re-express rich media content in new forms or products made possible through asset organization and collaboration.

Once a company has an ECM system in place to manage its digital assets, other components of the greater ECM suite can be added with greater results, as the content building blocks can be readily identified, accessed, catalogued, transformed and stored. For a news broadcaster, this can mean faster "time to story." For a magazine publisher, this translates into quick and inexpensive new content development through repurposing existing, approved and paid-for content. For a book publisher, it means not only streamlining the book publishing process, but also rapid distribution of ancillary assets associated with the book.

Regardless of the final product (book, music, television show, magazine, film), the most critical function for a media company is content production that is cost effective and efficient.

Production Asset Management

"Production" Asset Management within the context of ECM lets producers, editors, designers and Web developers access a central database of pre-approved digital assets (logos, photos, film, video, text, audio, animation) during the creative process. With assets securely stored in an ECM system, organized and intelligently tagged with appropriate metadata, the system not only provides an ability to search and locate desired content, it provides the user with relevant information about the asset. This allows creatives to understand how and where assets were used and lets them repurpose them in other materials and for other media.

At the heart of the "Production" Asset Management use case is allowing those developing creative content more time to focus on the creative process instead of being mired in non-creative tasks. Without a digital asset management strategy, creatives can literally burn

> Time Warner Book Group

With its rich history and vast holdings, Time Warner Book Group looked to digital asset management as a solution to support its publishing, marketing and new media activities. Time Warner Book Group required a solution to enhance its organizational efficiencies by enabling it to find and retrieve assets more quickly and easily. The solution also had to simplify the packaging of promotional materials for distribution to its internal Web sites and external eTailers.

The company's approach was to break its books into their digital components and establish a common meta-data standard to allow asset sharing across the company. Time Warner Book Group was able to bring formally outsourced processes, such as eBook production, in house. As well, the asset management solution enabled its sales force to create presentations in the field tailored to their customers.

For Time Warner Book Group, the benefits of establishing such a centralized repository include the elimination of redundancies and islands of information; the ability to repurpose core information; major efficiency gains in the distribution of content and marketing materials to online and brick and mortar trading partners; a vast reduction in hardcopy circulation, photocopying, large email attachments and scanning; and reduced time spent distributing and accessing online assets.

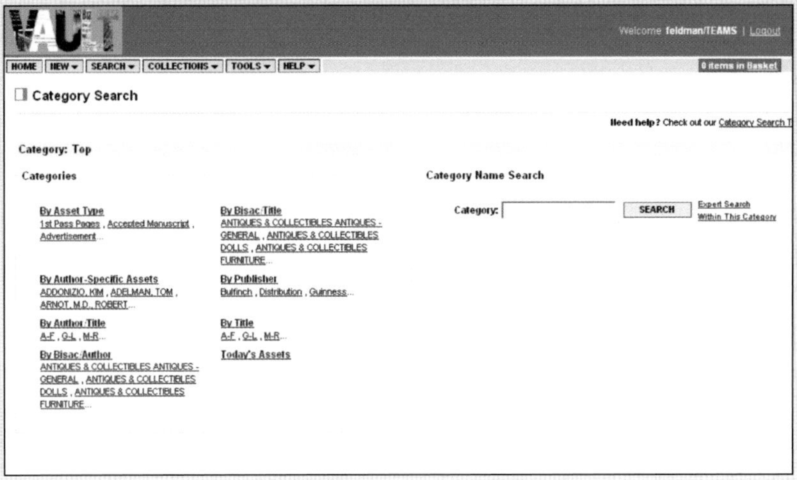

Figure 11.2: Time Warner Book Group's Digital Asset Vault

hours, if not days, simply locating content and determining the rights associated with it. Often the only solution is to re-create content that may already exist, which is time consuming and costly.

The review and approval process should not impede the process or add to the cost of the project. By storing work-in-progress in an ECM system, review and approval can be dramatically accelerated, as everyone involved in this phase of the project enjoys immediate access no matter where they are geographically. This approach also eliminates the time and expense wasted on shipping content for review.

At the conclusion of a project, all final content is stored, tagged with informative metadata and accessible for future use.

Brand Asset Management

To remain competitive and profitable, Media companies make significant investment in developing new products and identifying untapped markets. However, there is a less tangible but almost equally important aspect of their business that also requires investment – marketing of the brand. In the end, a company's brands may be among its greatest and most enduring assets.

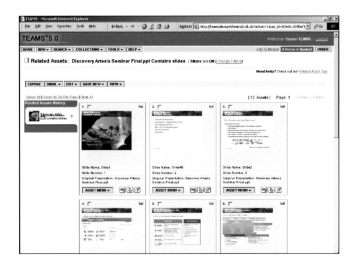

Figure 11.3: An ECM Solution Ensures Brand Integrity Across Projects

> Fox Filmed Entertainment

A business segment of Fox Entertainment, Fox Filmed Entertainment (FFE) is one of the world's top producers and distributors of theatrical, home entertainment and TV productions, and is especially known for their 20th Century Fox and Fox 2000 movies.

As a result, the marketing collateral that FFE develops for each production represents a significant investment for the company.

To streamline the management and distribution of brand assets and other marketing media, Fox Filmed Entertainment created an ECM-based secure central repository for rich marketing assets such as audio, video, images, graphics and text-based documents. The integration of the solution with third-party authoring applications enabled increased speed to market with most recent marketing materials.

"With each film generating hundreds of new assets that are in demand by our distribution, marketing, and communications groups, we needed...a way to streamline this process. ECM ...has met these needs by offering us world-class technology. As a result, rather than searching endlessly through disparate databases for the right asset, an authorized user can easily and securely access this important material," says the Vice President of Information Technology at Fox Filmed Entertainment.

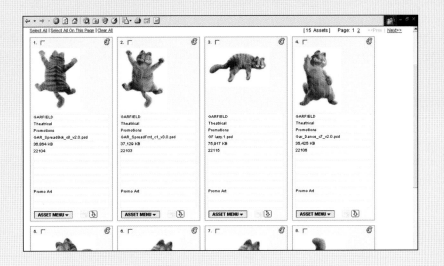

Figure 11.4: Digital Asset Management at 20th Century Fox

Ensuring the integrity and consistency of a brand is a highly specialized mix of both art and science. Media companies spend a substantial portion of their annual budget marketing and promoting the sale of their production media content, and trying to determine how their brand relates and moves their constituency. Once a brand has been successfully delivered to the marketplace, companies must ensure that the personality and essence of the brand is maintained. Therefore, it is critical to put in place policies, technology and workflows that protect the brand and make these marketing-related activities more efficient.

ECM for "Brand" Asset Management lets marketing, creative services, advertising and promotions access and collaborate around a central database of digital brand assets, including logos, photographs, commercials, promotional video, graphics, text, page layouts and completed campaigns. This saves time and money while ensuring brand integrity across an organization. Coupled with robust workflow, Brand Asset Management allows greater collaboration and control over a company's valuable corporate identity, which is reflected in countless materials and media. By doing this in real time, a company is able to reduce the approval process and get its materials working out in the market sooner.

Given the wide range of distribution channels available to media companies, the challenges increase. A company must ensure that its Web team is in sync with its ad agency, as well as those creating print materials. Often these groups do not work on the same team and can be geographically disparate. With a digital asset management system, the guardians of the brand can make sure that only approved branding is made available to them.

Distribution Asset Management

Once the challenges of producing rich media content have been addressed, the next major hurdle is to get content out to its point of consumption. For some media companies this means distributing new materials to a sales force or distributor. For others, it means broadcasting content to consumers or through third-party cable companies.

Leveraging an ECM system to address "Distribution" Asset Management offers producers and marketers the ability to make final products—whether original production content such as digital masters or promotional content such as short-form video and print-based advertising—available more cost effectively to their diverse distribution channels. In the television arena, Distribution Asset Management allows for broadcast operations personnel to more specifically automate the schedule and delivery of finished digital programming materials.

> Télévision Suisse Romande

Télévision Suisse Romande (TSR) is a company owned by SRG-SSR idée suisse, a private firm holding a public media concession. As Switzerland is a small country with less than 8 million inhabitants, TSR faces the stiff competition of over 35 other foreign channels. In response, the company adopted a broadcasting strategy based on two complementary channels and is evolving towards an additional multimedia-based offering.

The ECM-based Traffic system is a data-sharing solution at TSR. A data repository provides the foundation for centralization of decisions, decentralization of data entry and centralization of validations. The data shared at TSR includes the publication of programming grids, the distribution of the grids to the press, the acquisition of broad-casting data, the dissemination of financial management data, and more.

The show producers populate each project with basic required information, while the other participants of the work process provide or link additional information. This method provides access to rich information that does not have to be created from scratch. External users welcome the amount of information available through the TSR extranet, along with the ability to quickly access key information autonomously via this self-service method.

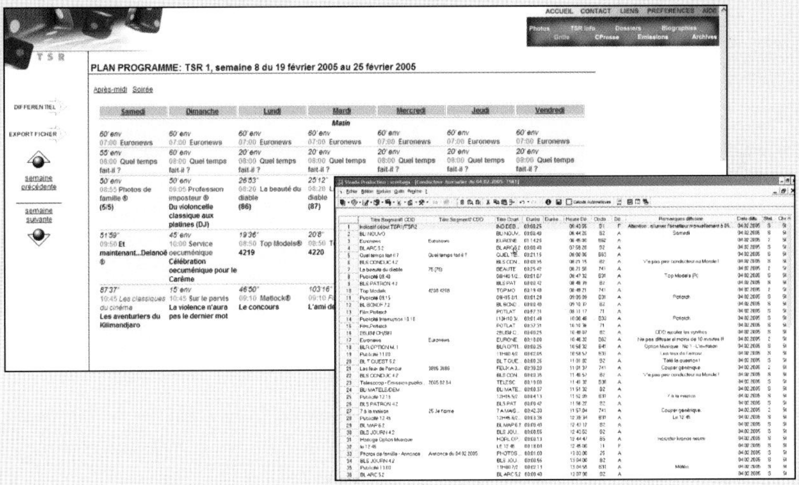

Figure 11.4: Publication of Programming and Broadcasting Data at TSR

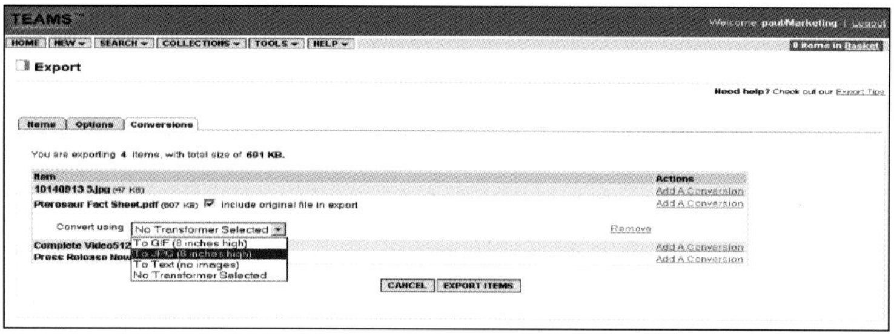

*Figure 11.5: Distribution Asset Management Facilitates
the Automation of Distribution Schedules*

As seen in the "Production" Asset Management discussion, media companies that embrace ECM as either a standalone technology or integrated with other components can increase the value of their content through reuse and repurposing of digital media. In addition, readily delivering digital content and expanding the access of content further elevates the value. Now, an entire organization, its partners, agencies and others involved in the creation and distribution of digital content have immediate access. To ensure that content is protected, an ECM system needs security features that allow departments to distribute and share content as broadly or narrowly as they see fit.

Leveraging an ECM system to address "Distribution" Asset Management lets producers and marketers make final products—whether original production content such as digital masters, or promotional content such as short-form video and print-based advertising—available more cost effectively to their diverse distribution channels. In the television arena, Distribution Asset Management allows for broadcast operations personnel to more specifically automate the schedule and delivery of finished digital programming materials.

ECM in Media

Managing digital assets is a key component of an ECM solution. This ability provides robust support for rich media content like video, images and formats from Quark and Adobe.

Typically integrated in between authoring and delivery platforms, ECM digital asset systems permit content to be managed once and then deployed to multiple delivery media including print, television and the Web. As it relates to Web development in particular, ECM systems act as a warehouse of digital "inventory," providing just-in-time delivery of digital content to software managing the digital storefront.

Lastly, metadata plays an important role. When richly described metadata is associated with content it becomes a true digital asset.

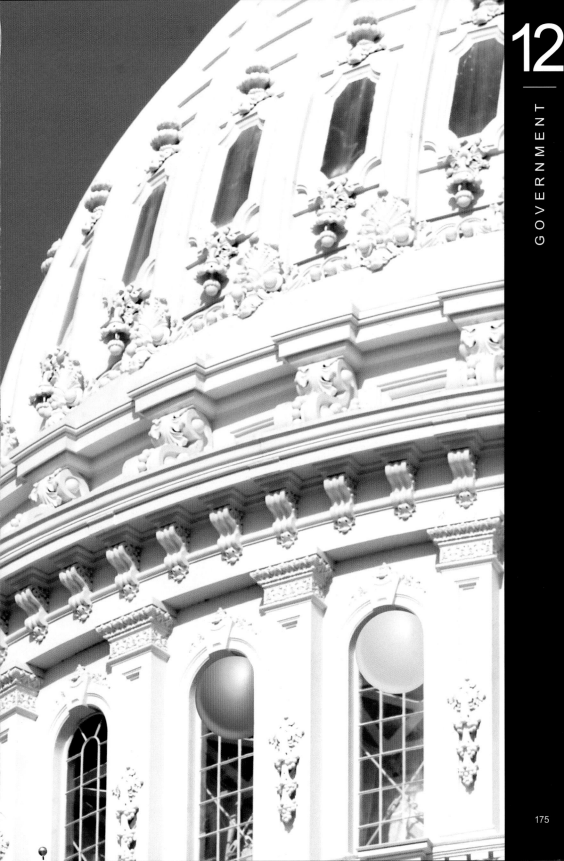

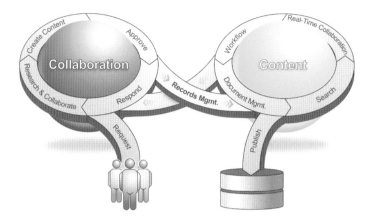

Figure 12.1: Information Management in Government Agencies

The major activities of a transformational government include sharing and publishing information interacting with citizens and agencies, and operating in a complete electronic environment. To successfully carry out these activities, government organizations rely on key integrated information management solutions to provide services online or share information and transactions horizontally. As correspondence or work **requests** enter an agency, employees must **collaborate** to respond to work and **create content** in a timely manner for **approval**. To ensure compliance or adherence to regulatory guidelines, some requests require that processes be turned into a case or lifecycle file, while others may require that regulated documents are reverse engineered once submitted. The government needs a solution that enables them to internally **respond** to and manage all these requests within a single application, enabling them to demonstrate certification and accreditation of architecture, technology and policy.

A Web-based ECM application can provide complete **document and records management**, project collaboration, **workflow**, and **search** and scheduling functionality for organizations in public services. Its centralized repository lets users access, collect and manage all types of information via any standard Web browser (allowing for **real-time collaboration**), while its Web-based interface integrates easily into existing information management systems, providing an integrated platform to manage the creation, flow and storage of unstructured information and structured data. The information is then **published** for reference.

GOVERNMENT

The Government sector is comprised of a worldwide system of agencies and departments with various roles, functions and missions, separated by more than geography. These agencies have requirements to share information with each other and their citizens in real time. The health of any government and its citizens depends on their ability to respond to changes throughout the world. ECM plays a key role in government by facilitating the acquisition, discussion and re-distribution of information timely and efficiently.

Today, with high bandwidth wireless Internet access and new devices that facilitate sharing information from anywhere, eGovernment has shaped the growth and future of ECM.

Government generally exists at three primary levels: federal, state and local. While each has their own constituencies, governing bodies, and unique challenges, an ECM solution can effectively assist each level in achieving policy and program success. This chapter will concentrate on the federal government level of two major countries: the United States and Germany.

In the federal government, communication between geographically disparate organizations in real and asynchronous timeframes is extremely important to the continuity of government. When crises arise, data must be quickly searched, assimilated, assembled and distributed in a secure manner to give officials information they need to make sound decisions. These decisions often affect federal, state and local governments as well.

Communication challenges also extend to government contractors, often located within the agencies or departments they serve. With the fast pace of government today, and the advent of performance contracting, defense contractors are under increased pressure to rapidly deliver solutions and have programs up and running while controlling costs and meeting compliance requirements. Government contractors also require secure collaboration tools to coordinate with sub-contractors on document and file sharing, reporting, proposal development and response, etc. These same secure collaboration tools are also used between contractors and government agencies themselves to deliver compliance reports, manage highly complex program documents and schematics, and provide mission-critical data in real-time from anywhere.

The Government Challenge

The major activities of a transformational government include sharing and publishing information, interacting with citizens and agencies, and transacting in an electronic environment. To successfully carry out these activities, government organizations rely on key integrated information management solutions to provide online services or to share information and transactions horizontally.

Increased pressure by internal auditors and offices of management and budget to justify information management projects is forcing government agencies to integrate and rationalize technology. Government agencies are forced to work with systems in place and innovate at the same time. Extreme pressure is placed on identification of cost containment issues such as total cost of ownership, lock-in cost and the switching cost of information management deployments.

In addition, government agencies face the challenge of succession planning and strategy for an aging workforce that lacks the resources to fill the roles of retiring senior management. Increasing performance with fewer, less-experienced people demands automated processes, the ability to develop rapid learning programs and the collaborative workspaces of an integrated information management infrastructure.

ECM Solutions for Government

ECM solutions can provide organizations with a fully compliant solution that helps government agencies manage information and exchange knowledge while enhancing productivity and performance. With a focus on reducing or eliminating paper-based processes, an ECM government solution is the only Web-based application that provides document and records management, project collaboration, workflow, search, and scheduling functionality for organizations in public services.

> Swiss Parliament

The Swiss Parliament's 5,000 Web pages provide Swiss citizens with a clear network of information about the parliament's members, business and activities. This unique Web service has proved extremely popular: around 5,500 visitors a day use it for an average of 25 minutes. In order to continue providing its citizens with the most up-to-date information at all times, the Swiss Parliament needed to replace its time-consuming and manual content management system.

Maintaining and updating the Swiss Parliament's Web site is now very simple and efficient with an ECM-based system. One of the highlights of this solution is the press release application, which imports XML files from the public relations department, formats them and publishes the text directly to the Web, enabling press releases to be generated dynamically.

Parliamentary Services can complete all necessary Web content updates with minimal effort. "Working with the solution is a real pleasure. It's easy to maintain and makes managing our Web site a quick and transparent exercise—even without any HTML knowledge," says the head of the Internet department at the Swiss Parliament.

Figure 12.2: Swiss Parliament's Web site

A centralized repository enables users to access, collect and manage all types of information via any standard Web browser while its Web-based interface integrates easily into existing information management systems. This provides an integrated platform to manage the creation, flow and storage of unstructured information and structured data.

For government, the compliance spectrum covers: correspondence or suspense tracking, case management, grants of issue management, regulated document submission and management, collaborative program management or certification, and accreditation. By combining all information management processes and requirements into an integrated architecture, a government solution supports this complex compliance spectrum. As correspondence or work requests enter an agency or department, employees must collaborate to complete work in a timely manner. To ensure compliance or adherence to regulatory guidelines, some requests require that processes be turned into a case or lifecycle file, while others may require regulated documents to be reverse engineered. A government solution enables government agencies to internally manage all these requests within a single application, enabling the agency to demonstrate certification and accreditation of architecture, technology and policy.

An effective solution complies with all current agency guidelines, providing organizations with a single integrated system that meets both the most open and the most restricted information sharing models. Security begins with user authentication; every user is given a unique user name and password. Using a nine-level permissions model, every object in the knowledge library—files, documents, workflows, discussions, tasks and more—has specific authorization levels for each user. Every project has an associated list of members, participants and guests who are involved in completing project tasks. Only members assigned to a specific project can access objects in that project.

The United States Government

As part of the institutionalization of the President's Management Agenda, and the continuing support of citizen-centric service delivery, U.S. President George Bush signed the E-Government Act of 2002 (Public Law 107-347, 44 U.S.C. Ch. 36) into law on December 17, 2002. E-Government is the use of information technology (IT) and the Internet, together with the operational processes and people needed to implement these technologies, to deliver services and programs to constituents including citizens, businesses and other government agencies. E-Government is designed to improve the effectiveness, efficiency and quality of government services.

> U.S. Office for Civil Rights

United States, Department of
Health Human Services

Through prevention and elimination of unlawful discrimination, the Office for Civil Rights (OCR) ensures that all affected persons have equal access to the many programs and services offered by the United States Department of Health and Human Services. Inundated by paper documents and burdened by a non-collaborative work setting, OCR wanted to improve its system for managing information and tracking correspondence.

A PIMS, or a Program Information Management System, has integrated OCR's business processes, correspondence and compliance information enabling direct, real-time access from a unified 'portal' interface. Users can now find what they need when they need it, reducing the time wasted in searching for information or in "reinventing the wheel."

Support for a collaborative work environment has enabled OCR employees to share in a community of knowledge with one another. PIMS has delivered a means for gener-ating and tracking correspondence and promoted a consistency of work methods and best practices sharing. OCR has also been able to improve the quality of service it provides to its customers.

Figure 12.3: An Example of Correspondence Management

The E-Government Act:

- advocates a more citizen-focused approach to current government-wide IT policies and programs;

- establishes an Office of Electronic Government in the Office of Management and Budget (OMB) to improve federal management of information resources;

- formalizes the establishment of a Chief Information Officers (CIO) Council;

- permanently reauthorizes and amends agency information security requirements through the Federal Information Security Management Act (FISMA);

- protects the confidentiality of certain types of data through the Confidential Information Protection and Statistical Efficiency Act (CIPSEA);

- supports activities that OMB and the executive branch are currently pursuing under the President's Management Agenda's Expanding Electronic Government initiative.

Under the Information Technology Management Reform Act (Public Law 104-106), the Secretary of Commerce approves standards and guidelines developed by the National Institute of Standards and Technology (NIST) for federal computer systems. These standards and guidelines are issued by NIST as Federal Information Processing Standards (FIPS) for use government-wide.

Depending on the government organization involved, various security accreditations or certifications may apply.

U.S. Government Regulations

The following is a brief summary of various agencies that have a mandate to develop and implement ECM intensive regulations within the United States:

Defense Department (Pentagon)

DITSCAP/DIACAP

The DoD Information Technology Security Certification and Accreditation Process (DITSCAP) helps users and security officers ensure that information systems operate at an acceptable level of risk. This includes the hardware, operating system, networks and software for the information system. The Defense Information Assurance Certification and Accreditation Process (DIACAP) will establish the standard DoD process for identifying, implementing and validating IA Controls, for authorizing the operation of DoD information systems, and for managing IA posture across DoD information systems consistent with Title III of the E-Government Act, FISMA and DoD Directive 8500.1.

DoD 5015.2

DoD 5015.2-STD, June 2002, defines basic requirements based on operational, legislative and legal needs that must be met by records management application (RMA) products acquired by the Department of Defense (DoD) and its components. Chapter 4 defines requirements for records management application's managing classified records.

DCTS

Defense Collaboration Tool Suite (DCTS) is a prioritized list of functional requirements that gives personnel the ability to link various command, control, communications and intelligence systems for sharing data, planning and consulting on information from worldwide locations.

Food And Drug Administration (FDA)

21 CFR Part 11

21 CFR Part 11 is the criteria under which FDA will consider electronic records to be equivalent to paper records, and electronic signatures equivalent to traditional handwritten signatures. Part 11 (21 CFR part 11) applies to any paper records required by statute or agency regulations and supersedes any existing paper record requirements by providing that electronic records may be used in lieu of paper records. Electronic signatures, which meet the requirements of the rule, will be considered equivalent to handwritten signatures, initials or other general signings required by agency regulations.

Federal Standards for Information Security

FISMA

FISMA utilizes NIST Special Publication (SP) 800-37, "Guide for the Security Certification and Accreditation of Federal Information Systems" as its compliance standard. NIST SP 800-37 provides guidelines for certifying and accrediting information systems supporting the executive agencies of the federal government. NIST SP 800-37 applies to all federal information systems other than those designated national security systems as defined in FISMA. The certification and accreditation package consists of the following documents: System Security Plan; Security Assessment Report; Plan of Action and Milestones.

The key document for the certification and accreditation process is the System Security Plan (SSP), detailed in NIST Special Publication 800-18, "Guide for Developing Security Plans for Information Technology Systems." The purpose of the SSP is to provide an overview of the security requirements of the system and describe the controls in place or planned for meeting those requirements and delineate responsibilities and expected behavior of all individuals who access the system.

Freedom of Information Act

FOIA

Enacted in 1966, the Freedom of Information Act (FOIA) was the first law to establish an effective legal right of access to government information, underscoring the crucial need in a democracy for open access to government information by citizens. FOIA generally provides that any person has a right to request access to federal agency records, except to the extent that records are protected from disclosure by any of nine exemptions contained in the law, or by one of three special law enforcement record exclusions.

Today, all agencies of the Executive Branch of the United States Government are required to disclose records upon receiving a written request for them.

Improving Inter-Agency Collaboration and Records Management

In compliance with the United States Government Paper Elimination Act (GPEA), organizations in the public sector are using ECM products to eliminate paper-based systems, streamline business processes, and mitigate risk and cost containment within existing programs. This will have a profound impact on ECM in the long term as agencies will only interact by electronic means. This has major implications for organizations that deal with the U.S. Federal government.

eGovernment in Europe

As we have discussed with the U.S. Federal Government, ECM technologies are increasingly being used by public authorities and organizations in Europe to save money and increase efficiency. At the same time they are adapting their processes to these technologies. The public sector fulfills an extremely important role in the European economic and social model by safeguarding a high level of prosperity amongst citizens, providing socio-economic cohesion and guaranteeing that competitive markets function. It performs numerous functions in a wide range of areas from education and health to social security and consumer and environmental protection. Europe's economic strengths—a qualified workforce and leadership in important industrial sectors—depend on the proper functioning of the public sector.

The public sector is accorded a key role in the modernization of the European economy and society. It enables Europe to become more competitive and dynamic, ensuring sustainable growth resulting in creation of more and better jobs and greater social cohesion. These are the Lisbon objectives for the year 2010.

> Irish Land Registry

Land Registry
Registry of Deeds

The paper records at the Irish Land Registry are stored at four different locations and are also replicated at the relevant county courthouses. Approximately 400,000 of those paper folios can be booked out for inspections, copying or other work at any time. As a result, the paper based system has often been extremely inefficient.

As part of the Irish government's Information Society initiative all government agencies were tasked to examine how they can deliver services electronically. Over 80 percent of customers listed the ready availability of Land Registry records as one of their top three priorities. It was decided that the implementation of an online search and retrieval system would meet both these criteria.

Currently, 12,000 folios a day are being scanned and added to the new system, which ensures the documents' ongoing protection and streamlines their use by customers. As a result, significant cost reduction has been forecast. Case work has been boosted by the fact that staff has instant access to document images.

Figure 12.4: Online Document Search and Retrieval at the Irish Land Registry

Public authorities now find themselves in a position where they are being asked to offer taxpayers "more service" for their money. Public administrations must provide more and better services with the same or reduced budgetary resources. In many member states, sluggish economic growth and the obligation to reduce budget deficits are resulting in drastic cuts in public expenditure. The most difficult task is to find a way of increasing productivity in the public sector to create scope for improving services at the same or reduced cost.

Furthermore, because of the ageing population authorities are having to cope with a smaller workforce and fewer gainfully employed taxpayers, while at the same time providing the same range of services but at an even higher quality.

Public service officials and employees want more interesting jobs with better opportunities for professional development and personal involvement; but guaranteed jobs, like life-long employment and social benefits, are increasingly under threat. The attractiveness of the public sector as an employer is at stake.

Today, the public sector in Europe stands at a crossroads; it faces formidable economic and social challenges, institutional changes and the dramatic impact of new technologies. Because of its importance as a promoter of economic growth, the public sector is expected to play an increasingly larger role in implementing the Lisbon strategy for economic, social and environmental renewal.

Within the public sector, administrations are being challenged to improve the efficiency, productivity and quality of their services. However, they must find a way to perform all these functions with the same or even reduced budgetary resources.

Information and Communication Technologies (ICT) can help public administrators face the numerous challenges. However, ICT must not be allowed to take center stage. Rather, ICT should be used in coordination with organizational changes and new skills to improve public services, and enhance democratic processes and the formulation and implementation of public policy. In practice, this means not only providing citizens with simplified official procedures and a citizen-friendly administration, but also facilitating contact between private enterprise and public administration, and improving the efficiency of cooperation between administrations. eGovernment is the key to modernizing public administration and encouraging stronger economic growth. Businesses benefit as the developers, providers, consumers and cooperation partners of eGovernment. This is what eGovernment is all about.

Prime examples exist from many countries showing how putting government services online creates better public services, reduces waiting times, improves price-performance ratios, increases productivity and transparency and reinforces responsible behavior. eGovernment is a central plank of the eEurope 2005 action plan. This is the only area where

> Federal Ministry of the Interior

BESCHAFFUNGSAMT
des Bundesministeriums des Innern

Trainloads of paper, pencils and computers, and larger items like police cars and helicopters—goods and services worth over 250 billion euros—appear on the shopping list of Germany's public authorities every year. The public procurement process should above all be fast, economical and transparent.

That is why the Procurement Agency of the Federal Ministry of the Interior is creating an innovative alternative to traditional procurement practices. Called "Public Purch@sing Online," the project allows contracts for goods and services to be awarded via the Internet. The electronic Tendering Module helps to establish a clear system for managing the placement of contracts. Moreover, the module automatically assists staff by taking over certain procedural steps. This has been made possible by the development of a workflow system which not only performs document management, but also handles work operations.

The German Federal Government mandated that all federal authorities use electronic tendering and a one-stop eGovernment shop by the end of 2005. This means that companies seeking public contracts can find all the tendering notices for the contracts of the federal authorities on the Internet. The project brings the Procurement Agency into compliance with the EU Directive on electronic commerce.

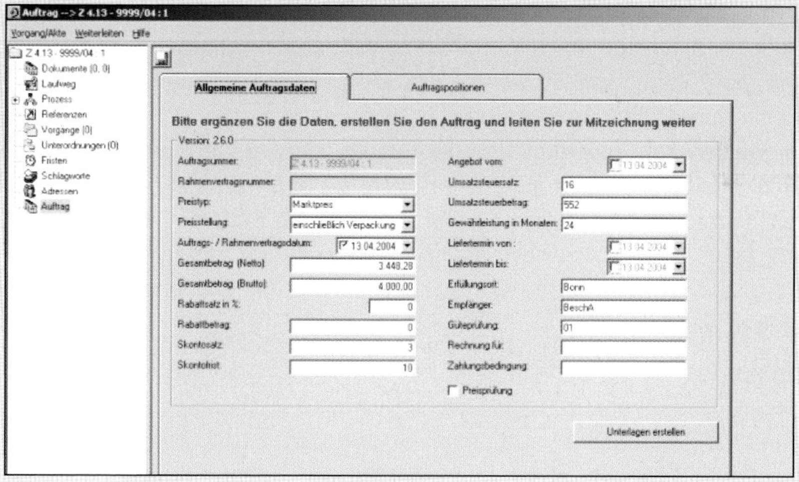

Figure 12.5: ECM Manages Online Procurement

governments are responsible for creating the basic conditions, and solely responsible for implementation. The recent eGovernment conference held as part of the eEurope 2005 action plan and its closing ministerial declaration, made clear the great advantages to be gained from implementing online public services in Europe.

Following this conference, the current state of eGovernment will be examined, highlighting the main problems and obstacles, and proposing cohesive measures to drive forward online services within the framework of eEurope 2005.

This communication makes clear the importance the Commission attaches to online public services as a means of creating a world-status pan-European public administration which, by offering new and better public services to citizens and businesses, contributes fully to the implementation of the Lisbon strategy. It calls upon Member States to clearly express their political commitment and leadership, and to join with all participants in the private and public sectors in intensifying their efforts.

eGovernment in Germany

By launching the BundOnline initiative at EXPO 2000, Chancellor Gerhard Schröder set the federal administration on a clear objective: all Internet-compatible public services should be available online by the end of 2005. The initiative took a significant step nearer to achieving this goal with the approval by the German federal government, states and municipalities of the joint eGovernment strategy "Deutschland Online", which networks federal, state and municipal projects with central coordination. The priority is to make the main administrative services at all government levels available over the Internet without any gaps in responsibility or changes of media. With BundOnline 2005, the German government has launched the largest eGovernment program in Europe. It is designed to ensure that each administration make approximately 440 public services available online throughout the country. For example, the Federal Office for Non-Military Service's decision to introduce new, standard software for community service training schools led to the creation of the BundOnline service for online registration for civic educational events.

BundOnline applies central coordination, but with local responsibility for implementing public services. This means that services are devised, implemented and enhanced by ministries and their subordinate authorities, while responsibility for overall coordination lies with the Federal Ministry of the Interior (FMI) and within it the BundOnline project group. The BMI also supports authorities with basic components and skills centers.

> Hessen

In the German province of Hessen, the provincial administrative centers are geograph-ically dispersed. In order to streamline document flow between the centers and accel-erate administrative processes, these geographical distances have been bridged with the help of an ECM-based document and process management system.

Preparation of files and documents, records management, file storage, archiving and searching are processes supported by the ECM solution. Incoming mail is scanned into the system, e-filed and electronically registered and archived. The employees at the administrative centers have direct access to the documents, independently of their location, while information can be forwarded within seconds. The files can only be accessed based on set permissions: as a result, access security has increased.

The integration of the solution with the back-end ERP system has fused two previously parallel running, heterogeneous IT-universes. All documents and data for current as well as future ECM and ERP applications are available to all employees from a single, province-wide, comprehensive archiving system. The new system is another milestone in the transition to an eGovernment in Hessen.

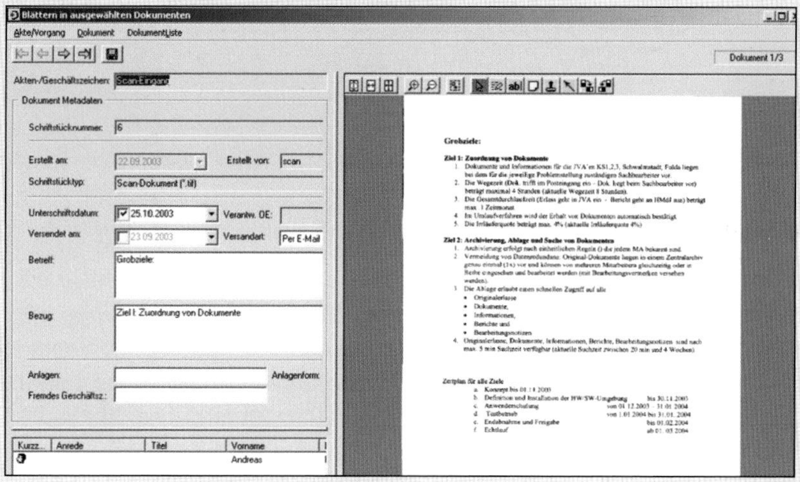

Figure 12.6: OCR Text Recognition at Hessen

Inter-Government Common Criteria

In June, 1993, the sponsoring organizations of the existing U.S., Canadian and European criteria started the Common Criteria (CC) Project to align their separate criteria into a single set of IT security criteria. Version 1.0 of the CC was completed in January, 1996. Based on trial evaluations and an extensive public review, Version 1.0 was revised and CC Version 2.0 was produced in April, 1998. This became ISO International Standard 15408 in 1999. The CC Project subsequently incorporated the minor changes that had resulted in the ISO process, producing CC version 2.1 in August, 1999. The CC defines a set of IT requirements of known validity which can be used in establishing security requirements for prospective products and systems.

Challenges in the Government Contractor Industry

Information challenges in the Government Contractor Industry include handling massive volumes of paper, data and documentation, collaboration, extensive security requirements for archiving, long-term archiving, legal requirements and government regulations.

As organizations grow, the task of managing thousands or even millions of paper documents is time consuming and costly. Much of this information becomes lost or buried within email systems or across shared drives. Without an effective means of organizing documents, the flow of knowledge becomes stagnant. Critical information might exist in a corporate knowledge base, but users cannot find it. As a result, multiple instances of outdated documents thrive in circulation, propagating new lifecycles of incorrect information. These inaccurate documents are often difficult to locate and eliminate. In order to remain agile in a competitive marketplace, organizations need to effectively store, share and disseminate corporate information.

In an economy where governments and regulatory bodies are creating new corporate governance and internal control regulations, organizations that are unable to effectively manage documents face increased risks. An advanced document management system can significantly reduce pressure on companies incorporating compliance with industry standards for document retention or complete regulatory submissions into their day-to-day activities.

Quality initiatives such as Six Sigma, ISO and GMP, as well as government regulations such as OSHA, require manufacturers to properly develop, document and ensure consistent processes that meet specified standards and government regulations.

The Aerospace Industry is an excellent example of a tightly regulated sector that has a critical need for an ECM solution to manage its complex and voluminous documentation. A complete paper copy of the regulations, engineering documents and test results required to manufacture an aircraft would weigh as much as the aircraft itself. The documents must be available for retrieval for a period of 99 years in order to receive the accreditation of the ATA (Air Transport Association). By developing special archiving formats and powerful search tools, ECM has revolutionized the management of documents required for this process by saving both retrieval time and physical storage space, providing excellent ROI.

Aerospace companies have to ensure just-in-time delivery of spare parts and services all over the world. Solutions like portals with customer access to all information such as price, availability, location and lead-time are essential to meeting customer requirements to save costs and time.

Government regulations drive the aerospace companies to establish maximum system availability. Dedicated back-up and recovery scenarios have to be implemented for all systems covering core processes and data. All information has to be accessible any time at any place in the world. System reliability has to be 24 hours a day, 365 days a year.

State Government

The primary responsibility of State (regional) governments is to provide services such as transportation, healthcare and education. The discussion in this chapter will concentrate on healthcare while the latter topics will be covered in the other chapters.

Within the Healthcare Industry there are specific process requirements which surround the treatment, management and development of patients. These are referred to in the industry as treatment pathways, which are comprised of automated workflow and knowledge management components. Pathways offer the best possible service and management of Electronic Patient Records (EPR) throughout the healthcare system or institution.

These new systems are replacing the inefficient paper systems that exist today. By streamlining and digitizing the monolithic number of processes and regulations associated with healthcare management, ECM is driving the advancement of the industry itself right down to the every day operations of a hospital.

When a patient gets sick and requires the facilities of a healthcare institute, a series of events occur which can be tracked, managed and automated by ECM.

The Healthcare Industry is composed of six major areas:

- Hospitals
- Private Healthcare Providers
- Public Healthcare Providers
- Academic Institutions
- Industry Consortiums
- Pharmaceutical and Research Groups

More so than ever before, these groups are now able to communicate and share infor-mation in ways which comply with government regulations, yet remain cost effective and intuitive. This means that all previous inhibitors of advancement through communication are gone. With the ability to share documents, communications and best practices, industry leaders can now utilize the information available to them in ways that were previously inconceivable.

Although large amounts of data in the healthcare industry are still stored in paper systems, the technology exists to revolutionize the efficiency, accuracy and adaptability of the medical industry. Although paper processes are still the norm in the healthcare industry, many tactical advancements have been made with respect to electronic information management. All of a hospital's systems—regardless of whether it's a diagnostic imaging system, patient monitor, scheduling application or prescription management system—gen-erate large amounts of electronic data. Where ECM enters this scene is the moment when all the data needs to be collected, managed, used for collaboration, or secured and archived. Generating a unified repository view, records management system, collaborative platform and general information archive makes gathering and using the large amounts of disparate information possible.

Managing the entire patient information cycle from diagnosis to final treatment is critical to eliminating the financial, geographical and technical barriers that have existed for generations. ECM is the enabling technology for this advancement. Not only can one hospital use this technology to run all of their process and information management, multiple facilities can use it to create regional information banks, which can be shared at the national and international level with research groups, pharmaceutical institutions and healthcare providers like never before.

Let's take a look at the components of this process and see how a proper ECM solution can serve both the healthcare institution and patient.

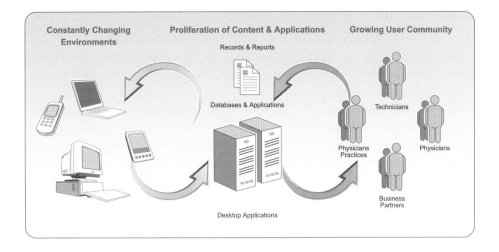

Figure 12.7: The Healthcare Industry

Doctor's Office

A patient visits their local clinic and is diagnosed with an illness. The doctor needs to be able to access their patient record from the regional healthcare institutes to refer to the patient's history. Additionally, if a new condition is diagnosed which requires further services from the healthcare institute, the doctor may choose to initiate a treatment pathway (workflow) to notify the hospital and even schedule the required diagnostic services automatically from their office. Any additional information the doctor has derived from this visit may also be included and added to the ECM healthcare system; when the patient arrives at the hospital they are greeted with the newest and most pertinent infor-mation immediately.

Outpatient Services

When a patient arrives at the hospital for day surgery, diagnostic imaging or any other outpatient service, a successful ECM deployment can track, manage and update their electronic records automatically, while managing them in a secure and searchable way. The technology currently varies from institute to institute or is handled through paper with great inefficiency. ECM can streamline the management of outpatient services by making records, process management and group collaboration services (doctor/hospital) easy and accessible.

Inpatient Services

When a patient is admitted for acute care, it is important to keep their records up to date and easily accessible in one place by means of a secure repository. The use of advanced workflow processes allow clinical staff to adjust and fine tune treatment pathways for inpatients easily and intuitively. This means that regardless of the patient's condition their treatment mechanism can be customized on a per patient basis by non-technical staff, which reduces errors in treatment and offers a secure auditable archive of treatments to date. This enhances the quality of care each patient receives and reduces administrative costs for the institution itself.

Treatment Pathways

Treatment pathways are workflow processes which recommend and track the best possible treatment and care for a patient. This could mean calculating and prescribing the appropriate medications, storing and managing diagnostic medical imaging, or discharge planning. More important than the ability to replicate a process is the ability to modify treatment pathways easily and on-the-fly. Every patient is different, though their treatment pathways may be similar. By using a set of defined treatment pathways as templates and putting the power of customization in the hands of the knowledge workers—in this case allied health workers, doctors and nurses—an ECM solution can reduce errors in treatment, speed up the process and make the entire administrative process more simple and cost effective.

Teleconsultation

Teleconsultation is an emerging area that couples the power of technology with the traditional concept of doctor house calls. By giving patients access to the healthcare solution and allowing them to update their own treatment pathways using off-the-shelf technologies such as digital cameras and collaborative meeting tools, doctors can assess, update and make judgments on treatment pathways without the patient having to come in to the office. This is particularly enabling in low service areas and with long-term care patients.

Electronic Patient Records

Every patient has a paper trail. In the context of the healthcare industry, this means an Electronic Patient Record (EPR). Unfortunately today, not every institution has deployed a solution such as ECM to handle these great volumes of information, and the consequence is reduced service quality for patients. By harvesting and making available all of the data collected on a patient, hospitals can share their records with other healthcare professionals and institutions, thus strengthening the quality of their network and exponentially improving

> Federation of State Medical Boards

Comprised of over 70 medical licensing and disciplinary boards in the United States and its territories, Federation of State Medical Boards (FSMB) is a recognized industry leader in medical licensure and discipline. One of the diverse services provided by FSMB is the Federation Credentials Verification Service, which obtains direct, primary source verification of credentials.

Requirements for the verification process are very complex and involve many workflow steps, third party collaboration and stacks of documents. A workflow engine and document management technology have enabled FSMB to streamline the associated processes through task and business process automation, reducing the time needed to process a file from request to distribution.

Management has more visibility due to integrated status reporting and follow-up procedures including personalized notification and audit functionalities. A business rules repository has aided FSMB in the enforcement of business rules while workflow technology has provided process consistency and improved time management. Fewer trade-offs are now required due to the ease of dealing with complex processes.

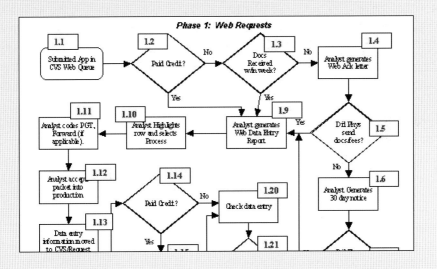

Figure 12.8: FSMB's Credentials Verification Process

the service they can offer their patients. Allowing specialists to collaborate on difficult cases or sharing an EPR to make complex diagnoses is critical to the advancement of the medical industry. More so than in other industries, keeping this information secure and highly available is critical—ECM solutions can make this a reality today.

Local Government

Local governments such as those at the City Council level are discussed here in various implementations at the city and metropolitan level. Most local government requirements are for online services delivery.

Program Management

Program Management (PM) solutions enable globally dispersed teams to communicate, collaborate, report project status, track project time, costs, progress and team performance—all from a standard Web browser. Organizations can form teams across geographical and departmental boundaries using corporate standard methodologies, best practices and information from previous projects.

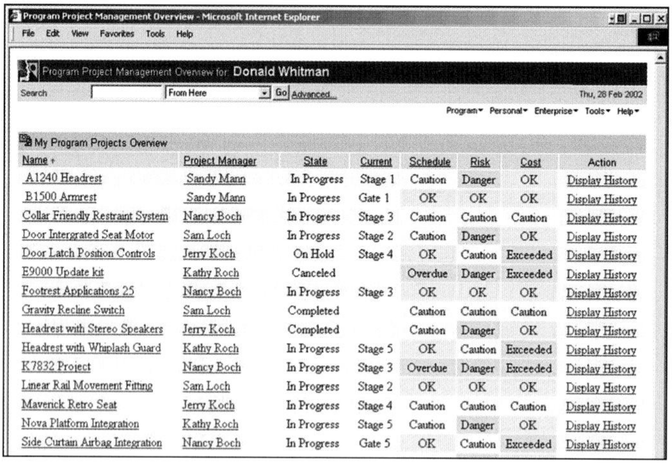

Name	Project Manager	State	Current	Schedule	Risk	Cost	Action
A1240 Headrest	Sandy Mann	In Progress	Stage 1	Caution	Danger	OK	Display History
B1500 Armrest	Sandy Mann	In Progress	Gate 1	OK	OK	OK	Display History
Collar Friendly Restraint System	Nancy Boch	In Progress	Stage 3	Caution	Caution	Caution	Display History
Door Intergrated Seat Motor	Sam Loch	In Progress	Stage 2	Caution	Danger	OK	Display History
Door Latch Position Controls	Jerry Koch	On Hold	Stage 4	OK	Caution	Exceeded	Display History
E9000 Update kit	Kathy Roch	Canceled		Overdue	Danger	Exceeded	Display History
Footrest Applications 25	Nancy Boch	In Progress	Stage 3	OK	OK	OK	Display History
Gravity Recline Switch	Sam Loch	Completed		Caution	Caution	Caution	Display History
Headrest with Stereo Speakers	Jerry Koch	Completed		Caution	Danger	OK	Display History
Headrest with Whiplash Guard	Kathy Roch	In Progress	Stage 5	OK	Caution	Exceeded	Display History
K7832 Project	Nancy Boch	In Progress	Stage 3	Overdue	Danger	Exceeded	Display History
Linear Rail Movement Fitting	Sam Loch	In Progress	Stage 2	OK	OK	OK	Display History
Maverick Retro Seat	Jerry Koch	In Progress	Stage 4	Caution	Caution	Caution	Display History
Nova Platform Integration	Kathy Roch	In Progress	Stage 5	Caution	Danger	OK	Display History
Side Curtain Airbag Integration	Nancy Boch	In Progress	Gate 5	OK	Caution	Exceeded	Display History

Figure 12.9: Program Management Tracks Important Aspects of Projects

> Hamburg Chamber of Commerce

In the digital age of e-commerce, the Hamburg Chamber of Commerce recognized the unlimited potential of the Internet to quickly interact and exchange information with its membership. As a result, the organization, along with the neighboring chambers of commerce and industries, created a project called HK24, a portal for business-to-business information.

The foundation for the portal is a Web content management solution, which enables the staff to present their editorial content on the intranet, extranet and Internet via a single user interface, which guarantees ease of use and automatic workflow formatting. No technical savvy is required to easily create and update content and place it in the portal.

Customers and prospects alike can now find all necessary contacts and role-based information using the HK24 portal. As a result of the project, Hamburg's virtual "House of Entrepreneurs" has become a business model for other German chambers of commerce and industries.

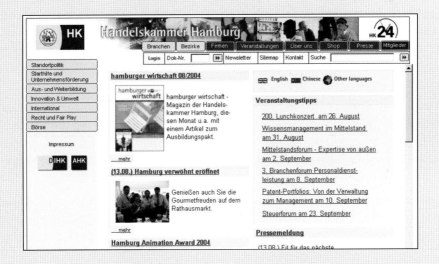

Figure 12.10: A B2B Portal at the Hamburg Chamber of Commerce

PM can be used to create formal process templates that define the activities, program tasks and deliverables that the team is to accomplish during any given stage of a project. The process template is also used to set up standard criteria by which each project can be evaluated. At each checkpoint, called a Gate Review, the project is measured against the template criteria to determine if it should continue to the next phase, be put on hold or terminated. Any number of process templates can be created and saved to the repository, allowing project managers to choose an appropriate template each time they create a new project. Once a template is selected, the program tasks, deliverables and Gate review criteria are automatically created in the new program project. All that remains is to choose a team and assign the tasks and deliverables to appropriate team members. The process templates act as the project workflow, guiding the team through multiple development phases, called Stages, and review cycles, or Gate reviews, of a program project. Establishing and using these templates ensures that corporate standards are met and best practices are followed. Every program project has its own secure project workspace that gives team members access to everything they need to coordinate all stages of a program project. Within this project workspace, all of the details that occur during the program project's life are captured. Notes from every project-related meeting are saved, allowing users to review what was discussed and what decisions were made. Issues that arise during the completion of a program stage or task are captured, enabling review of the cause of an issue, the action items instigated to resolve the issue and its final resolution.

One of the key benefits of PM is the rollup capability of all projects a user is managing. In a one screen view, the user can see the status of all projects they are managing. ECM providers understand the business of government and the transformational initiatives that the public sector is tasked with addressing—from managing public funds to mitigating risk and establishing partnerships.

Solutions are focused on information storage and exchange. This provides people who work in the public sector with the ability to communicate and interact to solve job-related problems and improve job performance.

One government organization identified the issue of ensuring the security of IT systems, networks and applications for their organization. Even a single security breach by terrorists or white-collar criminals could have devastating consequences in terms of financial loss, violations of privacy or even the risk of injury or death. This organization needed a clear, proven methodology to ensure their IT tools are being applied properly. U.S. federal and international governmental standards for systems already exist, such as the (NIST 1000) National Information Assurance Certification and Accreditation Process (NIACAP) 5-step process and the ISO/IEC 15408 Common Criteria methodology.

> The City of Calgary

A growing city means rapid property growth and an increase in the number of property and business assessments. These assessments are often the main revenue stream for municipal governments and it is critical to defend them in the event of a court dispute. Comprehensive supporting documentation must quickly be gathered and submitted in an evidence package.

Integrating ECM with other applications, The City of Calgary has developed a system for evidence package creation that monitors individual assessor's evidence package status; collects relevant documents from the repository and provides a case specific "workspace"; processes and converts files to required document format; automatically compiles all documents into one electronic evidence package and eventually distributes it to the complainant and the Review Board's repository.

The City of Calgary is now able to produce a better product within a shorter time, while meeting internal deadlines. Audit functionality provides track records vital for compliance purposes. Evidence package creation has been centralized and transitioned from a linear to a team approach, letting experts be experts. Assessors can finally focus on vital data analysis.

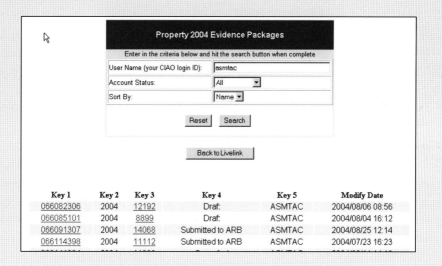

Figure 12.11: The City of Calgary's Electronic Evidence Package Viewer

Organizations use a PM solution to manage the many documents, test descriptions and templates involved in a System Security Plan, along with a database containing security requirements, configuration data and test results. The system includes a gated workflow that leads the security officers through each step of the process including information gathering, generation of the System Security Plan, tracking of test results and the creation of the final version of the System Security Plan. The system automates the Certification and Accreditation (C&A) process and infuses federally and internationally defined safety standards into the process, providing the organization with a standardized and managed approach for certifying and accrediting enterprise-wide classified and unclassified critical infrastructure assets.

As a manual process, the C&A cycle took 12 to 18 months from start to finish. The cost of the effort and time required impacts the ability to deploy needed systems. IT systems must also be re-certified every three years, which currently means starting over again.

With the use of document management functionality and workflow capabilities, the automated process reduced the timeframe to just weeks. The productivity improvements and associated cost savings were immediate; in side-by-side comparisons the C&A application required less than 10 percent of the time currently required.

A key strategic benefit is that over time the database will contain configuration data for all systems within a facility or across an agency, which will allow security officers to instantly determine which systems are affected by newly discovered threats or vulnerabilities and respond much faster than they can today.

Government customers are achieving ROI by using ECM solutions for applications such as Facilities Management, Case Management, Correspondence Tracking, Program Management, Proposal Management, etc.

Other Chapters Related to Government

The Government has natural similarities for benchmarking with other information intensive industries such as Education. These industries do not produce a product but rather satisfy a need that people have. In that way, the Services Department is also very similar to the issues faced by government organizations.

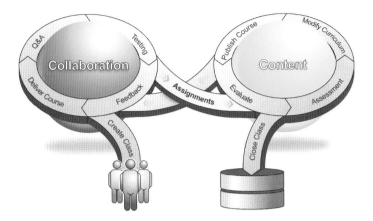

Figure 13.1: Course Creation and Delivery

The diagram above illustrates one aspect of the information lifecycle within a typical education e-learning environment; **creating a class**.

The initial key content—the courseware, which includes lessons, **assignments** and assessment pieces—is used to **deliver the course** to a specific set of students. Note that it is possible that these materials were created in a collaborative process with other teachers.

The students collaborate with the teacher (and each other) via **questions and answers** and are **tested** on the course material. **Feedback** on the course can be gathered at this point (from both teachers and students). **Assignments** and given and are evaluated by the course instructor. **Assessments** of the course are submitted as new content—the evaluation of this material is considered additional content.

The **feedback** that has been gathered at various times throughout the cycle of course can be to **modify the curriculum** for future course delivery. After the course is **published**, the class is **closed**. The course may be modified (using the feedback that was generated) or recreated.

EDUCATION

Leading education organizations around the world are focused on the concept of *sustainable improvement*. The primary goal is to create an environment that delivers better learning. The drive for improvement comes both from within the organization and often from government bodies that oversee and fund the organization.

A common theme that underlies many high-level strategies for improvement is enhanced communication and collaboration within and among the key stakeholder groups in the education environment – teachers, students, administrators, and, in primary/secondary education, parents.

This chapter explores how advances in technology have created new possibilities for significant sustainable improvements.

Over the last few years, it has become evident to many that significant enhancements to communication and collaboration within an education organization should be attainable by harnessing the power and ubiquity of computing and networking technology. Almost all stakeholders within an education organization now have ready access to personal computers and networks.

It is somewhat ironic that this potential for improved communication and collaboration is most evident to the students. They are the ones most likely to be using this kind of technology on a day-to-day basis as they exchange email, collaborate through instant messaging and electronically share music and digital photos.

Despite the strong desire to enhance communication and collaboration, and the strong belief that computers can provide a powerful way to achieve this, most education organizations are still grappling with how to make this happen effectively. This stems from the fact that the needs of the education community are fundamentally different from the needs of business or consumers. Unfortunately, the focus of most software offerings is either on meeting the needs of the business market or consumer market, making them a poor fit for education.

With the right communications and collaboration solution in place, an education organization can achieve significant improvements, including:

- more timely and effective collaboration on curriculum development;
- better sharing of teaching best practices to enable the teaching community to more effectively learn and benefit from the experience of their peers;
- better tools for managing day-to-day workflow of information between teachers and students;
- more effective ways to track student successes and challenges as they progress through multi-year, multi-teacher learning environments;
- enhanced communication with key stakeholders such as parents to more effectively bring them in to the learning process.

Some of this functionality is provided by what is often referred to as a "Learning Management System" (LMS) or e-learning solution. However, a more extensive communications and collaboration platform is required to more effectively address the broader set of needs of the complete education community.

What follows is a more detailed examination of the key factors that make an education organization different from an Information Technology (IT) perspective, and how these differences can be addressed. By effectively doing so, an education organization can achieve significant improvements in communication and throughout its community. This can provide both a foundation and a catalyst for the organization to create powerful new ways to achieve sustainable improvements in learning.

Collaborative Needs

Education organizations have unique collaboration needs that are very different from the typical business organization. Teachers are often spread across many different geographic locations within a school district or campus environment. Even within the same location, teachers have busy schedules that prevent the simple "let's have a meeting" approach to collaboration used in business. Students are often working at night as they do their homework after classes have ended for the day.

These realities create a demand for powerful asynchronous collaboration techniques that overcome distance and time restriction. These include:

> London Metropolitan University

The result of a merger, London Metropolitan University (LondonMet) is the United Kingdom's second largest conventional university. Faced with a variety of regulatory and operational issues, LondonMet has to manage millions of documents generated by staff and students. The organization comprises some 28,000 students, including 4,000 from overseas, distributed across a number of campuses with connections to European research and educational establishments.

The higher education landscape is changing and universities now operate in a tight regulatory framework augmented by frequent quality audits. Planning for these audits involves collecting and arranging copious amounts of documentation. Research is increasingly a multinational exercise with research teams from many institutions collaborating on research topics.

The solution selected by LondonMet to address its Enterprise Content Management issues not only provides the core document management capability needed for such a large organization, but it also provides an ideal collaborative environment for staff participating in large European research projects, often involving dozens of universities.

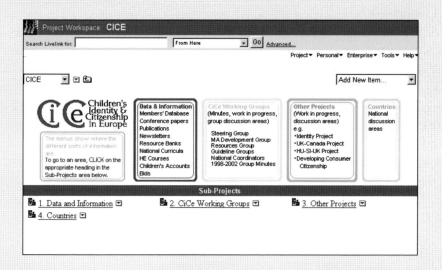

Figure 13.2: LondonMet's Interactive Information System for CiCe (Children's Identity & Citizenship in Europe), an interdisciplinary group of about 258 academics from some 79 different institutions in 29 nations in Europe

Teacher-to-Teacher Collaboration: Teachers have many different peer groups that they interact with regularly. Often, teachers in the same school need to collaborate on school-related issues, track school events, develop policies and procedures, and track project progress. Teachers with the same subject focus in schools or colleges across an entire district need to be able to collaborate to develop curriculum, share teaching techniques and promote best practices. They also need to be informed about district-wide, state or national initiatives.

Student-to-Student Collaboration: Students should be able to collaborate with each other in a secure environment that can be managed and audited as it supports joint work on team projects, peer-level mentoring, and communication and knowledge centers for social and sports organizations.

Teacher-to-Student Collaboration: Teachers and students need secure, managed collaboration capabilities to support a variety of activities, such as teachers providing lesson information, electronic reference materials, files, Web links, homework assign-ments, course calendars, and other electronic materials that supplement in-class teaching. Students need similar access to electronically submit homework assignments, reports and projects. Students should also be able to pose questions and ask for supple-mentary information.

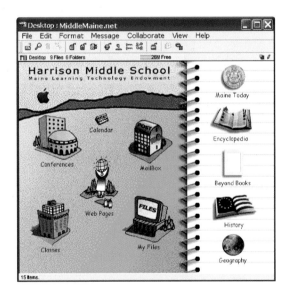

Figure 13.3: Online Teacher-to-Student Collaboration

> Clark County School District, Nevada

Encompassing the city of Las Vegas and a large surrounding area, Clark County School District (CCSD) is the 5th largest school district in the United States. It has over 275,000 students and 20,000 teachers spread across 275 schools.

Given their large size, CCSD knew that the organization would benefit from a powerful communications and collaboration solution that would enable staff to work together on curriculum development, sharing best practices, deploying district policies and procedures, and facilitating professional development.

Such a foundation would enable new teachers and new schools to get established quickly and effectively by tapping into a wide range of established and published knowledge bases—a vision shared by many school districts. CCSD also shares a common challenge with many other school districts—a tight budget with many priorities vying for scarce education dollars. CCSD met this challenge by deploying a cost-effective, scalable, education-oriented messaging and collaboration platform for their district.

This system now supports over 25,000 staff and over 25,000 students, with additional students being added as time goes on. Running on a very inexpensive infrastructure of four low-cost PC servers, the entire system is administered by a staff of three.

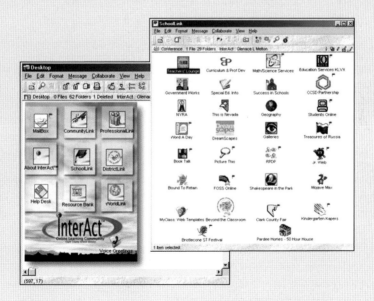

Figure 13.4: Clark County School District's Messaging and Collaboration Platform

Teacher-to-Parent Collaboration: Teachers in primary/secondary education need a secure, authenticated, easy-to-use facility to communicate key aspects of student progress, including attendance, homework assignments, field trips, school and course calendars, grades and subjective feedback.

All of the above can be achieved in a cost-effective, secure, reliable fashion with appropriate care in choosing an education-oriented software solution.

Education Sector Uniqueness

Education organizations often attempt to deploy popular business solutions as part of the core foundation of their communication and collaboration infrastructure.

A typical business solution for messaging and collaboration usually provides each user with an email mailbox, a calendar and an address book. Optional add-on systems may provide instant messaging capabilities and, potentially, document sharing capabilities.

In many cases, these business solutions are a poor fit, since they do not accommodate the special needs of education environments. Education organizations require support for the unique roles, workflows and information models associated with education environment as well as very diverse and relatively unmanaged end-user computing environments. These needs are often coupled with limited IT budgets and limited IT staff.

The following expands upon some of these unique needs of education environments:

Choice of Computer Type: In the corporate world, organizations typically dictate a standard for the entire organization and enforce this as the only accepted computing platform. This is almost always a Windows platform. In the education world, much more flexibility and choice is required; besides support for Windows, there is widespread use of Macintosh computers and a growing deployment of Linux desktops. These organizations need to know that all electronic capabilities will work efficiently on all types of computers.

Choice of Computer Vintage: The corporate world typically dictates that only recent Windows platforms will be supported. Today, this typically means support for Windows 2000 and Windows XP. This is viewed as a way to reduce support costs. In education, the organization has much less control over computers that the community will use. Students and even teachers may have older computers at home. Schools may have older donated computers that would be prohibitively expensive to upgrade. Education organizations need to know that their communication and collaboration solution will not exclude people who can't afford newer computers.

> Emory University, Atlanta, Georgia

EMORY
UNIVERSITY

Founded in Atlanta in 1836, Emory University specializes in a wide array of under-graduate and graduate areas of study including arts and science, medicine, nursing, theology, law, and business. Today Emory has over 11,000 students and 2,500 faculty members. Emory had a keen interest in taking advantage of the widespread availability of computers within their student and faculty population to create an online community that would enable their academic stakeholders to collaborate on a wide range of curricular and co-curricular topics.

This electronic community was named LearnLink. It has grown from its humble beginnings to encompass over 30,000 distinct shared knowledge bases, covering topics including online courses, faculty moderated discussions, fraternity and sorority conferences, sports clubs, social clubs, religious organizations, and other important campus presences.

"LearnLink has become an essential part of the student environment here at Emory," according to the Director of Academic Technologies at Emory. "It enables our academic community to collaborate and share knowledge on such a wide range of topics. We even provide access to new students before they arrive on campus so they can get a head start at learning about the history, culture, facilities, and spirit of Emory before even setting foot on campus."

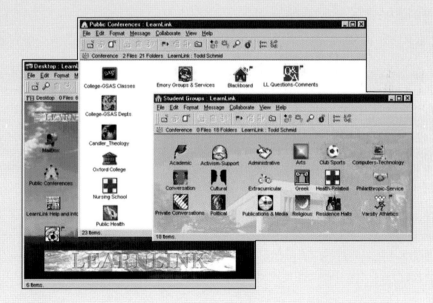

Figure 13.5: An Online Community Environment at Emory University

User Mobility: In the business world, each knowledge worker is issued a computer that is dedicated to them. If they move about doing their job they are given a laptop computer; otherwise they use a desktop computer. In many education environments, people don't have a permanent computer; computers are shared. A teacher or student might use one computer in the classroom, another computer at the library, and another computer at home. An education solution must support mobile users, not just mobile computers.

Limited Budgets: Education organizations typically have very limited budgets, with many priorities vying for scarce budget dollars. Studies paid for by Microsoft and IBM show that the typical deployment cost for large-scale business groupware systems (approximately 20,000 users) is in the neighborhood of $100.00 U.S. per user per year. It is possible to roll out feature-rich communication and collaboration solutions for as little as 1/10 the cost of typical business solutions. This is much more affordable for education organizations, and it lets them keep more budget dollars focused on core education needs and not on IT infrastructure.

Limited IT Staff: Typical business solutions are expensive to run in terms of support staff. According to studies funded by Microsoft and IBM, the average large organization (20,000 users) will need 13 to 16 dedicated support staff to run their business messaging and collaboration solutions. Education organizations (which often are much larger than 20,000 people) typically don't have (and don't want) large IT teams that are dedicated to running their messaging and collaboration infrastructure. They need solutions that require significantly fewer staff.

ECM in Education

The key needs of education organizations are similar around the world. They can benefit greatly from highly integrated messaging, collaboration and e-learning platform that is scalable, highly reliable, supports a wide range of computing platforms, is standards-based, and cost effective to deploy.

With such a platform in place, education institutions have the foundation they need to create a dynamic organization that effectively learns as it grows. This is the key to achieving continuous sustainable improvement.

Other Chapters Related to Education

The Education Industry is most similar to other industries that are knowledge intensive, and in which the output product is intangible, such as the Services Industry.

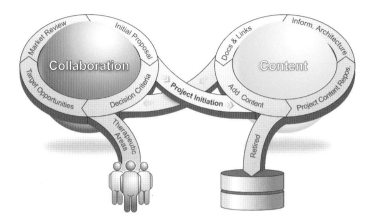

Figure 14.1: New Product Development

In directing Research and Development (R&D) efforts in the Pharmaceutical Industry, selecting from a range of product opportunities is an important and difficult process. The critical interplay between Collaboration and Content, shown above, is well illustrated in the early stages of establishing a research project. Generally companies have certain **therapeutic areas** such as cardiovascular or inflammatory diseases in which they focus their discussions. This collaboration among research scientists will help to define what **target opportunities** are available based on current scientific understanding of disease processes and potential molecular targets. However, to be successful, a wider audience from among marketing, medical affairs, legal and other departments must also provide **market review**.

After a particular R&D proposal is selected, an **initial proposal** is presented to senior management. If the proposal is rejected, **decision criteria** are shared with the team and the exploratory discussion starts again. If the proposal is accepted, a formal **project initiation** process is established and a **project content repository** is created. Companies often try to standardize the **information architecture** in the content repository so that users who participate in several projects can easily find information in a consistent location. **Documents and links** are added, providing background information, Standard Operating Procedures (SOPs), templates, and collaborative forums. Participants start to add **content** as the project starts and advances. Over time, a given project may go through several review stages and either be retired or continued, with revisions to the information architecture to allow downstream information to be accommodated.

CHAPTER 14

PHARMACEUTICAL AND LIFE SCIENCES

The Pharmaceutical and Life Sciences Industry depends on a steady pipeline of innovative new medications to sustain its traditionally robust growth and profitability. Over the last two decades a series of large-scale mergers and acquisitions have occurred by companies seeking the critical mass and global presence to rapidly introduce innovative, profitable new drugs in every major market. There are now only a few dozen multinational companies and for the first time, the larger companies are approaching global market shares of 10 percent or more. But huge risks remain even for the largest companies. Most drug candidates fail testing for safety and efficacy before they reach the market, and even for successful medications, R&D costs can be close to a billion dollars over timeframes of a decade or more. Once approved, successfully marketed drugs may have to be withdrawn because of unexpected side effects.

With human health and safety at risk, national governments have developed strict regulations governing pharmaceutical companies in every jurisdiction. These regulations require detailed documentation of every critical process and demand they be controlled and monitored.

While global pharmaceutical companies have grown fewer and larger, a web of Life Sciences companies such as Biotechnology and Clinical Research Organizations (CROs) have developed to provide key services through a range of collaborative interactions with Pharmaceutical companies.

The Pharmaceutical Industry is highly regulated and data and document intensive. Success depends on the safe execution of critical processes. Sharing key information with team members, making the best decisions possible based on all relevant information, and complying with government regulations is crucial.

Pharmaceutical Industry-specific regulations include the Food and Drug Administration's (FDA) Good Practices (GxP) requirements for laboratory, clinical and manufacturing processes, as well as 21 CFR Part 11 guidelines for electronic records in the United States. Comparable regulations can be found in other jurisdictions such as Japan, and Europe – where pan-European regulations are managed by European Agency for the Evaluation of Medicinal Products (EAEMP). Accurate and reliable documents are essential to show that critical processes that could impact human health, such as the manufacture of a drug, have been performed to industry standards.

In addition to these regulations, pharmaceutical and other life sciences companies must comply with other general corporate regulations. Given overlapping requirements and inconsistencies, achieving and maintaining compliance can prove to be a significant challenge. Companies must be able to show that they have tested their compliance through a validation process that can add as much as 40 percent or more to software system deployment costs.

The Pharmaceutical Industry depends heavily on partnerships at each stage of product development. Controlled and secure exchange of critical content between partners in support of collaborative processes is important. Biotechnology companies increasingly are the source of innovative new product candidates that are in-licensed by pharmaceutical companies for further development.

Outsourcing of services also requires secure content exchange. For example, clinical development, where promising new drug candidates are tested on human patients and volunteers, is often subcontracted to service organizations (i.e., Clinical Research Organizations). Manufacturing of test materials and final products is often outsourced to contract manufacturers.

While the Pharmaceutical Industry has the highest visibility and regulatory scrutiny, other Life Sciences companies such as manufacturers of medical and diagnostics devices face similar challenges.

Industry Requirements

Pharmaceutical and Life Sciences companies directly or indirectly produce and sell high-margin, high-value products. They depend on effective R&D programs to maintain their long-term competitiveness (see Chapter 7 for a review of R&D issues). As already described, these R&D programs are complex, expensive and time consuming. Within the industry, R&D is usually divided into four main stages:

Pharmaceutical product development cycles—from conception to marketing—require on average four to ten years longer than in most other industries. Increasing the efficiency at which global development teams cooperate is a critical factor in determining the speed at which new drugs can be readied for the market.

Roche's ECM-based platform for information sharing, entitled ShareWeb, supports the full lifecycle of global team projects. Providing a single point of access to training information, compliance programs and a broad range of documents, ECM helps improve efficiency at each stage of Roche's new product development cycles.

Since the launch of ShareWeb, access to documents is independent of format, knowledge from previous projects is available and updated at all times, international teams can be assembled faster and new team members are easily inaugurated. "ShareWeb brings the various countries in the Asia-Pacific region into one community," says Roche's Medical Director, Taiwan.

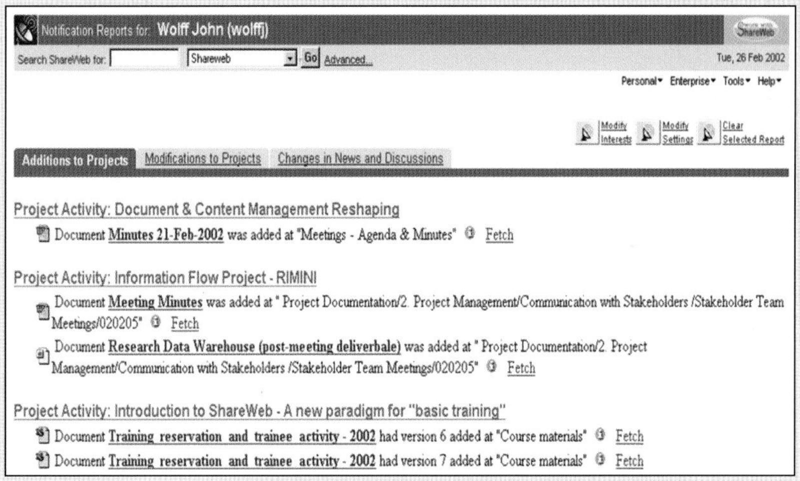

Figure 14.2: Roche's Share Web

1. Discovery Research – large numbers of potential drugs are tested to find a few promising Candidates that might be useful in treating a disease;

2. Pre-clinical Research – candidate drugs are tested in several animal species;

3. Clinical Development – the few remaining candidates are tested in humans;

4. Manufacturing Development – industrial-scale processes are developed for the safe and reliable manufacture of promising and successful drug candidates.

With the market launch of new pharmaceuticals, Marketing and Sales Departments must have documents and other materials that have passed the regulatory scrutiny of their product claims.

Each of these phases requires detailed documentation of processes and results – accordingly, the Pharmaceutical Industry has some of the most demanding requirements for document and other forms of content management.

Broadly speaking, pharmaceutical regulations require that documents either be submitted for formal review by regulators at key steps in R&D (such as prior to the beginning of clinical drug testing in humans), or that they be maintained in-house but be available for inspection at any time. Given the importance of these documents, companies typically have documented, internal processes that relate to meeting specific regulatory requirements, such as Standard Operating Procedures (SOPs).

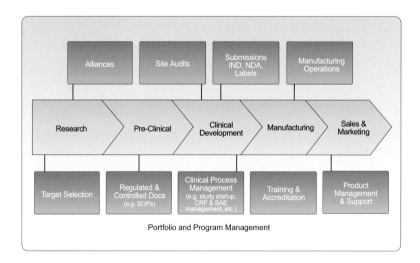

Figure 14.3: Pharmaceutical Product Development Stages

Managing Documents through a Full Lifecycle

Often before a new SOP is authored, management support is required. Many companies require consistency in their documents and issue document templates to authors following approval. Authors prepare one or more drafts, which they circulate through collaborative, electronic processes to colleagues for review. Review may include early, detailed review by a few colleagues, and later, high-level review, often by supervisors. The circulated document may be editable, such as in MS Word format, or in a secured form that cannot be changed but only marked with comments (such as a secure PDF format). Once a document has completed review, it must be approved by one or more managers. Increasingly, the Pharmaceutical Industry is moving to maintaining electronic documents as authoritative records, which allows for electronic signatures in place of traditional 'wet ink' signatures. The FDA's 21 CFR Part 11 regulations provide guidance on the acceptable use of e-signatures.

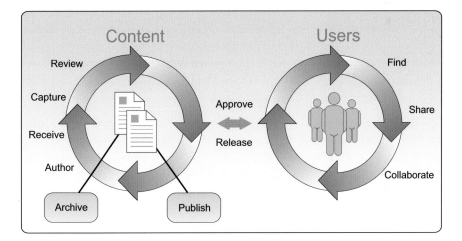

Figure 14.4: The Cycle of Electronically Managed Documents

Even when a procedure has been approved, often it cannot be released immediately. It is necessary to ensure that every staff member using the SOP (to operate a specific piece of laboratory equipment, for example) has fully read and understood the new procedure. Whereas once staff operated under an honor system to report when they had read a new procedure, companies now often provide short electronic presentations and other rich media to facilitate the learning of the new procedure. Electronic tests follow the presentations to ensure comprehension before staff certification.

Once SOP is in effect, it must be regularly reviewed to ensure that it does not require revision. Formal change management procedures are used to manage the review, replacement and withdrawal of specific versions of each procedure. But even after withdrawal, procedures involve critical corporate records that may have to be maintained for many decades, requiring that an ECM solution be extended to include formal records management and archiving.

Managing the Conduct of Clinical Trials

While every stage of the pharmaceutical R&D process involves considerable documentation, the clinical development phase produces the largest volumes. It can also present the greatest challenges to ensure effective collaboration among participants.

Drug candidates are usually tested in controlled clinical environments. Pharmaceutical and Biotechnology companies, as well as CROs acting on their behalf, identify clinical centers (usually hospitals) that can enroll sufficient patients with the targeted disease, and that have medical expertise to conduct quality clinical studies. For each center, approximately two dozen types of documents must be created and approved before any patient is enrolled. This 'study startup' documentation includes the résumés of all participating physicians, agreement on patient enrolment criteria, protocols to be followed during the trials, reimbursement rates, and so on.

When a patient participates in a clinical study, they must visit the clinical centre for initial screening and instruction on how to take the test medication. They also visit for follow up during and after the test period. Each of these visits is documented by physicians and study nurses in patient Case Report Forms (CRF), and usually associated laboratory test results are recorded. Originally, all of this documentation was in paper form, but Pharmaceutical companies now encourage participants to use electronic processes such as e-forms. However, for the foreseeable future, most studies will include at least some documents originally in paper form. Therefore, paper documents are typically scanned into the ECM system at high-volume scanning centers. Once scanned paper and electronic documents are obtained, they must be managed consistently using a single repository, so that staff do not need to be concerned with the original document. Document volumes can be huge; it is not unusual for late-stage studies to generate more than 100,000 documents each, most of which are automatically deposited.

But storage of documents is not enough. Many people are involved in conducting clinical studies. Some of these are internal to the sponsoring companies, some are in partner companies, and many are in hospitals. Even company staff may be at remote locations.

With revenues of over 5 billion euros and more than 10,000 employees, Sanofi-Aventis experienced the highest growth rate among leading European pharmaceutical companies. The rapid growth was inevitably accompanied by a rise in invoices to be processed: in response, Sanofi-Aventis embarked on an ambitious project—E@sy-Invoices—implemented in 20 countries across Europe.

Invoices are now scanned and archived, and a workflow notification is sent to the user. Integration of the system with other enterprise applications enabled the creation of dynamic links between accounting and archived documents. Access to documents is immediately available from any location, and numbers of circulating paper documents have been accordingly reduced.

Customer service has improved, as vendor queries and requests can be handled immediately, invoice discrepancies are easily dealt with, and approval workflows have been optimized. Sarbanes-Oxley compliance has been achieved due to complete traceability of the invoice flow. In the light of so many benefits and productivity gains, the E@sy-Invoices project has been a definite success.

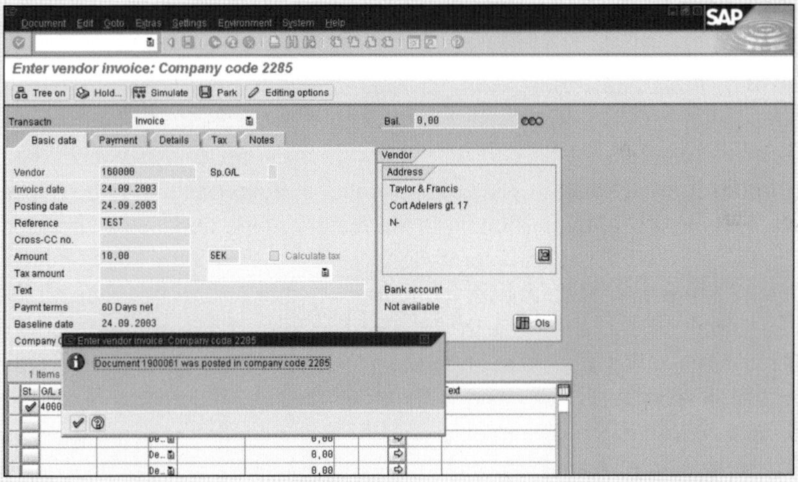

Figure 14.5: Handling Vendor Invoices at Sanofi-Aventis

Easy but secure access from any global location is very important. In typical ECM imple-mentations that support clinical trials, a great deal of effort is focused on designing an information architecture to accommodate all incoming documents and a security and a permissions model that controls which documents an individual can see and what they can do with them. Patient privacy and ensuring unbiased analysis of study results are two key factors in permissions model design.

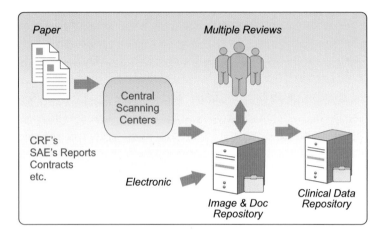

Figure 14.6: From Paper Documents to Tagged and Stored Electronic Records

ECM systems provide support for rich data or information about documents that is not included in the document itself. In clinical applications, documents may be tagged with 40 metadata fields or more, often relating to the history of the document and its state of review. Many people look at patient information for different reasons, including to extract data and enter it into a clinical database; to monitor whether protocols are being followed; and to ensure patient safety. Using search and reporting tools, it is possible to query all doc-uments in the system to find those that are waiting for their review. Such query tools can be easily optimized for individuals according to their job roles and incorporated into simplified role-specific dashboards, since optimal use of ECM systems often requires a streamlined, role-specific interface for efficiency and higher user acceptance and adoption.

No matter how well designed a clinical study is, there will always be exceptions. One of the most critical is when a patient experiences a Severe Adverse Event (SAE) such as a side effect or even death. In such cases, certain key people must be notified and timely decisions must be made, including notifying regulatory agencies and perhaps even sus-pending the trial. Such critical events are often managed using electronic workflow tools that provide a method to control and track a highly structured sequence of events, with automated staff notification and event escalation.

> # AtheroGenics

AtheroGenics is an emerging pharmaceutical company focused on the discovery, development and commercialization of novel drugs for the treatment of chronic inflammatory diseases. Clinical development at life science organizations such as AtheroGenics is a lengthy, highly regulated and paper-intensive process involving detailed case study reports, patient records, and clinical research and analysis documents.

The case study report forms, which capture clinical information in a study, are scanned and processed and stored as images in an ECM document repository at AtheroGenics. In use at 235 sites worldwide, 'ECM for Clinicals' eliminates filing and storing paper documents and manual document searching. A free flowing 'queue' of documents for transcriptionists lets them focus on essential data entry rather than document filing.

AtheroGenics has conducted a study comparing the paper-based processes to the 'ECM for Clinicals' use. Results demonstrate ECM has enabled an over 50 percent reduction in data entry time, and that the time for database lock has decreased by two-thirds. The costs of new hardware and software have been offset by the savings realized through decreased shipping and data entry costs.

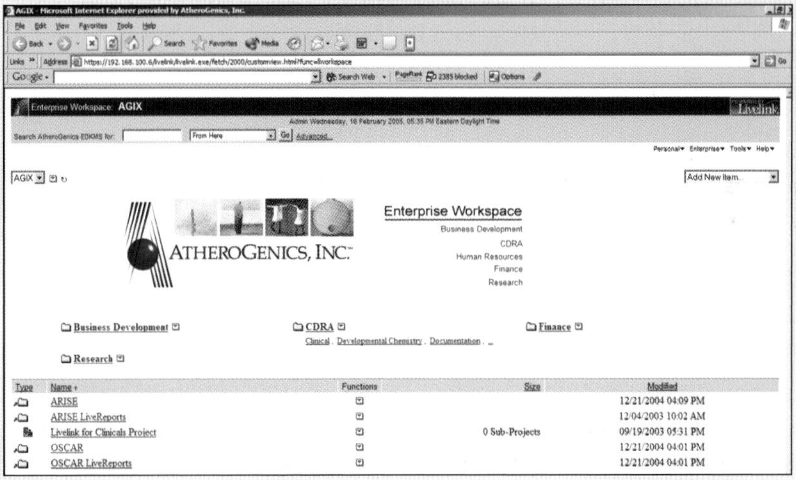

Figure 14.7: AtheroGenics' Enterprise Workspace

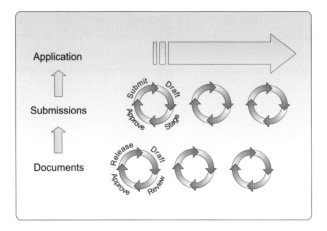

Figure 14.8: Hierarchical Lifecycle Management

Pharmaceutical companies strive to complete their clinical studies as quickly as possible – this requires that all necessary patient information be received and properly dealt with. Only then can data be analyzed to determine the effectiveness and safety of the candidate drug for incorporation into regulatory filings in support of additional clinical studies or approval to market the drug. ECM systems can greatly improve the efficiency and speed at which trials are set up, conducted and analyzed.

Making Regulatory Submissions

ECM systems can be used to manage documents that must be maintained for possible inspection by regulators, and can be used to streamline the conduct of clinical trials that generate key information to substantiate regulatory submissions. ECM systems can also be used to support the submission process.

Traditionally, components of ECM systems were used as key document repositories, but were incapable of supporting the preparation of regulatory submissions. These submissions summarize all of the information about a drug, including clinical study results, and support marketing approval requests for a new drug in a given jurisdiction. The challenge was that these submissions typically comprised hundred of documents, with up to a million or more pages in total, and required a unified page numbering scheme and tables of contents, all of which had to be printed and presented in multiple binders.

To make matters worse, there was no consistency across different regulatory jurisdictions. Specialty submission publishing applications were developed to address these needs.

The submission environment has changed. Regulators will now accept electronic submissions, and the format and content of them is much more consistent. With the move to electronic submissions, more frequent submissions and updates that require a tighter integration between the status of component documents and the resulting evolving applications are expected. A single application may consist of 200 or more incremental submissions over time.

As well, ECM systems have become more powerful and can publish document collections in a range of formats. Therefore, it is likely that a single end-to-end ECM system will evolve to manage all documents through every stage of their lifecycles, as well as the lifecycle of all multi-document submissions. ECM systems manage lifecycles effectively by tagging content with lifecycle stages that evolve, and by securely supporting a range of collaborative processes among staff members around the world.

The Pharmaceutical Industry in the Global Market

The Pharmaceutical Industry is active in all major markets globally and is increasingly dominated by fewer, larger companies. The key processes that support the development and testing of new drugs and manage existing drugs are similar in all markets – minimizing patient risk is paramount.

Pharmaceutical companies have pushed to deploy electronic processes that increase efficiency and responsiveness. At the same time, government regulators are under ever increasing pressure to provide more oversight as operating budgets are cut. As a result, global organizations such as the International Conference on Harmonisation (ICH) have encouraged more consistent pan-global formats and processes, but much more needs to be done.

The U.S. comprises some 40 percent of the global pharmaceutical market. Even if a company does not have R&D or manufacturing operations in the U.S., they must comply with FDA regulations if they wish to sell their product directly or indirectly in the U.S. Fortunately, the U.S. participates in ICH initiatives.

Given the global nature of the Pharmaceutical Industry, English is not the accepted language for submission in every jurisdiction. As such, providing multilingual access to common content repositories is not only challenging but essential.

ECM in the Pharmaceutical and Life Sciences Industry

As we have seen, the Pharmaceutical Industry is highly regulated and depends on many documents to support and record processes. As ECM systems mature and broaden their capabilities, they are better able to address the comprehensive and demanding needs of the Pharmaceutical Industry in ways that support cross-enterprise access and regulatory compliance.

A key ECM requirement is managing documents, whether they are maintained for possible inspection or submitted directly to government regulators. The largest volumes of documents and the greatest collaborative challenges are presented during clinical trials, but every stage requires content lifecycle support, including the management of large regulatory submissions.

Teams of people are involved at every stage of drug research and development, but the members of those teams change as projects advance over periods of a decade or more. Passing on critical information and ensuring that team members fully understand it requires effective collaborative support. But collaborative tools can also support critical time-dependent event management, such as monitoring and responding to events that endanger patient health.

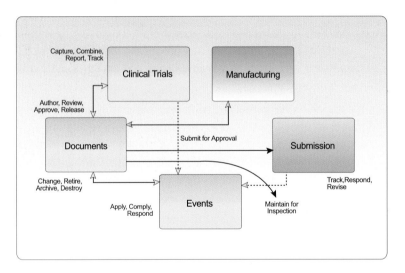

Figure 14.9: Solutions Related by Processes to Manage Content

Other Chapters Related to the Pharmaceutical and Life Sciences Industry

The Pharmaceutical Industry has a natural relationship to Healthcare. Due to the research-intensive nature of the industry, it also has many similarities to Telecommunications. The regulatory aspects of this industry are similar to the issues faced in the Financial Services Industry.

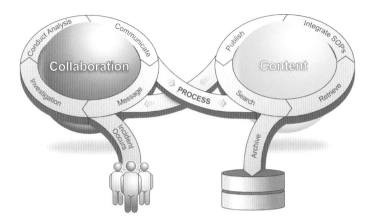

Figure 15.1: Case Management

In the Energy, Chemical and Utility Industries, when an organization experiences a Health, Safety or Environmental (HS&E) **incident** (such as a near-miss, spill, injury or death) the impact on numerous groups within and outside the company is immediate.

First, the company will form an incident **investigation team**. Usually this is a cross-functional team of different disciplines and organizational units. The team is responsible for determining the cause of the incident and recommending material changes to policy to prevent it from reoccurring. During the investigation, the team will set up its own investigation process and conduct activities such as **a root cause failure analysis**. As the investigation continues, the team will need to **collaborate** and share ideas. This collaboration incurs internally with employee interviews and the sharing of ideas within the team, and externally with vendors and regulatory agencies.

Ultimately, the group will determine the cause. To prevent reoccurrence, it will need to **investigate existing policies and procedures** which may need revision. During this process, the ECM **repository will be searched** from existing documents requiring revision. Once these documents are identified and the changes are made, the **alterations must be incorporated** into existing process workflows within the ECM system or training programs outside of it. Next, findings are **published** internally and, in some cases, externally to regulatory bodies.

The end result and the process steps and **discussions are stored** in an archive for future regulatory and litigation support.

ENERGY, CHEMICAL AND UTILITY

The Energy, Chemical and Utility Industries are a global collection of corporations and government entities that conduct large-scale operations that provide products needed by virtually everyone on the planet. The health of the Energy, Chemical and Utility Industries depends on its flexibility to respond within minutes to any changes in the environment which may occur. ECM plays a key role in the Energy, Chemical and Utility Industries by facilitating the acquisition of information, the discussion of this information and the re-distribution of the modified information.

Industry Requirements

According to the U.S. Department of Energy, world energy consumption is projected to increase by 54 percent from 2001 to 2025 (see Figure 15.2). While the mix of energy use will vary from region to region, the primary sources of energy (oil, natural gas, electricity and coal) are all expected to face an increase in demand during this period.

Energy companies today are challenged to efficiently match production to increased demand, and they must do so despite political turmoil, regulatory requirements (SEC and SOX), pressures for improved HS&E losses, and a workforce whose retirement is rapidly approaching.

The Energy, Chemical and Utility Industries comprise a global system of tightly integrated and highly complex relationships between corporations and government entities.

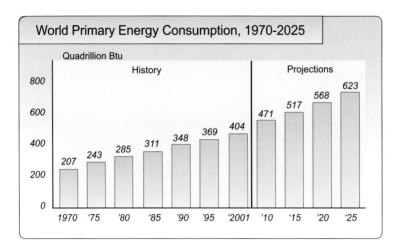

Figure 15.2: The Increasing Demand for Energy

The products, services and operations of the energy sector benefit or affect virtually everyone on the planet. These industries have a critical role in the world's economy.

This industry classification is generally categorized by segment:

• Upstream – This segment involves the exploration (discovery) and production (retrieval) of oil and natural gas resources.

• Downstream – This segment includes the refining, marketing and transportation of petroleum and related products (fuels, lubricants, petrochemicals, etc.).

• Midstream – This segment is defined as the gathering, transportation, storage and distribution of oil and gas products. Pipeline operations typically fall into this segment.

• Utilities – This segment comprises the generation and transmission of electric power and the distribution of natural gas. Utilities also include the management of water and wastewater operations.

Each of these sectors faces a unique set of challenges, and ECM plays a role in solving all of them.

The Royal Dutch/Shell Group of Companies has been finding and producing oil and gas around the world for over a century. With dozens of petroleum and natural gas exploration and production subsidiaries and approximately 90,000 employees, Royal Dutch/Shell recognized it had to reduce duplication of exploration efforts and minimize overlapping skill sets.

Royal Dutch/Shell opted for collaboration technology to combine expertise to manage the supply chain and improve efficiencies. Its British, Dutch and Norwegian exploration subsidiaries collaborate on exploring and developing oil and gas properties in the North Sea. A project for locating new oil fields requires the subsidiaries to work collaboratively and share key information such as geologic data. Most projects span six to nine months, although some can take as long as three years to complete.

ECM is used to share a wide variety of documents, from word processing files and spreadsheets to scientific data and CAD drawings. At any time, there may be 30 to 40 projects in progress. ECM keeps all the documents of a project together in one place. When a project ends, the associated documents are easily accessible in the corporate knowledge base as a learning resource, and for reuse and reference on other projects.

Type	Name	Functions	Status	Start Date	Due Date	Relationship
⊕	03_SIEP TR Workflow Map	⊡	Step Late	10/11/2002 03:09 AM	10/24/2002 03:09 AM	Manage
⊕	03_SIEP TR Workflow Map	⊡	Workflow Late	10/04/2002 02:21 PM	10/17/2002 02:21 PM	Manage
⊕	03_SIEP TR Workflow Map	⊡	Workflow Late	10/04/2002 02:38 PM	10/17/2002 02:38 PM	Manage
⊕	03_SIEP TR Workflow Map	⊡	Workflow Late	10/04/2002 02:46 PM	10/17/2002 02:46 PM	Manage
⊕	Rijswijk report nbr 1	⊡	Workflow Late	10/10/2002 04:14 AM	10/23/2002 04:14 AM	Manage
⊕	2002 8888	⊡	Completed	10/04/2002 10:12 AM	No Due Date	Manage
⊕	EP 2002 9999	⊡	Completed	10/04/2002 09:31 AM	No Due Date	Manage
⊕	JP Buckley Report	⊡	Completed	10/04/2002 08:31 AM	No Due Date	Manage
⊕	JPB Tech Report Test	⊡	Completed	09/29/2002 07:57 PM	No Due Date	Manage
⊕	JPB Tech Rpt 002	⊡	Completed	09/29/2002 08:13 PM	No Due Date	Manage
⊕	My Report - J Buckley	⊡	Completed	09/29/2002 05:23 PM	No Due Date	Manage

Figure 15.3: Managing Projects and Tasks at Shell

Upstream Oil and Gas

Despite record profits in recent years, upstream energy companies continue to face difficult challenges. With world energy consumption projected to increase over the next 25 years, upstream oil and gas organizations face added pressure to meet demand. Most of the easy-to-reach supplies of energy resources have been tapped, and future supplies will be located in places where it is difficult to operate.

Companies require policies and processes to accurately state reserves and to reliably produce against forecasts. They must be able to repeatedly meet stringent regulatory requirements. The recent passage of the Sarbanes-Oxley Act has only added to the complex compliance arena where the EPA, MMA, OSHA, SEC, FERC, and other regulatory organizations are involved.

In exploring for and developing new opportunities, companies frequently find themselves drilling in deeper water, on public lands sensitive to environmental impact, or with foreign governments interested in a portion of the profits, all of which lead to higher costs. With every new capital investment made, companies continue to search for ways to improve their rate of success and minimize risk.

Companies today frequently reduce their capital exposure by partnering with others on capital-intensive projects. While this activity reduces the risk for the parties involved, it also increases the number of people requiring information. The need for effective and efficient collaboration among owners, operators and vendors is critical.

With lifecycles that frequently span decades, oil and gas wells create significant data challenges for their owners, operators and partners. Well files, contracts, production reports, engineering drawings and many other electronic and physical records continue to be created at an amazing pace. Without an effective content management system, companies incur costs in locating or recreating information.

With the installation of Enterprise Resource Planning (ERP) systems largely in the rearview mirror, upstream energy companies struggle today to tie the structured data contained in these systems to the ever increasing volume of unstructured information. Whether you're linking the latest engineering drawing or safety procedure to a maintenance work order, or tying an invoice image or Authorization For Expenditure (AFE) approval to an accounts payable record, the merger of structured and unstructured content is increasingly important.

Upstream organizations are generally organized by project teams, leading to geographically dispersed workers. Members of technical disciplines (i.e., geologists, geophysicists, reservoir engineers, drilling engineers) frequently find themselves unknowingly working on similar projects. Companies today are encouraging collaboration within and across projects to improve the quality of decisions and minimize rework.

ENERGEN®

Energen Corporation is a diversified energy company that specializes in natural gas distribution and oil and gas exploration and production. The implementation of an enterprise-wide, scalable document management system was vital for the corporation's on-going success to reduce costs and decrease the time associated with storage and retrieval of electronic documents.

A Web-based, company-wide ECM system has provided Energen with the ability to create, revise and archive documents. Functionality such as keyword searching, full-text searching and optical character recognition for text searching, helps ensure the speedy retrieval of key information. Paper documents have been converted to electronic images for proper retention, compliance and security.

An association mechanism has been developed to link documents to proper transactions stored in a back-end enterprise application. Workflow technology enables documents to be routed between the systems, allowing for real-time retrieval of all necessary documents. As a result, costs associated with storing and retrieving documents have been significantly reduced.

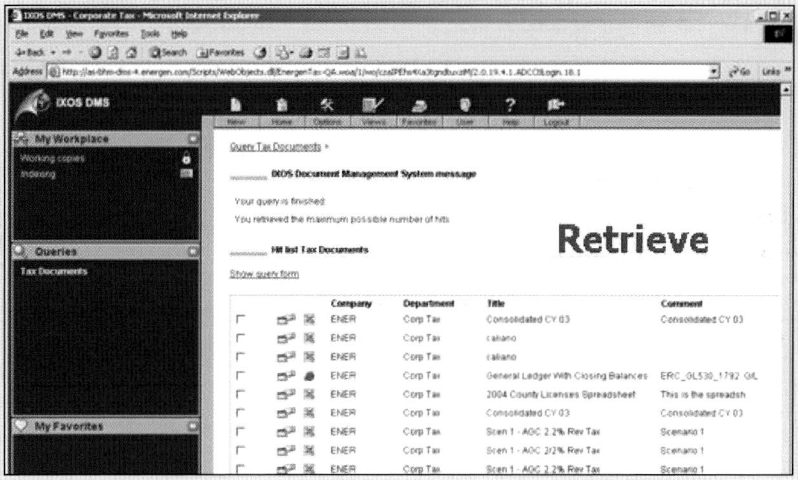

Figure 15.4: Document Management at Energen

The Energy and Chemical Industry is running quickly toward the major problem of lost knowledge. Recent surveys indicate that the workforce will be significantly impacted by retirement in the next five to ten years. In some fields such as engineering, geosciences and operations, hiring needs are expected to exceed 30 percent of the current workforce. Companies are looking now for ways to capture the tacit knowledge of their most experienced workers.

Productivity in Upstream Oil and Gas

ECM systems can solve many of the knowledge and process challenges faced by Upstream Oil and Gas. ECM solutions that manage document principles and practices save upstream energy companies hundreds of millions of dollars annually. Organizations across the globe leverage search, version control and document security as fundamental business process.

The exploration and production of oil and gas is a process-intensive industry. Organizations repeatedly perform critical business routines which, when administered incorrectly, can result in costly delays or penalties. The AFE process, for example, is a vital instrument that upstream organizations use to ensure capital expenditures are thoughtfully executed. Companies today leverage ECM systems to ensure the expedient and satisfactory completion of core business activities. These engines allow for the online completion and electronic routing and capture of PDF forms and other business documentation.

The upstream energy segment is a capital-intensive business with large-scale and expensive projects. Drilling and completion, facility design, construction and shutdown are but a few examples of the significant investments they undertake. With added investment comes the need for improved project management and reduced risk. Oil and gas organizations have at their disposal today strong project management tools which tie directly to their ECM repositories. With these tools, companies can focus on specific tasks, increase visibility and mitigate project risks, manage key documentation, leverage past experiences, and promote value-added collaboration.

From 50-year-old handwritten schematics to 3D seismic data reports to core drilling samples, well files come in a wide variety of forms. Regardless of size, format, content and age, well file information must be readily accessible through convenient means to innovate and stay competitive in today's upstream Energy Industry. Further, certain well file components need to be managed as official company records, with disposition schedules and location information prevalent. Upstream organizations today are leveraging ECM systems to identify, locate and manage their well files.

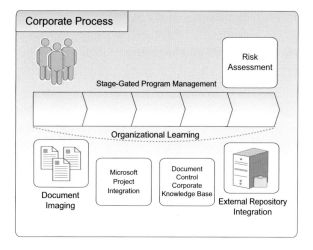

Figure 15.5: Upstream Process Flow

Geographic Information Systems (GIS) are designed to work with data referenced by spatial or geographic coordinates. These systems typically provide an interface to navigate to a suite of information by the only logical means for these applications, a map. The information contained in these systems, however, is often incomplete. Only when combined with unstructured data in the company's repository can an accurate situational assessment be made. Oil and gas companies today are improving the value of their decisions by linking their GIS viewers to their ECM repositories, allowing all relevant information around a specific spatial coordinate to be located.

Downstream Oil and Gas

Petroleum refining is a highly repeatable process that employs significant capital and operates on razor-thin margins. Profitability is driven largely by the ability to continually improve the operational efficiency of facilities. Downstream organizations rely heavily on methodologies such as Six Sigma to continually improve capabilities and reduce deficiencies in their manufacturing operations.

Operators in the downstream segment share some of the same challenges as upstream colleagues. Management of electronic and physical documents, increased compliance and a maturing workforce are examples. There are, however, some challenges which are unique to the segment. Producing fuel and lubricants from feedstock is a capital-intensive business which operates on tight margins. These margins are driven by three factors: the cost of feedstock, the price of produced product and the processes within the refinery.

Individual refineries have little influence over cost and prices, thus financial performance is driven by the ability to optimize the facility. Today's organizations struggle to leverage the collective learning of their workforce towards this goal.

The scheduled shutdown and maintenance of refining facilities is necessary but expensive. Scheduled maintenance is an effective deterrent to unpredicted and costly failures. But, given an average output of 100,000 barrels per day, it is easy to see the importance of minimizing time offline. Planning, control and education are all vital steps to ensuring a safe and efficient turnaround procedure.

In addition to refinery optimization and efficiently planned scheduled maintenance, downstream organizations must also prevent unplanned maintenance. Improving equipment reliability is a key focus of today's refining company. Companies are designing hand-held instruments that can detect impending failures, especially those in rotating equipment. Organizations will need a place to store the data from these devices to allow for investigation, analysis and reporting.

This challenge is faced by all energy segments. Still, the management of engineering drawings and documentation is of vital interest to downstream organizations. A significant percentage of refining organizations are faced with a costly challenge of locating, organizing and maintaining multiple revisions of engineering documentation. The challenge becomes more urgent and costly as external stakeholders are involved.

Productivity in Downstream Oil and Gas

Faced with these challenges, customers in the downstream energy sector generally gravitate toward ECM solutions. Downstream organizations today continue to investigate ECM solutions to manage the ever-increasing capacity of unstructured data. Many companies continue to scan and store physical documents and drawings so that they can be leveraged by the workforce.

Petroleum refining is a process-intensive industry. Like their upstream colleagues, they repeatedly perform critical business processes. One such process is the Management of Change (MOC). Driven by the desire to protect its employees and facilities, as well as the need to satisfy OSHA 1910.119 requirements, MOC is vital to downstream organizations. This important process requires that organizations establish and implement written procedures to manage changes, except "replacements in kind." Companies today leverage ECM systems to manage this process in an effective and efficient manner.

Murphy Oil, an oil and gas organization, found that non-integration of its front-end processes with the back-end ERP system caused time delays and cost accruals for the Accounts Payable department. Too much time was spent on invoice processing, complicating invoice status determination and resulting in dismal customer service.

An ECM solution provides Murphy Oil with a central repository, offering online access to documents and reports. The integration of the system with ERP software has automated workflow processes and instilled a greater process and resource visibility, reducing invoice cycle time, lowering average vendor inquiry resolution time, improving vendor relations and reducing administrative costs.

"Prior to the integration with the [ERP] software, vendor inquiries about invoices typically took about 15 minutes to complete; now it rarely takes more than a two-minute phone call. Our AP staff has more time to spend on activities that create value for our organization. The savings have added up," says the Systems Project Coordinator from the Controllers Department at Murphy Oil.

Figure 15.6: Three-way Invoice Matching at Murphy Oil

Refineries today must certify the delivery and understanding of new information. Take, for instance, managing the change process described above. The standard requires the work site and contract employers to train their employees on the changes prior to start-up. Today, using ECM technology, companies can efficiently create and deliver training based on information stored in their content repositories, and certify that the message has been received and understood.

Refining organizations continue to investigate tools that allow for revision and markup of CAD drawings while integrating with their ECM repository. The ability to search for drawings based on information contained in title blocks and markups is instrumental to engineering operations.

By using ECM collaboration technologies and allowing teams to work across facilities and time zones using disparate resources and pools of information, downstream energy companies can save millions of dollars annually. These savings can be attributed to improved plant efficiency, reduced downtime and improved HS&E compliance, allowing an overall improvement in competitive positioning.

Utilities

To stay competitive in a deregulated market, Utility and Nuclear firms increasingly need to focus on customer support and service. Furthermore, Energy firms need to leverage technical infrastructure investments while demonstrating solid economic fundamentals and eliminating inefficiencies.

Utility organizations maintain personnel and medical files in hard-copy form for tens of thousands of employees at multiple locations. Processing and maintaining these documents is costly. Files are physically transferred between local HR offices when employees change work locations, costing hundreds of thousands of dollars and lacking a proper audit trail.

Reducing the risk associated with storing and retrieving documents is vital in achieving compliance. Paper documents require conversion to images, allowing for retention, retrieval and proper security. A utility organization must have the ability to create, revise, search and archive documents. Keyword searching, full-text searching and optical character recognition for text searching ensure speedy retrieval of needed information and compliance.

According to industry experts, business process outsourcing will be required by Utility organizations to achieve optimal operational efficiencies and show equity growth to their investor community. These processes will likely be human resources, finance and information technology related functions.

> Pacific Gas and Electric Company

Pacific Gas and Electric Company (PG&E) is one of the largest combination natural gas and electric utilities in the United States, serving approximately 14 million people. Supporting more than 21,000 employees at more than 30 locations throughout California, PG&E's Human Resources staff faces the challenge of processing and maintaining a wide variety of documents.

Imaging and archiving technology electronically stores all relevant HR documents in electronic employee folders. Full integration with SAP has streamlined record-keeping processes and enabled significant reduction in the time spent on document filing, searching and storing, giving HR staff more time to spend on consulting activities.

"We not only eliminated inefficiency and the costs associated with paper documents, but the electronic images help ensure the accuracy and accessibility of important company information. A tightly integrated system means better security and data protection. Our new system supports the HR business objective of keeping all critical employee information in electronic form," explains the SAP Human Resources Team Lead at Pacific Gas and Electric.

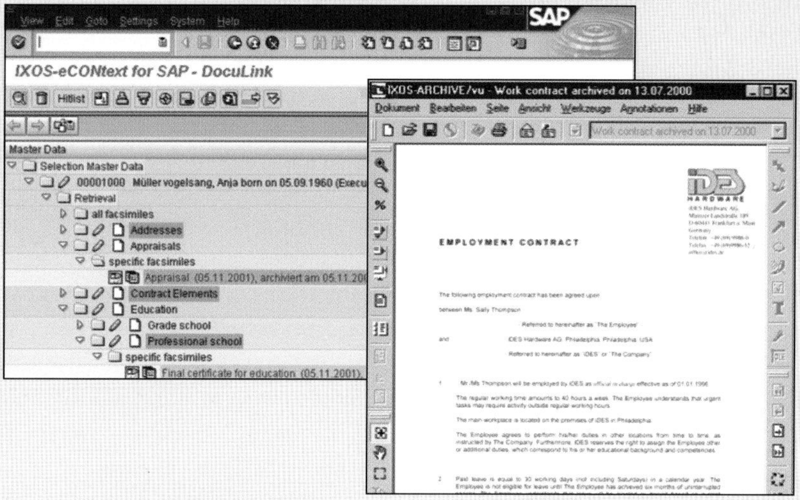

Figure 15.7: An Example of an Electronic Employee Folder

The industry is running quickly toward a major problem of lost knowledge. Recent surveys indicate that the workforce will be significantly impacted by retirement in the next five to 10 years. In some fields, such as engineering, plant maintenance and operations, hiring needs are expected to exceed 30 percent of the current workforce. Companies are looking for ways to capture the tacit knowledge of their most experienced workers. Additional capital will be required as facilities continue to age, requiring more sophisticated and integrated facilities management tools to achieve optimal equipment maintenance and performance.

Productivity in Utilities

Given the geographically and culturally distributed nature of Utility organizations, they face a chaotic collection of hundreds of Web sites scattered across the service area, with just as many individual content providers. This can result in a considerable amount of data duplication, lack of format and information standardization, and a weakening of a single corporate brand when bringing services to market. ECM solutions that manage Web content allow organizations to create a standard template for multiple languages, allowing for a stronger brand and delivering greater efficiency by enabling authoring permissions and review, eliminating duplication of data. Further ROI can also be measured by consolidation of disparate Web sites and multiple Internet Service Providers (ISP) into a single hosting solution and ISP, saving potentially millions of dollars annually.

According to industry experts, the top business challenge facing the Energy Industry today is regulatory compliance. To be compliant in this highly regulated industry, an organization must ensure that all relevant documents are available whenever and wherever required, vital information is archived, unstructured content, process workflows, and collaborative workspaces are managed, all within a central repository. Leveraging ECM systems to centralize this data achieves compliance with OSHA and other regulatory entities by allowing individuals to quickly find and share critical data. This allows the organization to focus on higher value activities while driving operational efficiencies. This data centralization also contributes to filling potential data gaps as people retire or leave the organization, ensuring a continuity of operation.

Other Chapters Related to the Energy, Chemical and Utility Industries

For related information, see the Manufacturing, Pharmaceutical and Life Sciences, and the Architecture, Engineering and Construction (AEC) chapters.

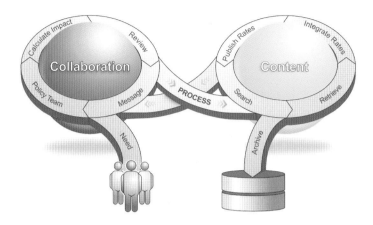

Figure 16.1: Lifecycle of Bank Rate Changes

In the financial services world, when the central **bank changes interest rates**, it has an immediate and material impact on all companies within the financial sector.

Typically, each bank will form a **team**. Usually this is a standing team since rate changes are recurring. The team must deal with a whole gamut of policy changes that are brought about by the rate change, from mortgages to business loans to derivatives. Sometimes the team will work together, but often they will be forced to work in parallel. The next step is to **share the work and calculate the impact** on each financial product, and to survey the competition. Next, the information must be **reviewed** and communicated through meetings and **messaging**. All of these steps involve extensive collaboration.

At the same time, documents are being **searched, retrieved and analyzed**. These might include those relating to previous policy decisions and those from company libraries. Once a decision on the rates has been made, the impact of these changes is **integrated** into the bank's ERP system to calculate new contracts and commission tables. The results are **published** on the Web so that customers can see the new rate offerings. Finally, the end result and the discussions that led to these decisions are stored in an **archive** for future regulatory and litigation support.

Taken together, these steps form the lifecycle of information within Enterprise Content Management.

INSURANCE AND FINANCIAL SERVICES

The Insurance and Financial Services Industries provide two essential services to a modern society. First, through the markets, they provide a mechanism to allocate and re-allocate resources to where they will be most productive. This requires the ability to redeploy capital quickly, take risks and accept the volatility of returns. Second, they provide—often through the same market mechanisms—a means for the accumulation and maintenance of wealth. The Securities and Investment Banking sectors generally focus on the allocation of resources to generate wealth, while the Retail Banking and Insurance sectors focus on the maintenance and protection of assets. But there is considerable overlap. There is always tension between the two goals; an investor, whether individual or corporate, must decide on the right balance between risk and the rewards.

The industry is a global system of products, revenue streams, corporations and governments working together to provide real-time transactions and information. The health of the Financial Services Industry demands the flexibility to respond effectively to any changes in the environment that may occur. Conflicts of interest are inherent to the industry. Establishing common standards for accounting and disclosure in the 20th century was intended to help keep these within reasonable bounds. In recent years, we have seen that it does not always work. There are many standards setting and regulatory bodies for financial services at international (for example, the Bank of International Settlements), national (SEC, BAFIN, FSA, etc.) and regional levels. Identifying and sharing information and ensuring compliance is essential to business operations. Regulators and legislators want to ensure high standards of behaviour from participants in the industry. To do this, they establish standards for business processes and monitor content to ensure compliance.

Earlier in this book, we showed that this intersection of people, processes, and content is where ECM comes into play. It also plays a key role in the industry by facilitating the acquisition of information, the processing of this information and the re-distribution of the modified information. Perhaps no other industry has been more revolutionized by the availability of real-time information than the financial services industry. Timely and relevant information is one of the most critical competitive advantages that banks can have.

Success depends on the ability to manage, preserve and leverage knowledge. It is inefficient to depend on uncontrolled email systems and shared network drives as a repository for corporate knowledge. Doing so can put an organization at risk of litigation or non-compliance with industry and government regulations. ECM enables financial services organizations to foster a knowledge-sharing culture that facilitates the flow of information throughout an organization in a compliant manner.

Financial Services as an industry is a mixture of innovation and conservatism. The core products of the industry, the interest-bearing bank account, the exchange-traded stock, the government bond, or the life insurance policy are centuries old. The methods by which they are accessed (ATM machines, Internet brokers, etc.) have changed; the products have not. At the same time, and often in the same corporations, the derivatives businesses continually create some of the most complex and innovative new products anywhere. As in any industry, mature products provide stability, but small margins; new products generate good returns but rapidly mature and lose differentiation in the marketplace.

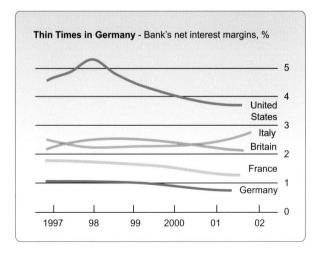

Figure 16.2: Tight Interest Rate Margins

Because wealth is created and managed by investing in businesses, financial services companies are closely bound to the business cycle. At the time of writing, most major economies are growing again, creating a positive business outlook for financial services. After years of cutting costs in response to weak business conditions, most financial service organizations anticipate revenue growth in the years ahead. Strict cost discipline will remain essential but banks and insurers also need to place greater attention on driving revenue growth.

Industry Requirements

The level of scrutiny of financial services firms varies widely. Business lines that deal with consumers are expected to provide comprehensive disclosures that might not be considered essential for another business that only works with highly qualified financial professionals. Financial services firms are vulnerable to the misrepresentation and misuse of information, and increasing emphasis is being placed on the need to understand the customer's identity and business profile. Risk-based assessments are another increasingly adopted feature of financial regulation—especially in guarding against money laundering and similar criminal or terrorist-related activities. Management of the complex tradeoffs in a risk-based model requires sophisticated ECM tools to tag and classify the information and provide structure and audited business workflows.

It is essential to establish what a financial product definition is, how it was sold, and to whom, on any day. This creates a demand for massive archives of automatically generated "high volume, low touch" content such as statements, web site snapshots, and so on, which must be maintained securely but equally may never be accessed again. Records management tools integrated into ECM applications ensure that information is retained as long as the business and regulators require it, but can then be disposed of.

One characteristic of Financial Services firms is their rapid adoption of technology to create new kinds of distribution channels. This has added to the complexity of information management, not only because there are more channels to manage, but also because content must now be repurposed for the different channels and taken through management and legal approvals. Companies in Financial Services, as in Media and Advertising, are finding that approval processes built around digital masters and coordinated workflows can reduce by months the time required to bring a new product to market.

Across the Financial Services Industry, technology budgets have been scaled back over the last several years to enable cost reduction. To remain competitive, banks and insurers must renew their commitment to investing in new technology strategically to reduce costs, improve efficiencies and strengthen revenue-generating initiatives.

Some of the greatest long-term gains in operational efficiency are achieved when firms reengineer business processes to fundamentally change how work is done. Benefits from re-engineering can be optimized by integrating with other cost reduction initiatives such as strategic sourcing and automation. These competitive dynamics are taking place against the background of unprecedented new regulatory requirements, rising corporate governance standards and stakeholder expectations, and an array of technology investments needed to remain competitive.

Of all these requirements, perhaps the most dramatic is the growth and impact of email. After the year 2000, email became the communication tool of record within many enterprises. It has been particularly acute in Financial Services, where the combination of mandated retention of large percentages of emails and extensive discovery requires a comprehensive ECM infrastructure and records management.

Placing the Customer Front and Centre

Pure economics means increasing the "share of wallet" among existing customers. Having learned from customer relationship management projects, banks in particular are emphasizing more targeted technology investments and better service. Defection rates remain high and cross-sell ratios remain low across much of the industry. At the same time, the pressure on margins drives companies to self-service models, especially in the mass market retail segments. Well designed, content-rich solutions that are responsive to users' needs add value by letting customers control where, when, and how they interact with their service provider, while minimizing rework in the financial institution. Both content and process are aligned by the ECM platform to deliver service.

Managing People

Despite its automation and adoption of technology, Financial Services and Insurance companies continue to be major employers. This is unlikely to change. This is a huge, complex and evolving industry, and also one that interacts directly with major personal and professional decisions. This requires skills, training, certification, reviews, reports and so on. Pressures on cost and responsiveness have led to the opening of operations in lower-cost locations such as India or China. For companies that can master the complexities and maintain high-quality customer relationships, the benefits promise to be substantial.

Integrated, rich-media-based training delivery solutions that track certification and regulatory reporting requirements manage the process and content for training. This enables companies to focus their efforts on the behaviours they want staff to practice. ECM systems provide a facilitation and coordination infrastructure that assures compliance by integration into the learning processes.

> Aargauische Gebaeudeversicherungsanstalt (AGVA)

Ihre Sicherheit – AGVA

The assessment of buildings and claims settlement lie at the core of AGVA's (Aargauische Gebaeudeversicherung) activities. To streamline the complex processes involved, and to link content to process, the insurance company implemented an integrated system made up of ECM and ERP.

Process and document management are entirely managed by a Business Process Management solution, which, together with an archiving solution, forms the ECM infrastructure at AGVA. All insurance products are managed using an ERP system and an inventory management system. Customer files are managed using the archiving solution, which is integrated with the ERP system for easy access to relevant information.

This integrated solution enables field staff direct access to up-to-date information about insurance coverage, claim benefits and premiums. Business processes at AGVA have been optimized, becoming more efficient and easier to manage. As a result, productivity has increased, resulting in cost savings, and customer service has improved, resulting in improved customer satisfaction.

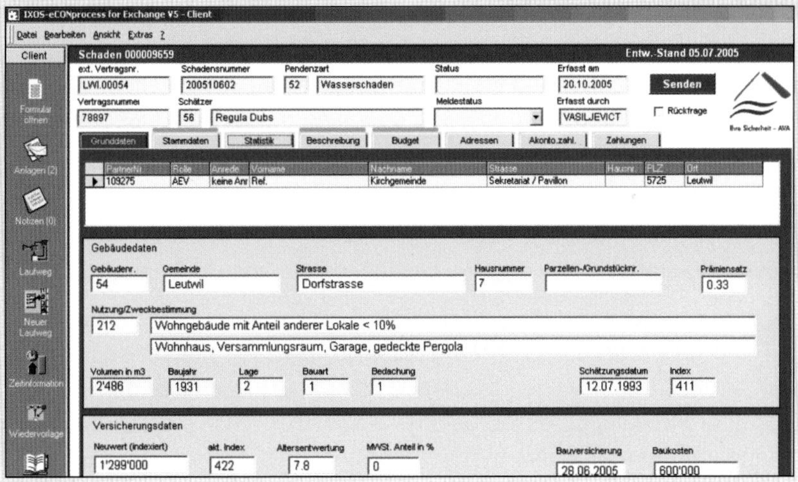

Figure 16.3: Claims management at AGVA

The growing regulatory burden and the introduction of new tools to accomodate the relentless innovation in products also has an impact. Although the rules are not yet complete, banks in Europe and many other parts of the world will need to adopt International Financial Reporting Standards in the coming years. The new standards, especially in insurance, will require substantially stronger financial reporting and controls. The impact will be widespread, affecting accounting, risk management and product development. Conversion may be costly, with fundamental implications for information technology, people and organizational processes.

Converting to International Financial Reporting Standards (IFRS) will also create major challenges in terms of educating investors, analysts and other stakeholders, so they can distinguish between accounting and economic changes. Companies that carefully explain how risk is monitored may be rewarded by both capital markets and policyholders for improved transparency and risk management, even if their reporting becomes more volatile. Customer education remains one of the most effective ways of developing and maintaining a position in the market.

Managing Processes

Many banks and insurance companies are shifting from cutting costs to holding expenses while growing revenue. Process and technology automation, shared services and moving business off shore to create a more efficient operating model help meet these strategic objectives.

Organizations are seeking to increase efficiency by automating key functions such as underwriting, sales and claims processing. Automated underwriting not only cuts expenses, it can increase sales by dramatically reducing the time needed to underwrite a policy.

The industry is seeking to maintain underwriting discipline as the hard insurance market comes to an end and rates fall. The temptation to increase market share may prove irresistible for some firms; however, insurance companies that have developed a more analytical and data-based approach to underwriting should be in a better position to hold their pricing and therefore preserve the profitability of each line of business.

Automating the quoting, policy issuance and back-end reporting processes also allows underwriters to increase production as needed, without having to add staff when demand rises. Automated underwriting is proving effective for mainstream applications such as auto policies. Although it has been harder to automate the customized underwriting required for large commercial risks, automated tools can speed the process and improve decision making.

> Winterthur Versicherungen

winterthur

The Winterthur Group is one of Europe's leading insurers and one of the ten largest insurance groups operating worldwide. The Group employs 27,000 staff, of which 70 percent work in thirty countries outside Switzerland. Together with the banking subsidiaries of Credit Suisse Group, it forms one of the world's leading integrated financial services companies.

The Winterthur Group had come to rely on highly qualified staff for maintaining their Web site. The company needed a content management system that would enable its staff to set up and run the company's Internet and Intranet Web sites with minimum costs and human resources. The new system met the company's needs for standard-ization, object base, functionality and user friendliness.

The software enabled content that was sourced from other systems to be dynami-cally integrated into the Web site. The ability to separate layout from content and re-use Web pages was directly beneficial for content authors. It is now possible to include various user groups in the maintenance and development of the system. The user-friendly handling of the system meant that many processes could be easily automated.

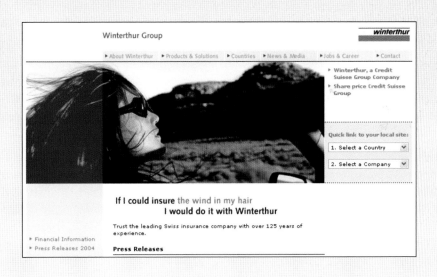

Figure 16.4: Winterthur's Web site

The insurance industry has lagged behind other financial service sectors in increasing efficiency because of the tendency to keep processes in house and design customized IT solutions. As companies seek to correct their recent under-performance, they will need to fundamentally rethink their operating models, use of technology and global footprint to remain competitive.

Insurers will also have to improve their processes. Often in reinsurance, companies revise agreements yearly without signing new contracts. Insurers using brokers will have to develop strict financial controls, processes and content around the payment of commissions.

Compliance and Corporate Governance

Banks and insurers face huge challenges in complying with new regulations. These include Basel II, International Financial Reporting Standards (in particular IAS 39), the Sarbanes-Oxley Act, and anti money laundering legislation.

There are many regulators (see Chapter 4 for a partial listing) that are reacting to the dawn of digital content as a legal form of information. Corporations began documenting their internal controls with desktop tools, then moved to databases as the set grew larger, and finally to ECM platform as it became clear that tracking and managing this information required structured data management and content and document tracking.

Even more important is solving the problem of integrating governance into the core operations of an organization. The rising tide of regulation is creating operational challenges for all companies, but especially insurers. Documenting the internal processes, risks, and controls identifies what the organization (and the regulator) wants to happen. Meeting these new regulatory requirements in an integrated way will be essential for success.

Companies have tended to manage regulatory change in silos, focusing narrowly on compliance and using compartmentalized regulatory controls. The greatest challenge is to make sure that this integrates into the core operations of the organization. Companies that choose to go beyond compliance and implement best practices through ECM solutions can achieve competitive advantage and protect their brands.

> AXA France

Traditionally an insurance company, AXA transformed its core business in 2003 to embrace the broader area of general financial protection. With over 50 million customers worldwide, AXA France needed a comprehensive tool to streamline customer relations and improve collaboration with both internal and external end users.

AXA implemented a Web-based personalized help system that enables document management to make their relevant business processes more efficient. The solution supports the management of user profiles and access rights, helps assure quality information, and capitalizes on the competencies and knowledge within the enterprise.

The online personalized help system facilitates collaboration between geographically dispersed end users and, as a result, AXA has been able to offer its services to a more dispersed audience. Re-use of information has saved time and resources, while the ability to measure new and returning visitor frequency allows AXA to evaluate customer satisfaction.

Figure 16.5: Document Sharing Environment at AXA France

Figure 16.6: Best Practices Make Things Happen

The U.S. insurer Progressive has made transparency of information a key part of its brand. In 2001, it became the first publicly held company to issue operating results monthly and in 2003, the first company to report earnings per share monthly. Adopting best practices in corporate governance and business practices can allow firms to strengthen their brand and distinguish themselves in the current environment of intense scrutiny and skepticism by investors.

In the past, both U.S. and U.K. insurance companies have been cited for selling inappropriate insurance products to consumers. Insurance companies will need to assure regulators and consumers that they are recommending products based on an objective assessment of what is in the best interests of their customers. By standardizing both marketing and contractual documentation and ensuring that only the appropriate document collections for a customer are assembled and delivered ECM solutions support this process and provide the audit transparency needed.

ECM in Insurance and Financial Services

Content and process management tools are essential to support regulatory compliance. Equally important is the value gained from ensuring that people work together more effectively.

Enterprise Content Management provides powerful tools for defining, organizing, and reusing business content, simplifying business process and helping employees coordinate with the organization and one another. ECM eases the creation, deployment,

A leading financial services provider and for two years running a Fortune 500 company, Capital One has a dynamic work culture that makes it difficult to maintain an organizational folder structure. As a result, its intellectual capital needs to be documented and tagged for easy access to reduce the learning curve associated with role fluidity.

New technologies or not, users have a natural tendency to continue with old habits. Capital One found that education about the benefits of a content management solution may increase usage. Based on user response, the organization implemented key system features that prompted more active usage. For example, integrating multiple applications into a single sign-on meant that users were more likely to log into the system at the beginning of the work day.

The enhanced ECM-based solution provides a higher degree of accessibility, centralized information, and new document composition and editing functions. Support for security requirements, provision of valid records and improved accessibility standards have enabled Capital One to increase user acceptance and system usage, thus enhancing performance.

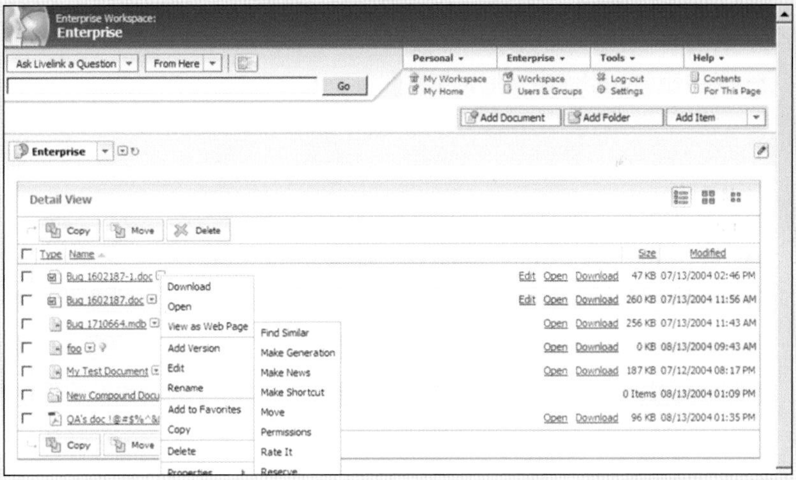

Figure 16.7: An Example of Document Management Functionality

modification and management of business processes—no matter how complex—with no programming needed whatsoever. This standardization of internal procedures yields higher employee productivity and process adoption.

Other Chapters Related to Insurance and Financial Services

Financial Services sectors are not yet subject to the regulatory rigor of Pharmaceutical Industry, but the issues are similar. As well, the structure of the Financial Services Industry is similar to that of the Manufacturing Industry.

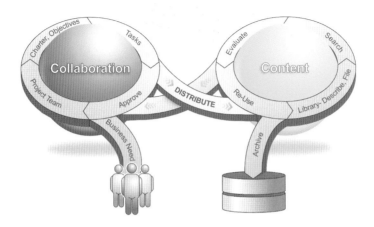

Figure 17.1: Business Improvement Project Process

A typical request in the Telecommunications Industry is for a business improvement project derived from a **business need**. An assigned project manager forms a **project team**, often from multiple disciplines and locations. A project **charter**, or **objectives** is formalized and **tasks** are defined. The team collaborates to produce documents which need **approval** to release funds to execute. Once approved, there is a need to **distribute** the plans, and guidance is required to execute the project. Once the project is complete, the documents are placed in a **library** containing searchable details. This enables team members from other projects to **search** the library, **evaluate** previously developed content and **re-use** some of the learning, avoiding wasteful duplication of effort. Eventually, the content is **archived**, allowing for potential future reference.

CHAPTER 17

TELECOMMUNICATIONS

The Telecommunications Industry is a trillion dollar (U.S.) per year industry. Spanning the globe, it acts as a central nervous system, transporting information at incredible speeds to the furthest reaches of the planet. Industry players include not only network operators but also equipment manufacturers, services and solutions providers. Telecommunications is an example of collaboration and fierce competition among subsidiaries within the same organization. It connects users to information like no other business and is increasingly mission critical to the operation of every organization— large or small, public or private sector.

The Telecommunications Industry is comprised of geographically dispersed organizations which face challenges posed by the need for information sharing, required not only to compete but to operate. After more than half a century in which giant monopolies, often enjoying "super-profits," could change gradually, the business has been cast into an era of tumultuous, rapid change as a result of the privatization and globalization which has fundamentally altered the landscape of the industry. This has created the simultaneous demands of exponential changes in capacity, price erosion (of more than 99 percent on some core offerings in less than 20 years), and the need for major new revenue streams. Massive technological changes result in radical new communications possibilities for customers personally and corporately. This often stimulates a customer's desire for more and ever improving services.

All of this must be achieved by workforces that, in some cases, have more than halved in less than 15 years, requiring gains in the speed, efficiency, cost effectiveness and security of all processes. Layers of regulation – from industry-specific to generic, from national to supra-national, call for auditable stewardship of information to execute and demonstrate compliance.

Industry Requirements

All of the largest players in the industry value chain – whether equipment manufacturers, network operators or service providers – have had to respond to unprecedented techno- logical change. The two largest fundamental changes in usage have been the convergent explosions of data communications (including mass Internet usage) and mobility. Richer content has driven exponential upgrades to user bandwidth at home and at work. Networks and computers of every size are inextricably integrated. The massive growth of Internet Protocol (IP) packet transmission has meant, however, that revenues have not expanded accordingly. Each major "win" in Internet Protocol Virtual Private Network (IPVPN) is also erosion of someone's traditional revenues. The revenue boom switched to mobile, which gained tens of millions of customers a year. In major developing economies like India and China, mobile now has more connections than traditional wire line.

In every major market, liberalization has brought with it regulation that constantly seeks to further the interests of the consumer by preventing the abuse of market power. In some cases, this creates obligations on one-time monopolies to prove the absence of such abuse.

The industry and its investors experienced the seismic consequences of the "dot com era," but in most key cases are now resurfacing. Those owning mobile networks saw uninterrupted growth in revenues and customers, but are now facing price erosion and the flattening or even decline of revenues per customer. The response is to find more and more applications and content partners to entice customers to take up new services to offset price erosion for voice services. While market penetration for fixed and mobile is high in all developed economies, there is room for growth in all the emerging economic powerhouses.

The huge growth in new services against the background of billions of dollars in price erosion globally calls for constant process improvements. This frequently calls for major systems updates, transitioning from legacy systems (often "home grown" for the older operators) and increasing integration to support the automation of end-to-end workflows that cross organizational and system boundaries.

The need to communicate and collaborate externally intensifies in line with market competitiveness. Partnerships have always been key since no one party fulfills the entire value chain. Distance collaboration to speed up the fruits of such partnerships is increas- ingly important, as competition for market share and new service launches intensifies. Customers of all kinds expect richer and more dynamic communication with vendors, and content, like services, becomes obsolete with increasing rapidity.

Even smaller players and market entrants have to question their effectiveness as the industry titans combine market power and portfolio depth with decreasing unit costs for transactions of all kinds.

> Cisco Systems

Founded in 1984, Cisco Systems is represented in 65 countries and has an estimated headcount of 32,500. Global development means geographically dispersed employees, extensive travel and high print and mailing costs. In order to reduce these costs and increase information sharing within the enterprise, Cisco turned to ECM technology.

Web-based communications tools support Cisco's networked virtual organization. Used for HR and e-sales business processes, the solution has enabled the automation of the executive speaker request process and the creation of a global Marketing Tracking System. It has also provided support for IT operations and created a portal for global e-sales.

The fast and cost-effective deployment of Web-based applications was largely culturally-based, enabling smooth change management. All information is now available on the Web and access to necessary data is possible anytime and anywhere. Employees at Cisco are more self-sufficient and productive, thanks to various self-serve applications.

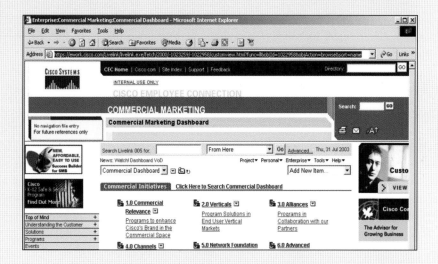

Figure 17.2: Commercial Marketing Dashboard at Cisco Systems

New Products Development

The multi-billion dollar investments have been made—20 times more bandwidth for users of landlines, up to 50 times more for basic cellular phone users. The race is on to conceive, design and bring to market new services, increasingly involving content, to promote bandwidth uptake and capture market share among new users. With a constantly evolving network of partners, the need for rapid, effective yet secure collaboration and information sharing is clear. As companies throughout the telecommunications value chain seek to leverage the collective power of global knowledge workers, the ability to make this possible with a high-performance platform and navigable information structure becomes one more weapon for competitive advantage.

Customer Relationships

Winning customers is one thing—keeping them is another. Sophisticated content and contact management help the holistic management of customer information—to show you know is to show you care. Even handwritten inbound customer contact needs to be part of the electronic customer record. What's more, this information may need to be shared across national boundaries, particularly to take advantage of the irresistible attraction of off-shore cost levels.

Increasing Efficiency

Price erosion is a constant and by no means an incremental trend. Existing services like a simple voice call often show dramatic price decreases and can be marketed as "free" with such technologies as Voice Over Internet Protocol (VoIP). New services replace and even outperform old ones at dramatically lower cost. In a market with many new entrants, this translates to much lower prices. The bigger players, built on conventional technologies, need to look at big cost lines and cut them. For a major telecommunications organization, people are one of the biggest costs, so processes that make better use of them are a constant goal.

Easing the Regulatory Burden

Major players are required to show they are competing fairly. At times, this gives rise to a duty of information discovery. If information is scattered across a plethora of desktop computer hard drives and shared network drives, proving the accuracy of such discovery in a reasonable lead time can be costly or impossible. Failure to meet the demands of regulators can lead to sanctions, which have major commercial impact.

A large and complex organization, BT is a UK communications solutions provider. Functionally diverse and geographically dispersed, BT sought to gain competitive advantage by enabling an integrated communications network for every stage of product development, spanning from discovery to post-launch evaluation.

In order to enable collaboration on such a large and diverse scale, BT turned to ECM technology. Centralized knowledge management has enabled the organization to capture, store, and re-use its intellectual assets, providing its employees with easy and quick access to wide-scale information and expertise. In addition, BT has established virtual communities, or e-communities, to increase collaboration across the enterprise.

Currently, increased communication ensures the facilitation of common understanding, clearer company positioning and increased process visibility, while enhancing corporate governance. BT employees feel increasingly self-sufficient and productive, and consequently report higher job satisfaction. In brief, the ECM solution has enabled BT to leverage intellectual capital from across the enterprise and to achieve business assurance.

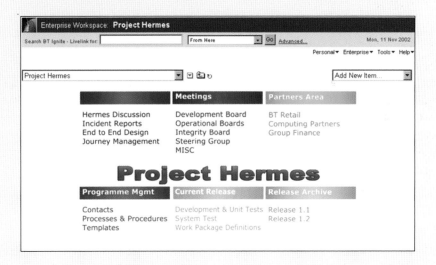

Figure 17.3: BT's Project Work Space

Information Sharing with Permissions

There is a need for information sharing with customers, suppliers, partners and even competitors (some parties can match all four descriptions), and a need to avoid sharing the wrong information with the wrong people. Separate platforms can lead to higher management, maintenance and even storage costs.

Telecommunication companies are unique in combining the geographic scope and pervasive reach of a utility with perhaps the highest transaction rates of any industry. They provide a bewildering array of products and services to literally every kind of customer from the biggest, most powerful corporation to the most vulnerable senior citizen. Parts of the industry have added tens of millions of customers per year for several years. These customers use services that transform their daily lives, from Broadband Internet use in a business environment to Text Messaging from the playground.

The competitive advantage required to succeed is neither simple nor one-dimensional. There is a need for high-speed, robust, cost-effective and customer-friendly processes for mass markets and mission-critical networks. Telecommunications companies must provide leading edge innovation for both consumers and corporations. In all cases, the challenge is to execute the value chain by teamwork in dispersed and often large workforces.

ECM in Telecommunications

ECM offers solutions throughout the value chain for the Telecommunications Industry.

There are opportunities to radically reduce the cost of core processes such as accounts payable (invoice verification), customer correspondence and order processing. These processes allow for the automation of low or semi-skilled processes. Many of them are effectively workflows which cross departmental barriers.

Large companies have shown how teamwork across processes, from development to deployment, can improve time to market. ECM solutions that make content visible to many help reduce time-consuming and costly duplication of effort. Field applications are emerging, making high-quality information available to field engineers, not only improving efficiency and cutting costs, but also ensuring workers receive the correct safety instructions.

From leading innovation units to the most established and mission-critical of processes, ECM is empowering the Telecommunications Industry to provide robust services, quickly and cost effectively to millions more users around the globe.

> T-Systems

······ **T**··Systems·

T-Systems is one of Europe's leading providers of information and communications technology for business customers. The geographically dispersed company — the Telekom Global Net is available in more than 50 countries with over 2,000 access points — had many small intranets, which resulted in high costs and did not provide the necessary collaboration support.

A central project repository with document management capabilities and a search engine, MyWorkroom is a collaborative environment integrated with the T-Systems portal for easy and direct single sign-on access. The development of virtual project rooms and team forums with role-based access has enabled collaboration in bound workrooms with 'doorways' in between, and business processes have received support from workflow technology.

The solution received high user acceptance, and at the end of 2003, myWorkroom became the standard system for 20,000 users. Both the organization and the users are benefiting from the solution, which has increased efficiency, improved the quality of collaborative work, enabled quicker project completion, and sped information retrieval and processing. These benefits allowed T-Systems to enjoy considerable cost and time savings.

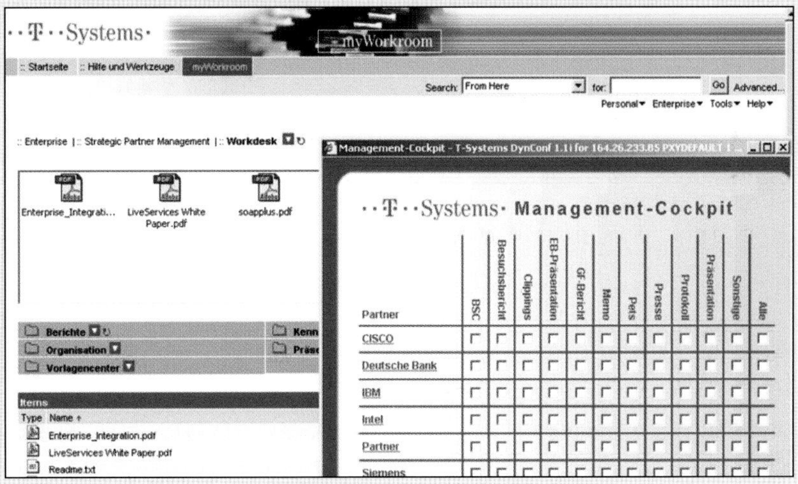

Figure 17.4: Partner Management at T-Systems

Quality Control

Quality Control is a critical factor for the telecommunications industry. Achieving and maintaining an ISO 9000 accreditation within the organization is a common challenge for a telecommunications company. ISO 9001 is a quality assurance model that is used by companies that design, produce, test, install and service items. At the heart of an ISO 9000 accreditation is the audit of the processes used to create and produce a product or service. Figure 17.5 is a diagram of a typical ISO 9000 process used in telecommunications. ISO 9000 quality implementation is an opportunity to streamline work processes within a department to achieve better productivity. Doing this makes processes or departments ISO 9000 compliant and results in greater efficiency and increased ROI.

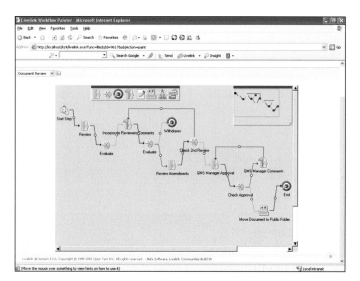

Figure 17.5: An ISO 9000 Approval Process

Other Chapters Related to the Telecommunications

The Telecommunications Industry is product-development intensive, and similar to the Pharmaceutical and Research and Development Industry. It is also services oriented, similar to the Services and the Government sectors.

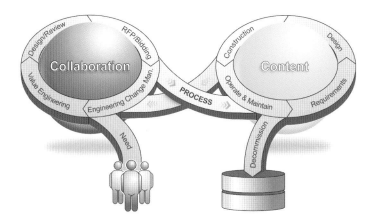

Figure 18.1: Construction Project Process

Construction projects begin with a **need**. A typical first step is to assemble a dedicated project team to share the tasks required to solve the problem and assess the feasibility. If the project gets past the feasibility stage, the collaborative process of initial design begins and more resources are added to the project. Starting with the design phase, **value engineering**, **design reviews**, and **engineering change management** are collaborative processes that continue through the remainder of the project lifecycle.

As the design phase progresses to begin finalizing budgets, the project team expands once again in the Request for Proposal **(RFP)/Bidding** stage, where general contractors, specialty contractors, suppliers and manufacturers start to have input in the final design and budgeting.

Once construction begins, the bulk of the design work is completed, but managing change becomes critical. Diverse conditions, availability of materials and equipment, and **requirements** changes are just a few of the events that can cause **design changes** that can delay projects and increase costs.

The Facilities Management phase starts as the **construction** phase ends, and must draw on the information compiled during previous phases. Easy access to as-built drawings, training and equipment manuals and documentation are just a few of the deliverables of the project team. Even in the Facilities Management phase, **operating and maintaining** as well as managing change is important as equipment is replaced or the facility processes change, until the facility is obsolete and **decommissioned**.

CHAPTER 18

ARCHITECTURE, ENGINEERING AND CONSTRUCTION

The Architecture, Engineering and Construction Industry (AEC) is a multi-trillion dollar (U.S.) per year industry. It is composed of a worldwide system of property owners and developers, regulatory bodies, architects, engineers, consultants, general contractors, specialist contractors, materials manufacturers, materials distributors and others who collaborate on millions of projects.

The success of any AEC Industry depends on having the flexibility to respond quickly to changes. ECM plays a key role in AEC by facilitating the acquisition of information, the discussion of this information and the re-distribution of the modified information. Managing projects and business is about managing information and communication.

Information comes in a variety of forms and its focus varies depending on the organization. For example, owners build and manage facilities to accommodate their core business, which typically has nothing to do with architecture, engineering or construction. Architects and engineers operate in a highly technical environment offering a variety of services throughout a project lifecycle. Contractors must build projects on time and on budget, needing as much information as possible to make critical project decisions.

The concerns of every party in an AEC or Facilities Management (FM) project relationship are different. Companies often operate using diverse and incompatible systems. Silos of information can exist, making management of the project difficult, from feasibility studies through to design, estimating, construction and on-going maintenance. In addition, each participating company has a business to run outside of the context of the individual project.

Industry Requirements

AEC is a fragmented industry. A typical project is made up of independent parties working together under a manager. Architects, designers, engineers, contractors, suppliers and manufacturers must coordinate their efforts across different locations, often using disparate technologies developed specifically for their professions. In addition, construction-related projects are typically a one-project-per-design process, unlike manufactured products which are built multiple times on a single design.

While technologies have advanced significantly within each stage of the AEC lifecycle, little has been achieved in unifying data across the entire project lifecycle. Islands of automation continue to plague the industry within and across the stages of a project. For any one company, this is compounded across projects, particularly if a company has not applied standards across projects.

As the Construction phase ends, contracts are closed out and responsibilities are handed off to operations and maintenance. Storing, accessing and mining data for claims resolution, ongoing operations and maintenance can continue to be a challenge even in this phase, not to mention finding data from previous phases when all the players have moved on to new projects.

Organizations in the AEC Industry are challenged to find ways to reduce risk, control costs and optimize project schedules. They must streamline the design, construction, operation and maintenance processes of construction-related projects while managing continuous change and improving the continuity and availability of information across the project lifecycle.

Optimization in Construction

Web-based ECM solutions promise to help coordinate design and construction activities to ensure compliance, provide better quality and shorter time to market.

To reduce risk, systems must increase the accountability of all project participants, and the transparency of all project interactions. Information must be accessible by all project participants. It must be maintained and current. Numerous studies show that incorrect and out-of-date information leads to unnecessary construction project costs of 2 percent to 5 percent.

DMJM**HARRIS**
AN AECOM COMPANY

Over 13,000 employees worldwide. Geographically dispersed project teams. Engineers. Suppliers. Construction managers. Owners. Contractors. All these groups need access to data warehouses and enterprise applications at DMJM + Harris, a global design, engineering and construction services company. Mega-projects require complex collaboration among different groups and companies, who often work on incompatible IT infrastructures.

An ECM-based central repository for all project information at DMJM + Harris enables direct document viewing, retrieval, editing and versioning using push and pull technologies for automatic and personalized notification. Documents can be created within the company and enabled for intra- and inter-company sharing with easy and fast access to information from anywhere.

The Web-based collaboration workspace provides a foundation for online document management, business process automation and team communication. Individualized accountability is achieved though workflow management, document review and approval processes, dynamic forms and reports, and notification functions. The core knowledge management function enables information visibility across all connected units at DMJM + Harris.

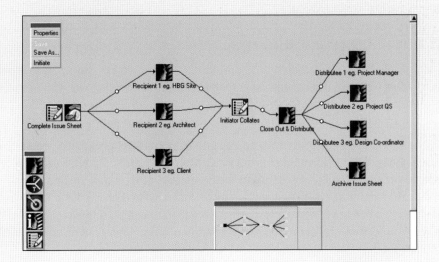

Figure 18.2: DMJM + Harris' Business Process Management

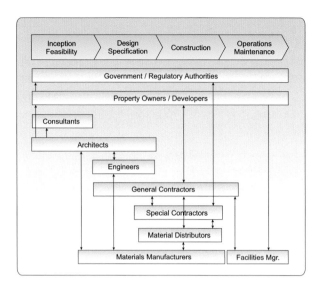

Figure 18.3: Functional Roles at Various Stages in the Construction Process

By shortening task completion times, reducing errors due to poor coordination and increasing accountability of project participants, project cost and schedules can be reduced.

ECM and Compliance in AEC

The mission of the U.S. Department of Labor's Occupational Safety and Health Administration's (OSHA) mission is to assure the safety and health of workers by setting and enforcing standards, providing training, outreach, and education, establishing partnerships and encouraging continual improvement in workplace safety and health.

Compliance to OSHA standards not only covers field situations and safety equipment, but require that proper documentation such as Material Safety Data Sheets (MSDS) be available on site as well as records of incidents and other safety issues. When an accident occurs on site, typically the first thing that OSHA will check is the project records. Having a solid document management solution to quickly find all required information when an OSHA inspector shows up is often a determining factor on whether a site is compliant.

In addition to managing OSHA-related documents, there are significant training requirements for personnel on site. A solution that can deliver rich media training while capturing records and histories of an employee's training can also play a significant role in avoiding OSHA compliance fines.

ARUP

Associated with famous structures such as the Sydney Opera House and Pompidou, Arup is an engineering design organization. With projects in more than 100 countries, a network spanning 70 offices and over 6,000 employees worldwide, Arup's vision of enabling staff to collaborate was a strategic necessity.

Project information can now be accessed directly anytime and anywhere using a Web-based repository. Documents can be viewed online, revised, printed and distributed. All key activities are automatically monitored and management reports generated, ensuring full audit-ability on all project communications. Extensive automation of business processes has reduced paper use at Arup and decreased storage costs.

Direct document access has reduced the time needed to find information and, along with versioning functionalities, ensured that employees work only with updated information. The increased transparency of communication promotes teamwork and helps to avoid disputes. With the ECM-based solution, Arup is well on its way to achieving a general improvement in efficiency and a reduction in costs, while providing better service to clients.

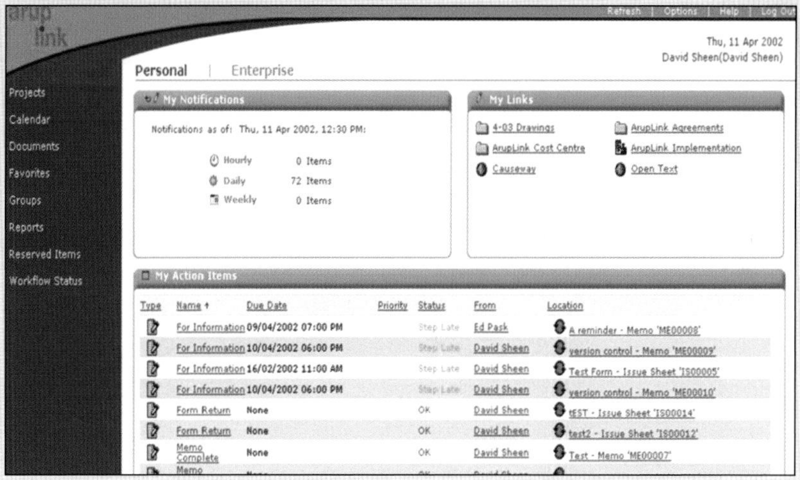

Figure 18.4: Arup's Personal Workspace and Notifications

Managing Global Teams

Engineering and Facilities Management projects face common issues globally. Although there may be regional variances in building codes and safety standards, the processes are fairly well defined.

As we become more of a global community, engineering-related activities are becoming more specialized. Engineering firms are building teams based on their expertise from across the globe, as opposed to working with regional teams. With ever increasing demands on reducing cost and timescales, a solid content and collaboration suite is essential for these firms to be competitive in today's environment.

Global Projects

Major construction projects are complex and their impact is often global. Consider the construction of an offshore oil rig. Specialists in a particular area of rig construction must be managed to ensure that quality, timely and cost-effective results are achieved. Complicating matters is the fact that no two projects are the same, and that different sub-contractors may be used depending on where the project is located. To maintain a high quality, on-budget construction project (which involves billions of investment dollars), an extranet of sub-contractors must be established. These sub-contractors are located in every part of the world and are therefore never in a common time zone at any given time. This emphasizes the need for asynchronous collaboration project management to ensure that all parts of the project are progressing on time. Figure 18.5 is a diagram of a typical RFP process used in global project construction. There are many other examples of global construction projects such as bridges, subways, tunnels and dams, all of which are immense in scale and can require up to a decade to complete.

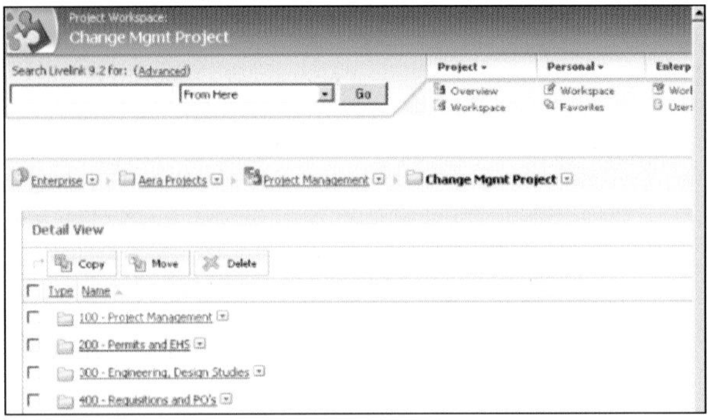

Figure 18.5: An RFP Site for Managing Global Project Sub-Contractors

Originating in Switzerland, Holcim has grown to become one of the world's leading suppliers of cement, aggregates and concrete. With over 100 cement production plants, more than 40 group companies and approximately 44,000 employees, the need for effective collaboration at Holcim was imperative to establish cost leadership and encourage faster learning.

HolSpace is an online communication space dedicated to the Holcim community. It provides easy access to solutions that facilitate intra-group communication and collaboration to support the 'faster learning organization.' Project workspaces support knowledge sharing and are ideal for international project work, while providing the foundation for Holcim's knowledge management efforts.

A document repository is easy to use and feature-rich with version control and audit functions. Communities of practice are now the key to knowledge management at Holcim by providing the day-to-day social setting where knowledge can be managed. Holcim's corporate knowledge is now in the best hands, as it is managed by the people who own, need, create and use it.

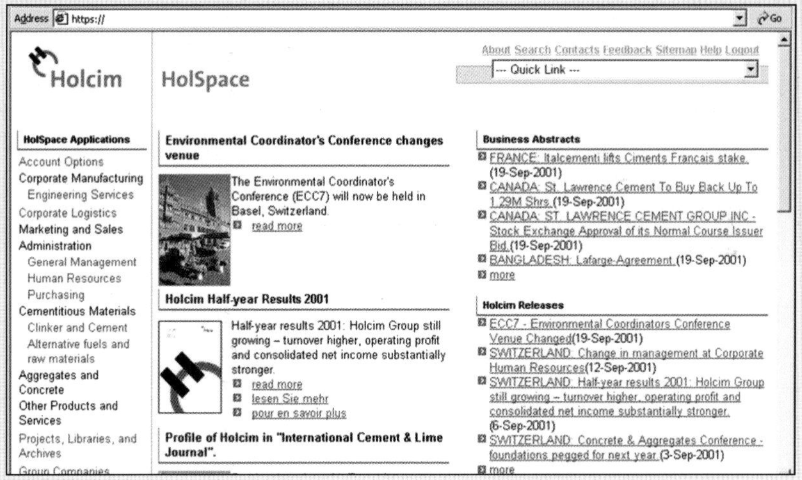

Figure 18.6: Holcim's Enterprise Workspace

ECM Solutions across Departments and Organizations

Success depends on the ability to manage, preserve and leverage an organization's knowledge assets. It is inefficient to depend on uncontrolled email systems and shared network drives as a repository for corporate knowledge, and can put an organization at risk of litigation or non-compliance with government regulations. ECM enables organizations to foster a knowledge sharing culture that facilitates the flow of information throughout an organization. The Architecture, Engineering and Construction Industry has some natural similarities for benchmarking with the Energy Industry as they both deal with large capital projects.

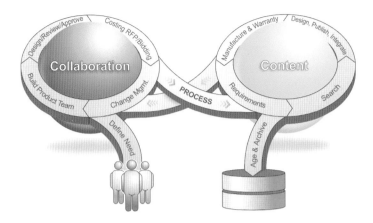

Figure 19.1: Information Creation and Storage Process

The Automotive Industry **defines market needs** and then designs, manufactures, assembles and warrantees automobile products to fill those needs. Once the market need is set, a dedicated **product team** is assembled. An ECM system manages market findings, product definitions and requirements, and manages any internal **review and approval** process regarding the initial product design. Other teams use the product information in the ECM system to build and manage Requests For Proposals (RFPs) for essential supplier products and to manage any related **costing**, **RFP and bidding** processes.

Customer, supplier and internal **requirements** are written, gathered and stored in the ECM system. Team members and permissioned members from other departments participate in the **review and approval** process and can access the ECM system via portal or search technology.

Once the product requirements are approved and the project is funded, product changes are managed by the ECM system's **change management** features.

The project team, along with other corporate departments, uses the ECM system to modify documents, and plans and tracks all changes with the ECM system's business **process** management features. Final documents are approved as part of a workflow, and **requirements** are prepared for **publication** and **integration** into various enterprise applications.

Content from product design is redistributed and published to the organization's Web sites. Finally, product documentation is classified, **archived** and tagged for disposition using the ECM system's ability to manage records and control a document lifecycle.

CHAPTER 19

AUTOMOTIVE

The Automotive Industry is a worldwide industry comprising vehicle manufacturing corporations and their suppliers. The strength of the Automotive Industry depends on its ability to quickly recognize trends in consumer transportation needs and rapidly fulfill them with durable, high-quality products. ECM plays a key role in the Automotive Industry by facilitating the creation and acquisition of vehicle information, its protection, categorization, discussion, modification, review, approval, re-distribution, retention, archiving and/or destruction.

Innovations in the Automotive Industry must be evaluated to ensure the safety of each passenger. Corporate cultures and the prosperity of companies in the industry are built on creativity and free thinking. Highly productive individuals with different nationalities, backgrounds and skills must be brought together in teams to ensure successful business operations. A powerful and strategic ECM platform best facilitates this.

Enterprise Content Management allows companies to better compete in a global market, easily collaborating with project teams located halfway around the world or right next door.

During the 1980s and 1990s, the Automotive Industry was revolutionized by the availability of real-time information from Enterprise Resource Planning (ERP) systems that drove inventory levels to record lows, creating a "demand pull" market that reduced product time to market and defined competitiveness. At that time, product development lifecycles averaged seven years. Industry leaders have recently been able to move this "concept-to-market" threshold to three years. And today, competitors are steadily moving this threshold toward 18 months—without sacrificing quality. Today's technology revolutions are systems that maintain volumes of structured information or fielded data about the many parts used in a vehicle's assembly. ECM systems have gone a long way toward reducing development timelines and improving manufacturing ability.

The Tiered Structure of Automotive

The Automotive Industry can be organized into three tiers:

• Automobile Manufacturers;

• First-tier suppliers that are direct suppliers and consultants to Automobile Manufacturers, including tire, paint, interior and lighting manufacturers as well as program management consultants and legal contractors;

• Second-tier suppliers, defined as suppliers and consultants to the first tier, and to a lesser extent, the Automobile Manufacturers, including tubing, piping and plastic manufacturers, as well as tool and die suppliers.

Automotive manufacturing companies and these suppliers, consultants and contractors, are constantly challenged to manage vast flows of information across globally dispersed organizations. With design, manufacturing and management facilities spread throughout the world, synchronous and asynchronous communication (collaboration) among a company's business units and its suppliers is extremely important to control costs, guarantee high quality and deliver products on time. There is also the ever-present need for faster access to high-quality information, all the way from a gaging station on an assembly line to warranty information from dealers and customers. Since most of these collaborations are in desktop application formats, companies are finding it difficult, if not impossible, to secure, manage, locate and age all of this important but complex and unstructured information.

The great problem the Automotive Industry now grapples with is relating structured information to massive stores of unstructured information. ECM products are the technologies helping the industry to secure, manage and age these two vast sources of critical information.

Increasing Efficiency with ECM

Each model year introduces new electrical and mechanical complexities to automobiles. Increased product complexity means increased development time and higher engineering requirements. New technologies like Computer Aided Design (CAD) and virtual modelling tools are a major focus here, but much more important is the networking and exchange among developers who use these tools, the rest of the company, and a company's suppliers. With high-powered design and simulation tools in place, collaboration and ECM systems have become another critical success factor.

BMW was one of the first companies in the Automotive Industry to embrace e-business technology to enhance corporate communications. It was no surprise when BMW turned to a Web Content Management (WCM) solution to make content available on its intranet as quickly as possible, while minimizing costs and complying with the highest quality standards.

The implementation of a WCM solution allows for the separation of content and layout, and for the provision of uniform templates, enabling BMW to achieve a consistent appearance for its intranet. In addition, the allocation of authors to groups simplifies work processes, assigning clear responsibilities and improving quality control.

The capabilities of the WCM solution significantly boost the efficiency of workflows from content authoring to publication, ensuring that content is delivered to the intranet in a timely manner, while considerably improving administrative tasks. Consequently, the intranet reflects the qualities that set the BMW Group apart: flexibility, speed and state-of-the-art technology.

Figure 19.2: BMW's Web Site

Lean Manufacturing is the continuous process of eliminating manufacturing steps to build a product. Implementing ECM can streamline manufacturing and manage the application of a Lean Manufacturing methodology.

Managing employee training, establishing certification processes and maintaining re-certification is essential to a company's quality processes and procedures. Poorly developed training content guarantees confused and low-skilled employees on a production line. ECM systems are perfect platforms for developing and maintaining high-quality, multi-lingual content for learning management systems and skills management systems.

Total Quality Management (TQM) and Six Sigma methodologies have become essential to automotive product quality. The main advantage of these methodologies is a closed-loop manufacturing process, where best practices and lessons learned are continuously combed from the completion of a product's lifecycle and fed back into the company's manufacturing process. An ECM system can capture the knowledge, manage the refinement and help re-apply the new methodology.

Industry Compliance

The Automotive Industry is governed by a number of regulatory compliances and standards such as OHSA, Quality Management (ISO 9000, Environmental Management) ISO 14000, Corporate Average Fuel Economy (CAFE), 49 CFR Part 571 - Transportation Recall Enhancement, Accountability and Documentation (TREAD), and SOX.

Consumer Demands

Organizations in the Automotive Industry are not only challenged to adhere to industry compliances, but they also face the competitive challenge of meeting the increasing consumer demands for design improvements in areas such as security. Active systems can dynamically help to avoid dangerous situations. Active traction systems automatically control the engine, transmission and braking systems to reduce wheel spinning and vehicle skidding. Passive systems such as airbags, seatbelts and seats protect passengers in the event of a crash.

Driver support systems control almost everything while driving: navigation, lights, phones, music, temperature, humidity, Internet, service and guidance. All these in-car service systems must be easily accessible and operable by the driver.

New technology must be maintained. The knowledge to do so must be documented, optimized, published, and distributed. Service product distribution and warranty feedback must be facilitated as well.

> Continental Automotive Systems

Continental Automotive Systems (CAS) is a leading technology partner in the global automotive industry. The company operates 44 sites worldwide, giving it a presence in all major markets. 163,000 wheel speed sensors, 130,000 brake hoses and 45,000 electronic brake and safety systems — each day CAS manufactures nearly 700,000 units for its nine main products alone.

To ensure quality manufacturing of components, the company needs to detect and eliminate potential defects early. Today, the large automobile manufacturing groups place their information (stock notifications, notes on deliveries and quality) on their Internet portals, meaning that suppliers like CAS have to access these portals several times a day. CAS has therefore set up identical continuous product monitoring and improvement processes based on their ERP system at all sites.

CAS also implemented a seamlessly integrated document management solution to include unstructured information to their quality processes. Now all documents accompanying customer complaints can be retrieved within the same database, enabling CAS to resolve quality issues fast. "We are well equipped to face future challenges with the combined ERP/ ECM solution. Moreover, its openness enables us to communicate easily with all the manufacturers' portals we need to access," says the project manager at CAS.

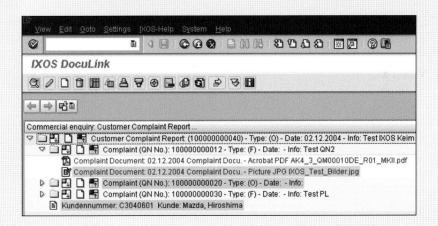

Figure 19.3: Customer Care at Continental

Complex Configuration Management

The Automotive Industry is highly competitive. Automotive manufacturers must be able to read the market and deliver a high-quality product before the competition. Automotive products are complex, and due to growing demand for quality and comfort, products are becoming more complex.

Integrated systems are controlling the complete automotive assembly process, including suppliers. Perfect, pre-configured and pre-mounted parts are arriving just in time at assembly lines to build a configured car as ordered by the customer (a standard car offers thousands of variants with all the different engines, colors, features and setups). Two absolutely identical cars are rare. The delivery processes of a complete secondary industry need to be synchronized from the design phase on—integrated communication, design, collaboration and production systems are the key. All these circumstance make the development of a new car more expensive, which diminishes revenues.

Global Competitiveness and Information Sharing

The Automotive Industry is one of the fastest moving manufacturing sectors. Consumers expect high quality automotive products. Sophisticated buyers demand the latest technological features, guaranteed safety and comprehensive services—all at a competitive price. To do this, automotive companies must be able to easily share critical product information across business units, their suppliers and contractors. Products must be manufactured to company and customer specifications. An ECM system can manage the event-driven, high-speed flow of critical specifications and information between Engineering, Manufacturing, and Sales Departments, and back to the customer, to ensure the best product is delivered in the shortest time. Simultaneously, key product information must be delivered to Accounting, Shipping and Management. Because the information is secured, aged and archived by the ECM system, other research and development can mine it for best practices and lessons learned—key bits of information essential to the development of future products and markets. Only an ECM system can deliver such a powerful closed-loop advantage to the Automotive Industry, now and in the future.

Global competitive pressures make it hard for even the largest companies to recover from small business mistakes. Each decision must be made with the best information available. Poor or incomplete information can mean the difference between being an industry leader or struggling for years to gain market share. ECM is the best platform to make a company an industry leader and maintain dominance.

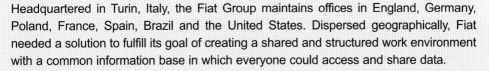

Headquartered in Turin, Italy, the Fiat Group maintains offices in England, Germany, Poland, France, Spain, Brazil and the United States. Dispersed geographically, Fiat needed a solution to fulfill its goal of creating a shared and structured work environment with a common information base in which everyone could access and share data.

In line with this strategy, ECM and email became the standard desktop for Fiat Auto, connecting over 5,000 employees and external consultants through an intranet. Fiat Auto's parent company, Fiat Capogruppo, implemented a group portal where all employees could access common resources and services, and create their own virtual project areas and communities.

Fidis, a Fiat Auto company that handles the financing of vehicle purchases, has created a Dealer Portal for over 600 Fiat Auto dealers in Italy who now have access to an uninterrupted flow of business information and activities. Thanks to the robustness of ECM technology, Fiat has been able to successfully create a shared environment capable of meeting the needs of its large, geographically distributed organization.

Figure 19.4: Online Collaboration Environment at Fiat

Selling into global markets makes products more expensive and complex due to governmental regulations and cultural differences. An ECM system is the ideal tool to gather and analyze the important information necessary to make the right product decisions in a global market.

Other Challenges Facing the Automotive Industry

Automotive manufacturers are finding the number of information systems they have and the number of software vendors they work with redundant and too large and expensive to manage. Many companies are mandating in-house programs to consolidate and reduce duplicate systems and vendors by up to 50 percent.

The management of information lifecycle is now mandatory, but most current systems are incapable of meeting the new requirements. The rate of document creation is far outstripping a company's ability to categorize, store, secure, search, effectively manage and age content.

Environmental pressures and global warming concerns are escalating the demands for "green" automobiles, and current technologies are too expensive to be realistic solutions.

An aging but highly skilled professional workforce will start retiring five years from now and few systems, if any, are in place to capture and maintain the knowledge they have accumulated throughout their careers.

Compliance with national and international governmental regulations is not only becoming more critical to a company's bottom line, its effects are also being felt throughout senior management and in the board room. Failure to achieve compliance is not an option, nor is failure to maintain compliance, as it risks the demise of an entire company.

Other Chapters Related to the Automotive Industry

This chapter is closely related to the Manufacturing and Media chapters, due to the consumer nature of the sales process.

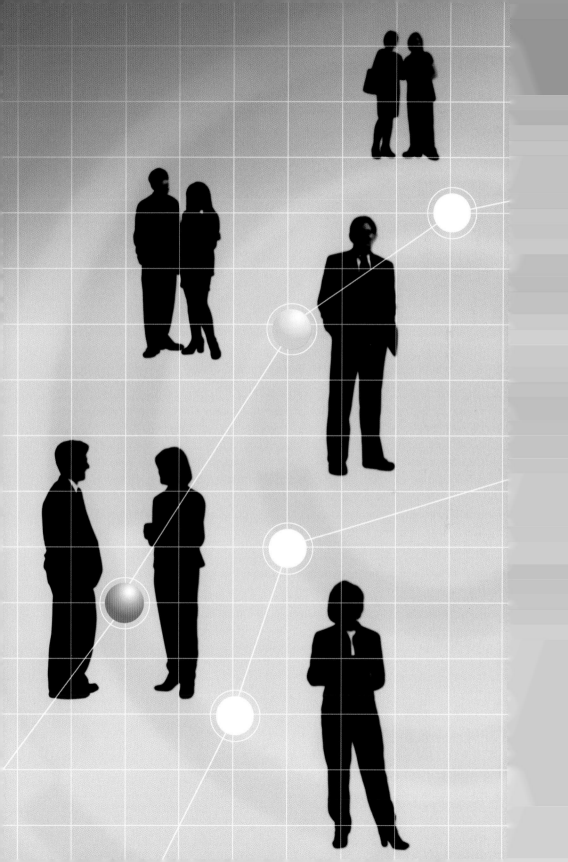

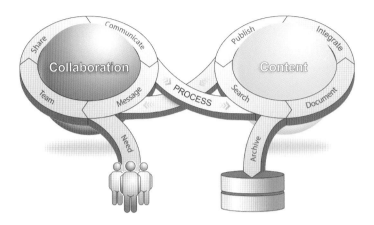

Figure 20.1: Customer Support Process

A customer calls in to the support line with a **problem** and a need to answer is established.

Typically, the **problem** is dispatched to someone in the **Support Group**. This individual researches the problem in the **support knowledge base, searching** for similar problems and known solutions. Failing this, they **collaborate** with others in the organization, such as R&D and Manufacturing or outside of the organization, such as third-party suppliers to find a solution. Additional collaboration may be required with Sales and Marketing. Legal may need to get involved should there be any liability issues related to the problem. During this collaboration, information is shared, and the individuals **communicate** using a variety of methods, typically generating large volumes of content. This content is very valuable, particularly for understanding how a decision was reached or for **regulatory** requirements.

Once a solution is found, it is documented and **published** in the support extranet and the customer is notified.

This type of problem handling very often results in further collaborative processes to find a general solution to the problem, once again involving others in the organization—another typical ECM lifecycle.

EXTENDED ENTERPRISE AND ONLINE MARKETPLACES

No organization today can survive on its own. Each exists within a network of customers, suppliers, business partners and other organizations.

Traditionally, an organization's value chain was seen as a linear process that included all of the activities necessary to design, develop, produce, market, sell and support the products or services offered. In this traditional view, customers and suppliers were seen as being 'outside' the organization. However, it is becoming increasingly clear in today's competitive marketplace that these 'outsiders' are an integral part of the organization's value chain, and that the relationships, collaborations and processes with these 'outsiders' should be recognized and managed according to their importance to the organization. The modern organization is flexible and adapts quickly to customer requirements by providing services and selectively extending the organization's knowledge base to those 'outsiders' who need access to the information.

There are many components of the Extended Enterprise, including outsourcing, distribution agreements, collaborative marketing, R&D program partnerships, alliances, joint ventures and preferred suppliers. These relationships can be permanent or temporary. The modern organization must be very agile to manage and take advantage of the constantly changing shape of the enterprise.

ECM technology is a critical enabler for these powerful extended enterprises, facilitating collaborative relationships and inter-organizational operations. In this chapter, we will review some of the issues and challenges faced by the Extended Enterprise in extending its ECM platform, and look at some examples of organizations that have done so successfully.

Expanding ECM systems beyond the enterprise to encompass customers, suppliers and other business partners has introduced significant technical, logistical and business challenges.

Ensure Data Security

The most prevalent area of concern has been around the security of the content being shared, ensuring it is only accessed by those intending to see it. The security of the other enterprise data when ports are opened to the outside world is also a concern. Security, access control and auditing are all key features of a good ECM system, but they become more urgent when extended beyond the organization.

Provide Appropriate Service

The scale and reach of extended ECM activities introduces technical, logistical and financial issues, especially in cases where ECM is extended to a large customer or partner base. Once outside the enterprise, the ECM system becomes an extension of the organization's brand, and the service provided to these external users reflects directly on that brand. A customer service extranet, partner portal or collaborative workspace for a merger can be business critical and must be available 24/7, 365 days of the year. There must be adequate bandwidth to accommodate much larger user numbers. Redundancy, scalability and performance all become key factors.

Minimize Additional Effort and Reduce Duplication

The effort involved in managing and maintaining an extended ECM platform needs to be kept to a minimum to ensure that the costs are contained, staff and other participants buy into the system, and duplication of effort is avoided. The more effort required to keep different ECM initiatives up to date, the greater the likelihood of failure.

The speed with which organizations are adopting these extended enterprise activities shows that providing ECM services to the extended enterprise is no longer a competitive advantage but a necessity.

Productivity and Security

Any organization with an existing ECM system will already be familiar with many of the security aspects of managing enterprise content. Beyond the normal corporate network, the right people need access to the right information at the right time. This can be challenging enough behind the corporate firewall—and it becomes that much more critical when extending the corporate knowledge base to partners, customers and suppliers.

> Dutch Ministry of Agriculture

Helicon Opleidingen is an agricultural educational center that operates under the Dutch Ministry of Agriculture. Because of the very specific nature of the center, the member group is small and geographically scattered, rendering the need for collaboration and knowledge sharing among students, teachers and researchers very high.

55,000 participants, ranging from ministers to farmers, can now collaborate and share knowledge using the 'Green Knowledge Center'—a Web-based, ECM-powered, centralized knowledge repository. E-learning functions offer students custom-tailored courses, and the creation of portfolios for participants allows for effective, Web-based Student Competence Management.

Helicon Opleidingen is deriving both business and educational benefits from the Green Knowledge Center. Cost and time savings have produced a return on investment, and online meetings have improved collaboration and project management, opening new possibilities on an international scale. Centralized knowledge capture is now assisting the center in its mission of turning the Dutch agricultural area into one of the best in Europe.

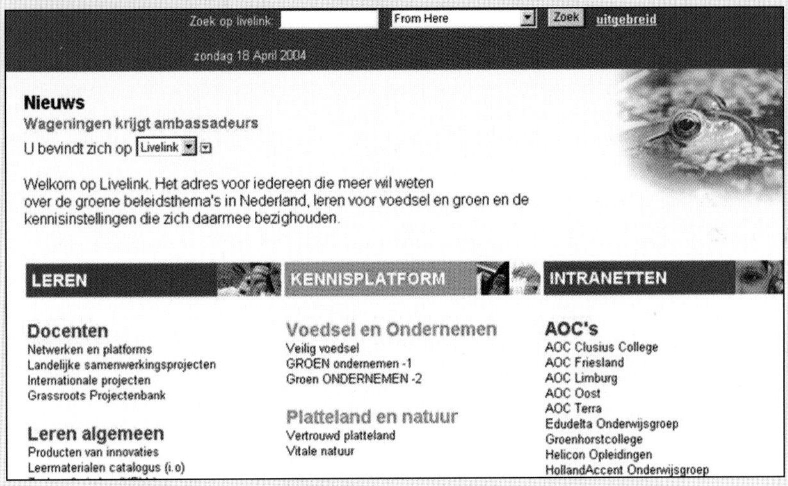

Figure 20.2: Ministry of Agriculture's Collaboration Environment

The most important consideration when establishing an ECM system is to ensure the security of sensitive corporate information. This may require creating a Demilitarized Zone (DMZ), a buffer zone that sits between your trusted internal network and the external network available to the outside world, protected by firewalls.

The ECM system should allow you to set many levels of permissions on a document or folder in the repository to fine tune the type of access that you want to grant to individuals and groups based on corporate policies. The system should provide access control lists on all objects and allow security settings to be modified globally.

The system should also offer comprehensive audit trail functionality to automatically record the date, time and performer of every type of event. Events that can be recorded include document creation, renaming, reservation and version control, content view, and so on.

Document management processes such as change requests and review and approval processes should be automated to ensure they are carried out accurately and consistently. You should be able to design processes according to your own requirements or according to those imposed by regulatory agencies.

Consolidated administrative interfaces ensure that security can be enforced, and that the necessary content management capabilities are available to users right when they need them. Administrators can quickly and easily provide users with access to different parts of Web sites and sections of content in various stages of development in the content lifecycle.

In cases where the external users include groups who should not be able to see each other but must access the same system, the ECM system should accommodate different areas or domains. This function ensures that users will not see each other or each other's content. It also ensures that the infrastructure and cost associated with system administration and maintenance is minimized.

Providing Service for the Extended Enterprise ECM Solution

Once an ECM system is extended beyond the enterprise to customers, suppliers or business partners, it becomes an extension of the brand. It is critical therefore that the system has the appropriate service and support. This applies not only to the business aspects, such as ensuring that emails from a Website are responded to promptly and appropriately, but also to the basic technical and logistical support for the system.

The most important factor is high-speed, reliable broadband connectivity to the Internet. The system should be monitored at all times (preferably from other points of the globe where users are accessing the system), and the IT Department should be able to guarantee over 99 percent availability and performance. Backups and disaster recovery procedures must be in place. Physical security features such as fire-suppression and smoke detection, temperature control and uninterrupted power supply are all essential to ensure the continued provision of superior service to the Extended Enterprise.

Enterprises wishing to extend their ECM solutions must decide whether to build up the necessary resources internally or outsource this. Outsourcing can be much more cost effective because it saves the organization from investing in networks, computer hardware, physical facilities or expensive IT staff. A hosted solution is particularly appropriate for those applications that are time limited (such as an extranet set up for a merger, for example), for smaller departments with niche requirements, or even for large applications where the system needs to be employed as quickly as possible.

Hosting with a professional company can mean getting the system up and running quickly, with limited IT resources and limited budgets, and can achieve a much quicker return on investment. It also eliminates the need for an enterprise to open up its own corporate networks or create a DMZ to protect the internal network.

Adding Value to the Extended Enterprise

In Chapter 11, Enterprise adoption of ECM was discussed and identified as having seven stages. The last two stages described the adoption of ECM outside the Enterprise. Extranets are Stage 6 of this adoption cycle, shown in Figure 20.3. The extranet stage is a natural evolution from an internal collaboration group that now wants to extend the definition of a team member to outside the organization. This is typically only done in limited cases in which the users are named users and well known to the organization. These groups are typically built around an existing internal application with a limited number of external users granted permission within the firewall. This is a natural extension since collaboration with business partners, suppliers and customers is already a large part of an employee's workload.

Extending the ECM system beyond the enterprise should add value and/or reduce costs. Any extended ECM initiative that requires a lot of additional effort on the part of the employee is doomed to failure. Fortunately, many processes can be automated to minimize the effort required.

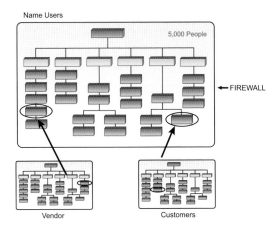

Figure 20.3: Stage 6 – Extranet

In many cases, content is already available within the organization as a result of existing business processes. The key is to reuse it and make it available to partners/customers/suppliers on a selective basis automatically. Processes that exist within the organization should not need to be duplicated for external applications; rather, technology should be harnessed to integrate external users to existing internal processes.

The solution is to ensure that the internal ECM system is extensible and scalable and can integrate seamlessly with other systems. The internal system should be the central repository to all content, applying standard document management functionality. Content should be sent to external sites or systems automatically without any human intervention. For example, a press release could be collaboratively authored by the Public Relations (PR) Department and the business unit responsible, and a workflow process would take it through the different stages of approval. Once marked for publishing, it would automatically be rendered to the appropriate format for the public Web site, the intranet and the extranet(s), where style sheets are applied. The same process should be implemented for marketing documents being shared with business partners and technical documentation being shared with distributors and customers.

Exchanging Information Via Online Marketplaces

The seventh and final stage of ECM adoption is the Online Marketplace, shown in Figure 20.5. In this stage, a series of extranets are extended to include a broad range of market participants, including competitors. An online Marketplace is a worldwide system of corporations and governments tightly integrated to provide real-time transactions and information. It functions as the main clearing house for all of the issues of that industry.

> General Dynamics

GENERAL DYNAMICS

Non-U.S. citizens and permanent residents who work at General Dynamics C4 Systems (GDC4) need to access unstructured data from the ECM system. Knowledge management, security, import/export compliance, information protection, information technology and internal controls created a data access system that provides ECM users with the citizenship information they needed to grant access appropriately. Consequently, GDC4 developed a Community of Practice (COP).

The COP organizes program/project data and controls access to it. GDC4 uses standard folders and sub-folders, which are needed for every program to ensure that new applications start with a standard setup. Access is controlled at the parent folder level to save data owners the task of determining who should access the data.

The GDC4 COP meets regularly to discuss issues and improve their access tools. The organization feels more confident that they are avoiding inadvertent access to their data. Since the penalties for non-compliance are serious, GDC4 relies heavily on their COP to bring new issues forward to be addressed immediately.

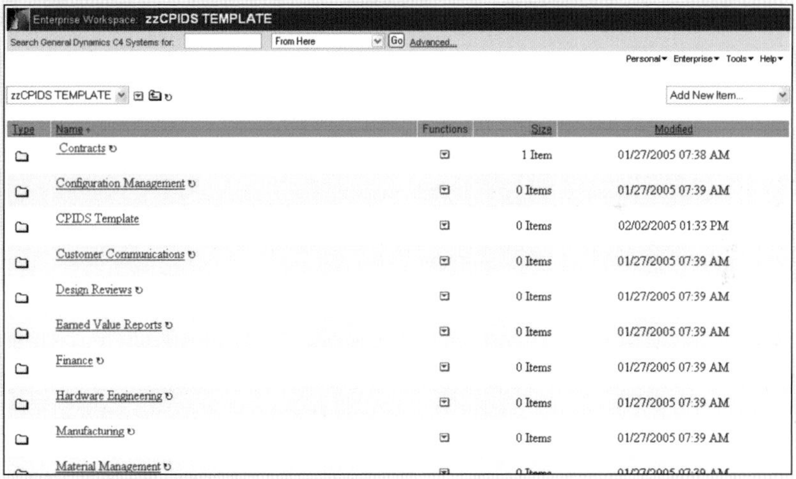

Figure 20.4: A Community of Practice at GDC4

When a marketplace is created around a major organization, that organization then acts as a "hub" and typically is responsible for the administration of that marketplace.

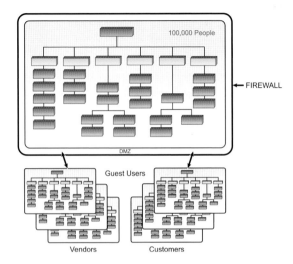

Figure 20.5: Stage 7 – Online Marketplace

The health of the Online Marketplace depends on its flexibility to respond within minutes to any changes in the environment which may occur. ECM plays a key role in the Online Marketplace by facilitating the acquisition of information, the discussion of this information and the re-distribution of the modified information.

The Online Marketplace is a term given to Web sites where buyers and sellers find and exchange information, collaborate and trade. Marketplaces can be operated by independent third parties or by an industry consortium. Often, these Marketplaces focus on a particular industry, although they sometimes focus on a particular region, function or process. The products most suited to this type of market are commodities. Examples include office supplies, automotive parts, building materials, chemicals and metals. Processes and services offered by Online Marketplaces include messaging, publishing, ordering, paying and integrating.

There are thousands of Online Marketplaces today, but few have the participation of the world's largest companies or handle large trading volumes. This final stage in the adoption of ECM has yet to achieve a wide acceptance, but this will certainly follow the trend set by the previous stages for which there has been broad acceptance.

> Salford City Council

Central UK government has set an ambitious target to local councils: 100 percent of appropriate services are to be available electronically or 'e-enabled' by December 31, 2005. Salford City Council embraced the e-revolution as a way of using new technologies to deliver improved and more accessible online public services to the community.

An object-oriented approach, full integration with back-end systems, and an intuitive Web content management for non-technical employees have enabled the council to raise public accessibility standards. As the consistent user interface, improved site navigation, design and content draw more and more visitors, Salford City Council has already realized a good return on investment.

"I am pleased that local people have discovered for themselves that the city council is already delivering on its ambitious e-Government agenda; in particular that our Web site makes it possible for Salford's citizens to interact with us at a time that suits them," says a Councilor on the Salford City Council.

Figure 20.6: Salford City Council's E-Services

Maximizing Productivity with Accreditations

One of the best solutions for achieving ROI in extranets or online marketplaces is through the online education of partners. In today's heavily regulated climate, global organizations operate under increasingly strict requirements to ensure that employee-training and accreditation programs meet compliance demands. This also extends to partners (integrators and other contractors) that are outside of the organization.

Regulations such as Sarbanes-Oxley and Basel Capital Accord II, as well as industry-specific regulations, are introducing a series of new challenges for firms. Ensuring that employees understand regulatory requirements, and being able to prove it, while maintaining competitive edge and maximizing productivity, requires a dedicated employee accreditations solution. An accreditations solution lets you improve the quality of partner training services by ensuring that your training courses and materials are delivered to the right contractors in an organized manner. A comprehensive course calendar lets employees coordinate their courses and work schedules, ensuring maximum ROI on learning initiatives, without sacrificing job productivity.

Global enterprises can have thousands of geographically dispersed partners, often separated by time zone differences and language barriers. Organizations need a solution that manages every step of the partner accreditations process, reliably, consistently, and across the enterprise, without compromising productivity.

Ensure Regulatory Compliance

With an ECM system designed to manage accreditations, you can create internal processes that ensure your organization can manage and respond to risks in a compliant manner. Business reputations can be irreparably damaged if organizations cannot respond to inquiries or subpoenas. The inability to produce proof-of-compliance documents in a discovery process during arbitration or litigation can create significant legal expense, including default judgments, undesirable settlements and compliance fines. An ECM system mitigates the risks associated with being unable to retrieve employee certifications information quickly, reliably and transparently.

You can also manage, view and report on your organization's accreditations and licensing activities so that you are always aware of how your organization measures up to industry standards. To any level of detail, you can quickly analyze various metrics, including the effectiveness of classes and the courses.

The results of continuing education initiatives are generally qualitative—it is difficult to measure the overall success and improved efficiencies of your organization as a whole.

With an ECM system, however, you can define robust, precise competency and compliance objectives, providing a long-term goal for your training initiatives and enabling you to measure overall success over time against that goal.

ECM Provides Powerful e-Commerce Solutions

As increasing numbers of businesses are starting to rely on the Internet, and as e-commerce is escalating, more customers are looking to purchase goods and services over the Web. This increase in Internet usage prompted the International Standards Organization (ISO) to reconsider its Web store interface that offers customers products such as certification standards documents, manuals and topical materials. The organization found that the interface was difficult to navigate and that customers experienced difficulties finding required information.

The Web store presented other challenges as well: the standards documents ordered online had to be sent as email attachments, causing mailbox limitation problems for larger files; statistical reports could not be generated; and for each order, multiple order copies and invoices were generated.

In addition, the Web store was not integrated with the existing back-end SAP financial system that ISO used to process customer orders. The separation of the system and the front-end Web site meant that duplicate processes had to be performed, such as inputting customer information and order details into the back-end system. Whenever a customer made any changes to personal details or the order, this information had to be manually input into the SAP system as well.

As a consequence, the order delivery process was frequently lengthy and the customer help desk was overloaded with rising numbers of queries. In addition, the organization suffered large cost upsurges because of time and resources spent on duplicate business processes.

The ISO Central Secretariat already has a long history of working with ECM solutions, having selected ECM as its document management system in 1995. Since then, the use of ECM has grown within ISO and today, every international standard is developed using the ECM platform. For instance, the ISO Web site was developed using the ECM content management software. "ECM already provides a robust document management base, plus openness and seamless integration of all the collaborative working tools we need," says Pasi Rinta-Filppula, Director of Information Processing Services at the ISO Central Secretariat. Consequently, when the time came to evaluate the Web store and design a system to replace it, the organization did not hesitate to consider ECM solutions.

A project team was formed to develop a commerce solution to meet ISO's front-end needs. In this case, it was simply a matter of extending the investment in the Web site that already used an ECM content management platform. The employed ECM module separates the styles, presentation and navigation elements of the site from the content, and ensures that the Web store is tightly integrated with the rest of the Web presence.

Now, visitors to the Web store can view existing standards documents as well as other relevant materials available for purchase, such as books, magazines or CDs. The documents and applicable metadata are stored in an ECM repository. Visitors can look for products using powerful search engines. Any chosen product can be added to the shopping basket, which can be viewed and edited at any time. In addition, existing customers can log in to a personalized area to view more order details. The ISO Web store uses a secure credit card transaction system that allows for immediate credit card authorization and payment.

The store is now fully integrated with the existing back-end SAP financial system, which processes the orders, calculates the shipping charges, and passes the information back to the front-end Web store, eliminating the need for paper-based copies.

The new Web store has eliminated the need for human intervention in the online ordering process. Customers are now enjoying an improved user interface that supports a secure log-in to a personalized area, where orders can be placed and downloaded, purchase and transaction details retrieved, electronic invoices obtained, delivery details chosen, and personal details updated. As a result, the ordering process has improved dramatically, becoming quicker and more secure. The improved online delivery means that more customers are selecting electronic delivery, so ISO saves printing costs and overhead for physical documents.

The Web store has significantly decreased the number of processes involved with customer order handling, such as eliminating the need for manually inputting customer and order details, sending or faxing invoices, or dealing with delivery details. For instance, electronic documents are now delivered immediately, on-line and in real time, and invoices are generated automatically and emailed to the customer. Such processes are now handled exclusively by the customer—saving the company time and resources.

A new knowledge repository is available to customers, allowing them to solve a majority of inquiries quickly using the Internet instead of the phone. This has significantly reduced the number of telephone-based customer queries and complaints allowing for shorter waiting periods, letting customer support staff focus on urgent and more complex customer problems. As well, the current integration of the front-end Web store with the back-end SAP system allows the Customer Service staff to immediately access all user and product details and payment reports.

The International Organization for Standardization Central Secretariat (ISO) is a worldwide federation of national standards bodies from 120 countries. As more customers turned to the ISO Web store to purchase the requisite standards, the organization found that the interface needed to be more user friendly, while the lengthy delivery system and the non-integration with the back-end ERP financial system needed to be addressed.

ECM is already the foundation for ISO's Document and Web Content Management. It was simply a matter of expanding on the existing platform to create a solution that featured an improved user interface, a personalized user area and online delivery. In addition, the solution is integrated with ISO's ERP system.

The new ISO Web store has eliminated the need for human intervention in the online ordering process. Customers can now place, track and retrieve orders, update personal details and find answers to queries online at their convenience, resulting in increased customer satisfaction. For ISO, the new Web store has meant lower costs and more time to focus on its core business.

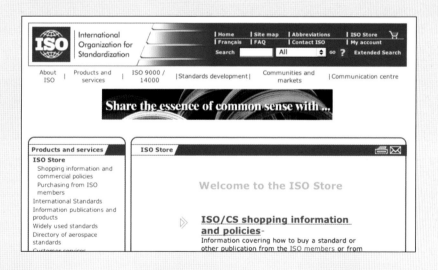

Figure 20.7: ISO's Web Store

Extending Beyond the Enterprise

Traditional, closed, hierarchical organizations are giving way to inter-organizational operations. This organizational model is known as the Extended Enterprise. Organizations partner and collaborate and form joint ventures and alliances to increase the value delivered to customers and shareholders.

ECM plays a key role in the Extended Enterprise, enabling the extension of information sharing, collaboration, and service offerings to others in the organization's value chain.

An organization's worth resides largely in its knowledge assets. Success depends on its ability to manage, preserve and leverage its assets. It is inefficient to depend on uncontrolled email systems and shared network drives as a repository for corporate knowledge—and doing so can put an organization at risk of litigation or non-compliance with government regulations. ECM gives organizations a knowledge sharing culture that facilitates the flow of information throughout an organization.

CHAPTER 21

ECM AND THE FUTURE

In the future, all components of current ECM technology must be seamlessly integrated. The value will lie in the business solutions enabled by ECM technology, not the technology itself. The approach to these solutions will be revolutionized by advances in ECM, broadband and wireless technologies, and tighter integration with desktop productivity tools for information workers. In addition, the nature of ECM will change as content, collaboration, and processes begin to blur the traditional lines that separate applications.

When it comes to investing in technology, the rush to get on the Internet has been replaced by a more thoughtful and fundamental approach. Companies are asking themselves: What procedures must our company comply with to ensure that we can continue to do business as a trusted partner? Why is my company investing this much money? Where is the return on investment for this project?

These are valid questions that indicate the market is now entering a long-term, sustainable investment track for ECM-centric business solutions.

The future of ECM will also be driven by the growth and sophistication of enabling technologies such as rich media and mobile technologies. In the organization of tomorrow, creating a document will not happen in isolation and meeting with someone in an office on the other side of the world will be only a click away. In many ways, the combination of productivity applications is already occurring at the personal and group levels: content is currently being created and saved automatically to a company intranet and global meetings are coordinated from the desktop. By integrating the functionality required to create, share and distribute a document (or other forms of media), people can achieve the highest level of productivity and effectiveness.

Future Trends

All of these issues are driven by six fundamental trends that will greatly affect the future, not only in ECM but in computing and society as a whole:

Content Aggregation	Easy access to all enterprise information available in desktop productivity applications
Increased Legislation	Compliance and governance features as demanded by increased legislation and internal controls
Security	Server-based architecture models for safeguarding the quality, integrity and recoverability of intellectual property
Higher Bandwidth	Rich media collaboration made possible by increased bandwidth
Online Mobility	Presence-awareness within all ECM applications through "always on" online mobility

While each of these trends is important, their simultaneous occurrence represents an important period in the development of the ECM industry.

Content Aggregation

In recent years, enterprises have made large investments in IT infrastructure and enterprise applications, such as ERP, CRM, email and ECM. Information relating to core business processes is often spread across these multiple applications, but there is no single point of access. To streamline business processes, improve information worker productivity and reduce risk, there is increasing demand to provide easy access to all information from enterprise applications directly from desktop productivity tools and portals.

This aggregation of content is achieved through the ECM framework's "Enterprise Library." The Enterprise Library does not require content to be moved from its existing locations, but is a metadata layer that indexes and enables information workers to access content wherever it lives. The Enterprise Library layer makes it easy to retrieve information from multiple enterprise systems with a single search and to present the results in any interface, including Web-based portals and desktop applications. The Enterprise Library is connected to long-term storage devices to enable the use of records management rules to archive content for compliance purposes.

Increased Legislation

Perhaps the single biggest trend affecting ECM is the global increase in legislation. As discussed in the Chapter on Compliance and Corporate Governance, new legislation has had a profound impact on many industries. Regulators are seeking good governance and accountability through transparency. Such transparency is achieved by the diligent recording of all decisions made, including the collaborative processes and documents involved. We will see this diligence extend across every form of corporate communication—from email to instant messaging (IM) and recorded online meetings. Virtually everything will be digitized and recorded with a proper audit trail.

Most organizations will need to demonstrate that they are compliant with all regulations, both old and new. The amount of work required to comply is enormous. The Sarbanes-Oxley legislation, for example, has created an immense change in the way public corporations monitor and record decision making and reporting. Increased regulation means that organizations will receive more inquiries in the form of discovery orders, audits and so on. The information required for the response can span multiple applications and storage devices. The Enterprise Library provides a consolidated window into all enterprise content, enabling a timely and cost-effective response to such requests.

Regulations increasingly specify how organizations store information, and are particularly concerned with ensuring that it is tamper proof. The Enterprise Library enables organizations to automate the process of storing content relevant to a particular regulation appropriately. For example, most inland revenue regulations require a ten-year retention period for all cost or revenue-related documents on non-rewritable storage media, such as WORM (write once, read many).

Many industries are now subject to old and new regulations that regulate digitized content in the same way that paper-based content was regulated in the past. Going forward, this means that ECM will be mandatory for running a business. In the future, ECM deployments must assist an organization in meeting governance requirements, in addition to the basic requirements for higher productivity and a better return on investment.

Security

Security is another factor that will dramatically impact ECM and the rest of the computer industry. Intelligence theft, virus attacks and internal tampering are all threats to the quality and integrity of an organization's intellectual property. We all know that information on the desktop can be vulnerable to electronic attack and theft, but this information is also physically insecure—for example, when a laptop is stolen. With laptops containing more than 100 GB hard drives, the loss of content can seriously compromise an organization.

Organizations must also store backup copies of content in secure, offsite locations for disaster recovery. The Enterprise Library automates the process of storing vital or official documents on high-availability media servers that are located at a specified minimum distance from a main office.

These security issues can be addressed most cost effectively by a server-based architecture, which consolidates all active data on secure central servers, where it can be shared via a document management system. With heightened awareness of security issues, this type of architecture—content stored on central servers with user access via desktop GUIs—will become the standard in the near future.

A server-based architecture also makes it easier to control the information needed for regulatory compliance. Many regulations require an audit trail of information and actions. This involves enforcing higher levels of security for content storage and access.

Higher Bandwidth

Bandwidth will reach a satisfactory level once reasonable resolution (100x100 pixels) and VOIP (Voice Over Internet Protocol) can be delivered reliably. When this occurs, virtually all real-time collaboration, along with a substantial amount of asynchronous collaboration (email or blogging, for example), will advance from document to audiovisual formats. Instead of writing letters or sending emails, we will be sharing our ideas in face-to-face conversations hosted by rich media technology.

This evolution will improve productivity as the technology becomes more intuitive and easier to use. As a result, ECM technology will be available on a mass level, heralding the final stage of ECM adoption throughout the computing world. Because rich media places greater demands on bandwidth, storage and CPU power than other forms of media, it will become an increasing challenge for organizations to manage.

As rich media develops, ECM architecture will be required to integrate "slow zone" collaboration with "fast zone" bandwidths until the transition is complete. The ability to search on these objects will also require further advances to be made in retrieval algorithms. While this is achievable, it remains a growing challenge in the implementation of ECM solutions.

Online Mobility

Perhaps the most revolutionary of all future trends affecting ECM is the advent of "always on" computing. In its earliest form today, personal digital assistants (PDAs) or cell phones with SMS are letting users always be connected to the Internet. The next step in managing these online users is to enable collaborative groups to be aware of the presence of other members online. This presence-awareness creates a transition for users, from individual productivity tools such as writing a document to the ability to instantly initiate a dialog with other parties online.

Users can invite others into a real-time meeting area to review and discuss material as if they had just gathered physically around a whiteboard. In the virtual world, there will be as many hallways and whiteboards as there are users in the system, bringing Metcalfe's Law one step closer to the ultimate value of complete interconnectedness.

A Better Way to Work

Perhaps the most complex issue that ECM users face is the demand to achieve compliance via the transparency of content and action, while simultaneously supporting a security structure that restricts access. Balancing these conflicting requirements with the ability to deliver features and remain cost competitive will be the true measure of success for future ECM implementations. Implementing a secure and scalable infrastructure in the context of a larger ECM strategy will determine an ECM solution's effectiveness over the long term.

As more transactions become Internet based, accounting will be faster and more precise. Transparency and compliance with such regulations as Sarbanes-Oxley will simply be built into the system and take place almost effortlessly.

Sales and marketing departments will receive critical information in record time, so they will be able to influence their markets at just the right moment. Direct mail information will be automatically collected and combined with individual consumer buying patterns to create customer profiles that can be used in email or targeted direct mail campaigns.

Research and development departments will be able to stay in tune with the changing needs of customers by having access to tailored information, sent along with each sale or Web search that occurs. Collaborating online using rich media will enable global teams to brainstorm ideas on a shared whiteboard.

Collaborative bid proposals and contract administration will streamline development cycles and improve time to market. Suppliers will add significant value by understanding the context in which a material is to be used if it is easily accessible.

CEOs will have incredibly accurate and timely information and make better decisions to pilot their enterprises. They will know that their teams have the right resources assigned and will be able to make the best decisions autonomously. They can be assured that their accounting practices and fiscal reporting are compliant. They will recognize how research and new product development meets regulatory requirements. They will know what their risks are and manage them effectively. Most importantly, they will know what their opportunities are and the precise moment to seize them.

Today, the ECM industry has taken the opportunity created by regulatory compliance to extend its leadership within the IT world. Leveraging the information within the organization has never been more important. Businesses today have to deal with large amounts of internal and external information—much of this brought about by the growing importance of the Internet. Organizations have to turn information overload into competitive advantage. Downsizing during economic hardship, the retirement of experts, the need for flexibility in the workplace and critical demand to better service customers are factors that drive companies to adopt an ECM strategy. Soon, the impossible will become an everyday reality as we log into a seamless system to find relevant information, meet online with colleagues from all over the world, collaborate on critical projects, share best practices, and effortlessly manage processes and the lifecycles of corporate information. ECM solutions will evolve in parallel with progressive Internet technologies. People will be more productive; companies will be more efficient. Because it defines a better way to work, the ECM industry will continue to expand the scope and scale of ECM solutions. In the future, millions of ECM users will become hundreds of millions of users as ECM solutions become commonplace.

So now you know that the next great idea, the next breakthrough, the next innovation, resides within the collective knowledge of connected people. This is the motivation that has driven ECM innovations from the start. By enabling great minds to work together across organizational and geographical boundaries, ECM unleashes potential and gives businesses room to grow. It ensures that companies evolve according to defined procedures and in accordance with standards and regulations. For this reason, ECM will be used by every sector of the economy, by all industries and by firms of all sizes. It will make global companies as nimble as start-ups and give small firms the global reach to deliver sophisticated, professional products and services using virtual networks.

GLOSSARY

Alliances - A formal agreement establishing an association or alliance between organizations to achieve a particular aim.

Application - Software or programs used to execute tasks on computers.

Architecture - The design concept for a software system that describes the overall philosophy of how the components interact.

Architecture, Engineering and Construction (AEC) - The industry involved in the construction of all major infrastructure projects in the global economy such as roads, bridges and office towers.

Archive - A component of ECM. Systematic transfer to alternate storage media of digital data that is no longer required to be immediately accessible. Often stored via Computer Output to Laser Disk (COLD) systems. Also a collection of historical records and documents, especially about an institution.

Archiving and Retrieval - See Records Management.

ARMA - The trade association of information management professionals

Asset Management - The tracking of physical assets

Automated Classification - The technology and methodology of automating the classification of information to improve retrieval accuracy.

BLOG (Web Log) - A Web site that provides updated headlines and news articles of other sites that are of interest to the user; also may include journal entries, commentaries and recommendations compiled by the user; also written web log.

Browser - See Internet browser.

Business Applications - Software programs used to solve business needs such as word processing, accounting or customer relationship management.

Business Intelligence - The focal point for improved end-user performance, enabling knowledge workers to synthesize a myriad of information sources (for example, data marts, real-time feeds, Web content, groupware, email).

Business Practice Improvement - A specific part of continuous improvement in management. It involves the actual flow of work in order to achieve an objective.

Business Process Management (BPM) - Refers to aligning processes with an organization's strategic objectives, designing and implementing process-centric tools or architectures and determining measurement systems for effective process management. BPM also refers to automation efforts, including workflow systems and ERP systems. A component of ECM.

Case Management - The management of case books in an organization.

Claims Processing - The processing of customer-driven requests for action. Typically found in industries such as insurance.

Clinical Research Organizations (CROs) - A firm hired by a pharmaceutical, biotechnology or medical device company to conduct clinical trials.

Clinical Trial - A research study involving human subjects, designed to evaluate the safety and effectiveness of new therapeutic and diagnostic treatments.

The Code of Federal Regulations (CFR) - Maintained for every government agency and usually updated annually.

Collaboration - The technology and methodology of supporting work between people.

Collaboration Software - Programs that link processes and individuals across different locations and time zones to create an environment where team members work together to circulate ideas, experiences and knowledge. A component of ECM.

Collaborative Document Management (CDM) - The technology and methodology to manage documents created in desktop systems.

Collaborative Knowledge Management (CKM) - Software that allows users within an organization to manage documents, projects and processes, and transparently store the by-products of collaboration into a knowledge base.

Committee Management - The governance and support structure of a formal committee. Often associated with NGO or trade associations.

Committee of Sponsoring Organizations of the Treadway Commission (COSO) - A set of definitions that describe how an organization controls their environment.

Communities of Practice (COP) - The process of nurturing communities of employees having like interests. A method of sharing information from a common web site instead of using email. Can also be referred to as a "virtual water cooler."

Compliance - Adherence to a body of regulations, government legislation or standards (for example, ISO 9000).

Computer-Aided Design (CAD) - The use of a computer in industrial design applications such as architecture, engineering and manufacturing.

Content Management - Storage, maintenance and retrieval of HTML and XML documents and all related elements. Content management systems may be built on top of a native XML database and typically provide publishing capabilities to export content to a Web site, CD-ROM and print.

Contextual Information (Collaboration) - Small services/objects that can be embedded in business applications.

Corporate Governance - The relationship between all the stakeholders in a company. This includes the shareholders, directors and management of a company, as defined by the corporate charter, bylaws, formal policy and rule of law.

Corporate Training - The internal education of employees and related partners within an organization.

Cross-Departmental Application - The implementation of a corporate activity that crosses over between major reporting departments to create an activity whose leadership is shared among organizations within the overall entity.

Curriculum - The set of materials and lessons that constitute a set of knowledge to be taught on a particular subject.

Customer Relationship Management (CRM) - Enterprise-wide software applications that allow companies to manage every aspect of their relationship with customers. The goal of these systems is to assist in building lasting customer relationships, and to turn customer satisfaction into customer loyalty.

Database - A collection of data (normally numeric) arranged for ease and speed of search and retrieval.

Demilitarized Zone (DMZ) - Taken from the military term, the area of a network between the Internet and the internal network. This zone is NOT in the internal network, but is NOT widely open on the Internet. A firewall or a router usually protects this zone.

Digital Asset - Any subdivision or collection of content and meta-data that holds value to the owner. Digital asset may include photos, video, audio, Web page, text document, Microsoft® PowerPoint or graphic.

Digital Asset Management (DAM) - A set of coordinated technologies and processes that allow for the efficient storage, retrieval, and reuse of digital content files. DAM provides the business rules and processes needed to acquire, store, index, secure, search, export and transform these assets and their descriptive information. A component of ECM.

Document - A piece of work created with an application, such as by a word processor. A computer file that is not an executable file and contains data for use by applications.

Document Management (DM) - Involves the capture and management of documents within an organization. The term traditionally implied the management of documents after they were scanned into the computer. Today, the term has become an umbrella under which document imaging, workflow, text retrieval and multimedia fall. A component of ECM.

Document Repository - A database that includes author, data elements, inputs, processes, outputs and interrelationships. A component of ECM.

Due Diligence - The process of carefully confirming all critical assumptions and facts presented by one party to another usually as a condition of finalizing an agreement.

ECM Applications - Applications that are usually tailored to address line-of-business problems or customized for specific vertical markets. Core technology elements include an RDBMS, a suite of component services, and an access layer (Web browser or rich client). In addition to the platform infrastructure, solution components can encompass a combination of software, hardware, or even a process methodology.

eLearning - The technology and methodology of supporting the online learning objectives of an organization.

Email - One of the first and most popular uses for the Internet, email (electronic mail) is the exchange of computer-stored messages by electronic communication.

Email Archiving - The technology and methodology for managing the exponential growth of email storage. A component of ECM.

Email Management - The technology and methodology for managing emails as business records. A component of ECM.

Email Monitoring - The technology and methodology for monitoring email traffic passing through an organization. A component of ECM.

Employee Accreditations - The practice of giving employees an online test to ensure that they have mastered a subject area.

Engineering Change Management - The process of controlling changes to an engineered product or infrastructure, enabling approved changes with minimum disruption.

Engineering Document Management - The technology and methodology to manage engineering documents.

Engines - Software that performs a primary and highly repetitive function, such as a database, graphics or search engine.

Enterprise - Typically refers to the entire organization.

Enterprise Applications - The contextual integration of unstructured information with structured numerical data.

Enterprise Content Management (ECM) - Systems that capture, store, retrieve, print and disseminate digital content for use by the enterprise. Digital content includes pictures/images, text, reports, video, audio, transactional data, catalog and code.

Enterprise Portals - See Portals.

Enterprise Resource Planning (ERP) - Any software system designed to support and auto-mate the business processes of medium and large businesses. This may include manufac-turing, distribution, personnel, project management, payroll and financials. ERP systems are accounting-oriented information systems for identifying and planning the enterprise-wide resources needed to take, make, distribute, and account for customer orders.

Expertise Location - The technology and methodology for locating experts within an organization.

Exploratory Projects - Those projects initiated by an organization to investigate and explore a topic of interest.

Extended Enterprise - The ecosystem of suppliers, customers and partners surrounding an organization.

Extranet - A private network that uses the Internet protocols and the public tele-communica-tion system to share a business's information, data or operations with external suppliers, vendors or customers. An extranet is usually viewed as the external portion of a company's Intranet.

Facilities Management - The coordination of many specialist disciplines to create the optimum working environment.

FDA Compliance - The steps required by the Food & Drug Administration in the United States prior to marketing a drug for use by patients.

Financial Accounting Standards Board (FASB) - The rulemaking authority for financial accounting and reporting.

Firewall - A physical boundary that prevents unauthorized network traffic crossing from one area into another.

The Freedom of Information Act (FOIA) - Protects the rights of the public to information and makes provisions for individuals to obtain information about the operation of federal agencies. Adopted in the USA in 1966.

Generally Accepted Accounting Principles (GAAP) - The common set of accounting principles, standards and procedures.

George Boole - Mathematician and philosopher of Boolean logic, which underpins many information searching algorithms

The Health Insurance Portability and Accountability Act (HIPAA) - Passed in 1996 to help people buy and keep health insurance, even when they have serious health conditions. The act sets basic requirements that health plans must meet.

Hosting - The service offered to organizations to house, equip, secure, and maintain a web presence for an organization.

Index - In data management, the most common method for keeping track of data on a disk. Indexes are directory listings maintained by the operating system, RDBMS or the application. An index of files contains an entry for each file name and its location. A component of ECM.

Information Lifecycle Management (ILM) - A component of ECM.

Instant Messaging (IM) - Exchanging messages in real time among two or more people. Instant messaging requires that both parties be logged onto a network, such as the Internet, and their IM service at the same time in order for an exchange to be initiated. A component of ECM.

Intellectual Property (IP) - The general term for intangible property rights which are a result of intellectual effort. Patents, trademarks, designs and copyright are the main intellectual property rights.

Internet - An interconnected system of networks that connects computers around the world via the TCP/IP protocol.

Internet Browser - The program that serves as the client front end to the World Wide Web.

Intranet - An "internal Internet" configured behind a firewall, potentially connecting departments, customers and trading partners

ISO - International Standards Organization

Joint Ventures - An agreement between two or more firms to undertake the same business strategy and plan of action around a specific business initiative.

Knowledge Delivery - The technology and methodology to deliver targeted information to targeted audiences.

Knowledge Discovery - The technology and methodology to proactively discover information based on pre-defined interest profiles.

Knowledge Management (KM) - An umbrella term for making more efficient use of the human knowledge that exists within an organization. The major focus is to identify and gather content from documents, reports and other sources and to search that content for meaningful relationships. A component of ECM.

Knowledge Repository - A database of information about applications software that includes author, data elements, inputs, processes, outputs and interrelationships.

Libraries and Archives - see Knowledge Management

Multimedia - Integration of text, voice, video, images, or some combination of these types of information. See also Rich Media.

NIST - National Institute of Standards and Technology

Online - Connected to or accessible via a computer or computer network. Typically refers to being connected to the Internet or other remote service.

Oracle - An enterprise software vendor providing ERP applications.

OSHA - The Occupational Safety and Health Administration of the U.S. Department of Labor or Occupational Safety and Health Act.

Patriot Act - USA legislation passed in October 2001 in response to terrorist attacks that required an increased set of compliance rules surrounding the handling and provisioning of information.

PeopleSoft - An enterprise software vendor providing ERP applications.

Permissions - Management of who can access information on a computer or network. The Access Control List (ACL) is the set of data associated with a file, directory or other resource that defines the permissions that users, groups, processes or devices have for accessing it.

Personal Digital Assistant (PDA) - A lightweight, hand-held, usually pen-based computer used as a personal organizer.

Pharmaceutical - An industry that researches and produces drugs for health care patients.

Portal - Within the enterprise, software that provides access via a Web browser into all of an organization's information assets and applications. Portals provide a variety of services, including Web searching, news, white and yellow pages directories, free email, discussion groups, online shopping and links to other sites. A component of ECM.

Pre-Clinical Research - A research study not involving human subjects, designed to evaluate the safety and effectiveness of new therapeutic and diagnostic treatments.

Process Automation - The orchestration of work activities having a specific sequence.

Production Document Management - The technology and methodology supporting a high-volume, low-touch production process (e.g., claims processing). A component of ECM.

Production Imaging - The technology and methodology of capturing paper to digital images.

Productivity - A measure of the efficiency of a particular individual, business practice or organization.

Program Management - A structured repeatable business process that is often cross-functional, multi-disciplinary, operated from a program office, and owned by a program manager.

Project Selection - The assessment and decision process for advancing projects or new product ideas.

Public Web Sites - The technology and methodology to support a public web site.

Real-Time Collaboration - Tools that provide a way for people to collaborate simultaneously. The primary data collaboration tools are electronic whiteboards, which is a shared "chalkboard," and application sharing, which lets remote users work in the same application together. A component of ECM.

Records Management (RM) - The creation, retention and scheduled destruction of an organization's paper and film documents. Email and computer-generated content also fall into the RM domain. A component of ECM.

Regulatory Compliance - Overseen by various governmental agencies throughout the world to ensure compliance with laws, regulations, and established rules. Examples relevant to content management applications include: U.S. FDA 21 CFR Part 11, U.S. DiD 5051.2 Standard, U.S. Sarbanes-Oxley Act, Basel II, KONTRAG, DOMEA and HIPAA.

Regulatory Submissions - See Regulatory Compliance.

Relational Database - A database (typically numeric) in which all the data and relations between them are organized in tables. A relational database allows the definition of data structures, storage and retrieval operations and integrity constraints.

Report and Output Management - The process of verifying the delivery of business reports and output to target groups. A component of ECM.

Return On Investment (ROI) - Traditional financial approach for examining overall investment returns over a given time frame (supports indexing and scoring).

Rich Media - Information that consists of any combination of graphics, audio, video and animation, which is more storage- and bandwidth-intensive than ordinary text.

Rights and Permissions - Identifies the circumstances under which a particular asset may be used. For instance, indicates who legally owns the asset, in what mediums it may be used (Web, print, TV), and the financial liabilities incurred to include the asset.

SAP - An enterprise software vendor providing Enterprise Resource Planning (ERP), CRM, and business applications.

Sarbanes-Oxley Act (SOX) - Passed by U.S. Congress to protect investors from the possibility of fraudulent corporate accounting activities. Also known as SOX. This act prescribes actions such as controls and the transparency of reporting that all major public companies must adhere to when reporting their financial results.

Search - To look for specific data in a file or an occurrence of text in a file or on a page. Implies sequential scanning of content or indexes in order to find the results rather than a direct lookup. A component of ECM.

Securities and Exchange Commission (SEC) - The SEC was established by Congress to help protect investors, by administering the Securities Act of 1933, and the Securities Exchange Act of 1934.

Security - The act of restricting access to certain information or programs. See also Permissions.

Siebel - An enterprise software vendor providing customer relationship management (CRM) software.

Software - The programs, routines, and symbolic languages that control the functioning of a computer and direct its operation.

Stage-Gate - A specific business process, often used for new product decision making, broken into stages and specific gate criteria to advance to the next stage.

Standard Operating Procedure Management (SOPM) - The process of managing a collection of operating procedures.

Standard Operating Procedures (SOP) - Documents describing how to perform routine operations.

Storage Management - The technology and methodology to optimize storage requirements to storage devices.

Storyboarding - The process of creating a rough outline of what a video will look like using a selection of video clips. This process helps a user visualize the whole video and how it will look when it is completed.

Structured Data - Data that resides in fixed fields within a record or file. Relational databases and spreadsheets are examples of structured data.

Suppliers - The vendors and manufacturers from which a business buys the products and services necessary to operate.

Taxonomic Classifications - Laws or principles of classification; systematic division into ordered groups or categories.

Team Support - The technology and methodology to support effective teamwork.

Unified Messaging - The technology and methodology of unifying voice, email, and faxes into a single inbox.

Unstructured Data - Data that does not reside in fixed locations. Free-form text in a word processing document is a typical example.

Value Chain - A collection of business entities, each of which adds value to a product or service that makes up a finished good (or service) purchased and used by a customer.

Web - A shorthand way to refer to the World Wide Web and possibly its complementing technologies. For example, a Web authoring tool might be used to create documents that contain Hyper Text Markup Language (HTML).

Web Conferencing and Meetings - The technology and methodology for effective virtual meetings. A component of ECM.

Web Content Management (WCM) - Systems designed to drive Web sites by separating content from presentation and providing the following capabilities: capacity planning, site design/layout, look/feel navigation, content development, production, delivery, session tracking, and site evolution. A component of ECM.

WIKI - A community Web site where both the content and organization are open to editing by the community.

Work Orchestration - The orchestration of work activities lacking a specific sequence.

Workflow - Using applications and technology to automate the execution of each phase in a business process. For example, a workflow may contain the automatic routing of documents and tasks to the users responsible for working on them. A component of ECM.

World Wide Web (WWW) - An HTML-based Internet system developed at the European Center for Nuclear Research (CERN) in Geneva. Also relates to the complete set of documents residing on all Internet servers that use the HTTP protocol. The Web is accessible to users via a simple point-and-click system.

BIBLIOGRAPHY

Basel II: Revised international capital framework. Bank for International Settlements.. http://www.bis.org/pub/bcbsca.htm. June 26, 2004

Cain, Matt. *Mapping Collaboration Maturity.* META Group Report: ©October 16, 2003

Chapman, Merrill R. In Search of Stupidity: Over 20 Years of High Tech Marketing Disasters. Apress, ©2003

Cotton, Bob and Richard Oliver. Understanding Hypermedia. London: Phaidon Press Ltd. ©1993

Cracks in the Pillars. Economist.com. http://www.economist.com. ©April 15, 2004

Frappaolo, Carl. Knowledge Management. Oxford, UK: Capstone Publishing. ©2002

Hanser, Kathleen. *Amazing Technology Facts from Boeing Commercial Airplanes.* http://www.boeing.com

Hayward, Simon et al. *Hype Cycle for e-Workplace Technologies.* Gartner Report: ©June 6, 2003

IAS Plus, Deloitte Touche Tohmatsu ©2005 http://www.iasplus.com/standard/ias39.htm

Logan, Robert K., and Louis W. Stokes. Collaborate to Compete. Canada: Wiley ©2004

McGrath, Michael E. Product Strategy for High Technology Companies, Accelerating Your Business to Web Speed. New York: McGraw-Hill Book Co. ©2001

McLuhan, Marshall. Understanding Media. New York: McGraw-Hill Book Co. ©1964

Monks, Robert A. and Nell Minnow. Corporate Governance. 3rd Edition. Blackwell Publishing Ltd. ©2004

Moore, Connie and Robert Markham. *Market Leaders Emerging in Enterprise Content Management.* Forrester Research: ©August, 2003

Moore, Geoffrey. Inside the Tornado, Marketing Strategies from Silicon Valley's Cutting Edge. HarperBusiness: Reprint edition ©1999

Moschella, David C. Waves of Power, The Dynamics of Global Technology Leadership 1964-2010. New York, NY: American Management Association, ©1997

Open Text Corporation. Ten Years of Innovation: 1991-2001. Canada: ©2002

Open Text Corporation. LiveLinkUp Conference Proceedings. Volumes 1 – 7. Canada: ©1999-2001

Peters, Tom. *The Wow Project, Excerpts,* Fast Company. Issue 24. ©1999

Rao, Ramana. *Bridging Structured and Unstructured Data.* Knowledge Management Online. Line56 Media: ©April 01, 2003

Saint-Onge, Hubert and Debra Wallace. Leveraging Communities of Practice for Strategic Advantage. New York: Butterworth-Heinemann. ©2003

Stewart, Thomas A. *The Case Against Knowledge Management,* Business 2.0. February 2002, Vol. 3, pp80-83

USER CASE STUDY BIBLIOGRAPHY

Aargauische Gebaeudeversicherungsanstalt. *AGVA implements Business Process Management.* Success Story. Open Text © 2006. http://www.opentext.com/ecmtrilogy/solutionsbook/innovator/agva

Arup. *Enterprise Collaboration & Document Management at Arup.* LiveLinkUp Europe Proceedings 2002. Open Text © 2002. http://www.opentext.com/ecmtrilogy/solutionsbook/innovator/arup

Atherogenics. *Livelink in Pharmaceutical and Life Sciences Industries.* LinkUp Phoenix Proceedings 2004. Open Text © 2004. http://www.opentext.com/ecmtrilogy/solutionsbook/innovator/atherogenics

AXA France. *Intradoc, le référentiel documentaire métier d'AXA France.* LinkUp Europe Paris Proceedings 2004. Open Text © 2004. http://www.opentext.com/ecmtrilogy/solutionsbook/innovator/axa

bioMérieux. *bioMérieux using Livelink as its corporate document management platform.* eyeforpharma.com © 2003. http://www.opentext.com/ecmtrilogy/solutionsbook/innovator/biomerieux

bioMérieux. *Livelink in Pharmaceutical and Life Sciences Industries.* LinkUp Phoenix Proceedings 2004. Open Text © 2004. http://www.opentext.com/ecmtrilogy/solutionsbook/innovator/biomerieux

BMW. *Applying principles for success to intranet management.* Success Story. Open Text © 2004. http://www.opentext.com/ecmtrilogy/solutionsbook/innovator/bmw

BMW. *BMW's Spartanburg, S.C. Plant Fosters Efficient Operations.* Success Story. IXOS SOFTWARE © 1999. http://www.opentext.com/ecmtrilogy/solutionsbook/innovator/bmw

Booz Allen Hamilton. *Livelink Enterprise Server Integration with PeopleSoft at Booz Allen Hamilton.* LinkUp Phoenix Proceedings 2004. Open Text © 2004. http://www.opentext.com/ecmtrilogy/solutionsbook/innovator/booz_allen

BT. *ECM in BT — Vision and Realisation.* LinkUp Europe London Proceedings 2004. Open Text © 2004. http://www.opentext.com/ecmtrilogy/solutionsbook/innovator/bt

Cable & Wireless. Open Text © 2005. http://www.opentext.com/ecmtrilogy/solutionsbook/innovator/cable_wireless

Capital One. *Nature vs. Nurture: Livelink Usability Research and Planning at Capital One.* LinkUp Phoenix Proceedings 2004. Open Text © 2004. http://www.opentext.com/ecmtrilogy/solutionsbook/innovator/capital_one

CBC. Open Text © 2005. http://www.opentext.com/ecmtrilogy/solutionsbook/innovator/cbc

Cisco Systems. *Web-Kultur — Wie schafft man kulturelle Voraussetzungen für vernetztes, webbasiertes Arbeiten.* LinkUp Europe Munchen Proceedings 2004. Open Text © 2004. http://www.opentext.com/ecmtrilogy/solutionsbook/innovator/cisco

City of Calgary. Open Text © 2005. http://www.opentext.com/ecmtrilogy/solutionsbook/innovator/calgary

Clark County Nevada School District. Open Text © 2005. http://www.opentext.com/ecmtrilogy/solutionsbook/innovator/clark_county

Columbia Sportswear. Open Text © 2005. http://www.opentext.com/ecmtrilogy/solutionsbook/innovator/columbia

Continental Automotive Systems. *Qualitätsmanagement für Kundenbeanstandungen.* LinkUp Europe Munchen Proceedings 2004. Open Text © 2004. http://www.opentext.com/ecmtrilogy/solutionsbook/innovator/cas

Distell Limited. Open Text © 2006. http://www.opentext.com/ecmtrilogy/solutionsbook/innovator/distell

DMJM+Harris. *Mega-Project Web-Based Project Collaboration*. Live LinkUp Chicago Proceedings 2002. Open Text © 2002. http://www.opentext.com/ecmtrilogy/solutionsbook/innovator/dmjm_harris

Dow Corning. *Dow Corning Realizes Improved Service, Lower Costs and Streamlined Operations with IXOS Enterprise-Wide*. Success Story. IXOS SOFTWARE © 2001. http://www.opentext.com/ecmtrilogy/solutionsbook/innovator/dow_corning

E.ON Energy. *E.ON Energy. Success Story*. IXOS SOFTWARE © 2001. http://www.opentext.com/ecmtrilogy/solutionsbook/innovator/e.on_energy

EcoRecycle. Open Text © 2005. http://www.opentext.com/ecmtrilogy/solutionsbook/innovator/ecorecycle

Emory University. Open Text © 2005. http://www.opentext.com/ecmtrilogy/solutionsbook/innovator/emory

Energen. *Document Management Implementation*. LinkUp Phoenix Proceedings 2004. Open Text © 2004. http://www.opentext.com/ecmtrilogy/solutionsbook/innovator/energen

E-Plus Mobilfunk. IXOS Services Optimizes Processes at E-Plus. Success Story. IXOS SOFTWARE © 2002. http://www.opentext.com/ecmtrilogy/solutionsbook/innovator/e-plus

Federal Ministry of the Interior. *Federal Government Procurement Goes Online*. Procurement Agency of the Federal Ministry of the Interior © 2003. http://www.opentext.com/ecmtrilogy/solutionsbook/innovator/fmoi

Federation of State Medical Boards. *Complex Livelink Workflow Implementations*. LinkUp Phoenix Proceedings 2004. Open Text © 2004. http://www.opentext.com/ecmtrilogy/solutionsbook/innovator/fsmb

Fiat. *Driving knowledge management*. Success Story. Open Text © 2003. http://www.opentext.com/ecmtrilogy/solutionsbook/innovator/fiat

Fluor Hanford. Open Text © 2006. http://www.opentext.com/ecmtrilogy/solutionsbook/innovator/fluor

Fox Filmed Entertainment. *Digital Asset Management & Global Marketing at 20th Century Fox*. LinkUp Phoenix Proceedings 2004. Open Text: © 2004. http://www.opentext.com/ecmtrilogy/solutionsbook/innovator/ffe

Fraunhofer OIC. *Collaborative research for future innovation*. Success Story. Open Text © 2003. http://www.opentext.com/ecmtrilogy/solutionsbook/innovator/fraunhofer_oic

General Dynamics C4 Systems. General Dynamics © 2005. All Rights Reserved. http://www.opentext.com/ecmtrilogy/solutionsbook/innovator/gdc4

Hamburg Chamber of Commerce. *The Gateway of the Hamburg Economy*. Success Story. Open Text © 2003. http://www.opentext.com/ecmtrilogy/solutionsbook/innovator/hamburg_cc

Holcim. *Livelink At Holcim's Intranet*. LiveLinkUp Europe Proceedings 2002. Open Text © 2002. http://www.opentext.com/ecmtrilogy/solutionsbook/innovator/holcim

HP Singapore. Open Text © 2005. http://www.opentext.com/ecmtrilogy/solutionsbook/innovator/hp

Industrial Technical Research Institute. *Advancing in the race for technological leadership*. Success Story. Open Text © 2005. http://www.opentext.com/ecmtrilogy/solutionsbook/innovator/itri

International Tracing Services. *Timely Processing of the Past*. Success Story. Open Text © 2005.
http://www.opentext.com/ecmtrilogy/solutionsbook/innovator/its

Irish Land Registry. *IXOS Document Management System streamlines and simplifies the search for information*. Success Story. IXOS SOFTWARE © 2002. http://www.opentext.com/ecmtrilogy/solutionsbook/innovator/irish_land_registry

ISO Central Secretariat. *Building a worldwide extranet with Livelink*. Success Story. Open Text © 2005. http://www.opentext.com/ecmtrilogy/solutionsbook/innovator/iso

Johnson Controls. *Paperless Approvals with Livelink Workflow and eForms*. LinkUp Phoenix Proceedings 2004. Open Text © 2004.
http://www.opentext.com/ecmtrilogy/solutionsbook/innovator/johnson_controls

LawPro. *Achieving a (Mostly) Paperless Office*. LiveLinkUp Orlando Proceedings 2003.
Open Text © 2003. http://www.opentext.com/ecmtrilogy/solutionsbook/innovator/lawpro

London Metropolitan University. *Bringing resources under control*. Success Story. Open Text © 2004. http://www.opentext.com/ecmtrilogy/solutionsbook/innovator/londonmet

Lufthansa Cargo. *Lufthansa Cargo*. Success Story. IXOS SOFTWARE © 2001.
http://www.opentext.com/ecmtrilogy/solutionsbook/innovator/lufthansa_cargo

Mercer Human Resource Consulting. *The Overwhelmingness of Compliance*.
LinkUp Phoenix Proceedings 2004. Open Text: © 2004.
http://www.opentext.com/ecmtrilogy/solutionsbook/innovator/mercer

Meredith. Open Text © 2005. http://www.opentext.com/ecmtrilogy/solutionsbook/innovator/meredith

Miele. *Konstruktionszeichnungen auf jedem PC*. Success Story. IXOS SOFTWARE © 2002.
http://www.opentext.com/ecmtrilogy/solutionsbook/innovator/miele

Ministry of Agriculture – Helicon Opleidingen. Open Text © 2005.
http://www.opentext.com/ecmtrilogy/solutionsbook/innovator/ministry_of_agriculture

Motorola. *Consolidating Content and Collaboration Across the Enterprise*. Motorola Compass: Availability, Scalability and Performance for the Enterprise and Beyond. LiveLinkUp Orlando Proceedings 2003. Open Text © 2003.
http://www.opentext.com/ecmtrilogy/solutionsbook/innovator/motorola

Motorola. *Motorola Extends use of Open Text's Livelink*. Press Release. Open Text © 2003.
http://www.opentext.com/ecmtrilogy/solutionsbook/innovator/motorola

Motorola. *Using COMPASS to find the way*. Success Story. Open Text © 2003.
http://www.opentext.com/ecmtrilogy/solutionsbook/innovator/motorola

Murphy Oil. *J.D. Edwards Integration Case Studies*. VIP Conference 2003.
http://www.opentext.com/ecmtrilogy/solutionsbook/innovator/murphy_oil

Nortel. *Nortel Networks: ROI 635%. Return On Investment Study*. Open Text © 2000.
http://www.opentext.com/ecmtrilogy/solutionsbook/innovator/nortel

Novartis Pharma. *Expediting Order Processing*. Success Story. Open Text © 2005.
http://www.opentext.com/ecmtrilogy/solutionsbook/innovator/novartis

Pacific Gas & Electric. *Pacific Gas and Electric Co. Creates Paperless HR Solution*. Success Story. IXOS SOFTWARE © 1999. http://www.opentext.com/ecmtrilogy/solutionsbook/innovator/pg_e

Reebok. *Reebok Revolutionizes Information Systems*. Success Story. IXOS SOFTWARE © 1999.
http://www.opentext.com/ecmtrilogy/solutionsbook/innovator/reebok

Roche. *Roche Streamlines Pharmaceutical Development with Livelink*. Press Release. Open Text
© 2003. http://www.opentext.com/ecmtrilogy/solutionsbook/innovator/roche

Roche. *ShareWeb — Integrating Collaboration with Content Management*. LiveLinkUp
Paris Proceedings 2003. Open Text © 2003.
http://www.opentext.com/ecmtrilogy/solutionsbook/innovator/roche

Salford City Council. *E-enabling public services*. Success Story. Open Text © 2005.
http://www.opentext.com/ecmtrilogy/solutionsbook/innovator/salford

Sanofi-Aventis. *Easy Invoices Project*. LinkUp Phoenix Proceedings 2004. Open Text © 2004.
http://www.opentext.com/ecmtrilogy/solutionsbook/innovator/sanofi-aventis

Sanofi-Aventis. *Enabling instant email access*. Success Story. Open Text © 2005.
http://www.opentext.com/ecmtrilogy/solutionsbook/innovator/sanofi-aventis

Sasol. *Using Livelink to Support Controlled Documents for ISO and OSHA Regulatory
Environments*. LinkUp Phoenix Proceedings 2004. Open Text © 2004.
http://www.opentext.com/ecmtrilogy/solutionsbook/innovator/sasol

Shell. Rapaport, Lowell. *Team Collaboration Unites the Workforce*. Transform Magazine.
United Business Media Company © 2003.
http://www.opentext.com/ecmtrilogy/solutionsbook/innovator/shell

Siemens. *Global Network of Knowledge*. Live LinkUp Chicago Proceedings Open Text © 2002.
http://www.opentext.com/ecmtrilogy/solutionsbook/innovator/siemens

Siemens. *Siemens Achieved Efficiency with Livelink an SAP R/3 Integration*. Case Study Interview.
Open Text © 2002. http://www.opentext.com/ecmtrilogy/solutionsbook/innovator/siemens

Sinclair Knight Merz. *Global Collaboration Using Distributed Livelink Servers*.
LiveLinkUp Orlando Proceedings 2003. Open Text: © 2003.
http://www.opentext.com/ecmtrilogy/solutionsbook/innovator/skm

Sony Global Treasury Services. *Faster Return on a SAP Investment*. Success Story.
Open Text © 2005. http://www.opentext.com/ecmtrilogy/solutionsbook/innovator/sony_gts

State of Hessen. *Einführung eines Dokumentenmanagementsystems im hessischen Justizvollzug*.
LinkUp Europe Munich Proceedings 2004. Open Text © 2004.
http://www.opentext.com/ecmtrilogy/solutionsbook/innovator/hessen

State of Hessen. *Forcierte eGoverment Umsetzung in Hessen*. Open Text © 2004.
http://www.opentext.com/ecmtrilogy/solutionsbook/innovator/hessen

Swiss Air. Swiss.com—ein wachsender Vertriebskanal. LiveLinkUp Europe Munich Proceedings
2005. Open Text © 2005. http://www.opentext.com/ecmtrilogy/solutionsbook/innovator/swissair

Swiss Parliament. *Keeping Citizens Informed*. Success Story. Open Text © 2004.
http://www.opentext.com/ecmtrilogy/solutionsbook/innovator/swiss_parliament

Time Warner Book Group. Open Text © 2004.
http://www.opentext.com/ecmtrilogy/solutionsbook/innovator/time_warner

Télévision Suisse Romande. Open Text © 2005.
http://www.opentext.com/ecmtrilogy/solutionsbook/innovator/tsr

T-Systems. *Collaborative Environment bei der T-Systems International: Erfolgsfaktoren bei der
Einführung von myWorkroom*. LinkUp Europe Munich Proceedings 2004. Open Text © 2004.
http://www.opentext.com/ecmtrilogy/solutionsbook/innovator/t-systems

U.S. Army Aberdeen Test Center. Open Text © 2005.
http://www.opentext.com/ecmtrilogy/solutionsbook/innovator/aberdeen_test_center

U.S. Office for Civil Rights. *The Office for Civil Rights Dramatically Improves Its System for Managing Information and Tracking Correspondence*. Success Story. Momentum Systems, Inc. © 2003. http://www.momentumsystems.com/pdf/casestudy_HHS_PIMS.pdf.
http://www.opentext.com/ecmtrilogy/solutionsbook/innovator/ocr

U.S. Office of Naval Research. *United States Office of Naval Research*. Success Story. Formark © 2003. http://www.formark.com/case_studies/onr/index.html.
http://www.opentext.com/ecmtrilogy/solutionsbook/innovator/onr

U.S. Office of Naval Research. *U.S. Office of Naval Research Implements Open Text's Livelink Software Suite*. Press Release. Open Text © 2004.
http://www.opentext.com/ecmtrilogy/solutionsbook/innovator/onr

UBS. *Achieving corporate compliance with s.o.c.r.a.t.e.s.* Success Story. Open Text © 2004.
http://www.opentext.com/ecmtrilogy/solutionsbook/innovator/ubs

Vintage Petroleum. *Vintage Petroleum Improves Financial Processes, Advances Sarbanes-Oxley Compliance with Open Text's Livelink*. Press Release. Open Text © 2005.
http://www.opentext.com/ecmtrilogy/solutionsbook/innovator/vintage_petroleum

VSP. Open Text © 2005. http://www.opentext.com/ecmtrilogy/solutionsbook/innovator/vsp

Volvo Aero. *Volvo Aero gains control with IXOS over massive data growth*. IXOS SOFTWARE © 2003. http://www.opentext.com/ecmtrilogy/solutionsbook/innovator/volvo_aero

Winterthur Versicherungen. *Efficient Content Management at Minimal Costs and with Minimal Human Resources*. Success Story. IXOS SOFTWARE © 2004.
http://www.opentext.com/ecmtrilogy/solutionsbook/innovator/winterthur

INDEX

K, L

M, N, O

P, Q

R

Get the complete set of Enterprise Content Management (ECM) books for your reference library.

The ECM book trilogy (Solutions, Technology, Methods) covers all the important aspects of identifying and deploying ECM solutions. The books explain how to turn content into competitive advantage.

ECM Solutions

The ECM Solutions book is the first in the trilogy. It is intended for the non-technical reader who has a business challenge involving electronic information such as email or Web pages. The issues described in this book mainly concern regulatory compliance and increased productivity. Learn about effective ECM solutions for every major department in your organization and benchmark the most effective deployments by industry.

ECM Technology

The second book in the series describes the primary technologies that comprise ECM. Technologies discussed include search engines, knowledge management, workflow, collaboration, Web publishing and email archiving. Find out which ECM technologies are appropriate for a particular problem and discover the most effective deployments.

ECM Methods

The third book in the trilogy reviews the most effective methods for deploying ECM applications. Methods are described for every type of situation from a simple deployment to the creation of a large online marketplace. One of the key aspects of any ECM deployment is the management of people in a changing environment. Establish your competitive advantage by modeling your ECM solution on some of the most innovative organizations in the world.

For more information about these books visit www.opentext.com or www.amazon.com.